CW00545237

Contemporary British Television Drama

Contemporary British Television Drama

James Chapman

BLOOMSBURY ACADEMIC
LONDON • NEW YORK • OXFORD • NEW DELHI • SYDNEY

BLOOMSBURY ACADEMIC
Bloomsbury Publishing Plc
50 Bedford Square, London, WC1B 3DP, UK
1385 Broadway, New York, NY 10018, USA

BLOOMSBURY, BLOOMSBURY ACADEMIC and the Diana logo are trademarks of Bloomsbury
Publishing Plc

First published in Great Britain 2020

Copyright © James Chapman, 2020

James Chapman has asserted his right under the Copyright, Designs and
Patents Act, 1988, to be identified as Author of this work.

For legal purposes the Acknowledgements on pp. viii–ix constitute an extension
of this copyright page.

Cover design: Charlotte Daniels
Cover image: Olivia Colman and David Tennant
in *Broadchurch* (© BBC Pictures)

All rights reserved. No part of this publication may be reproduced or
transmitted in any form or by any means, electronic or mechanical, including
photocopying, recording, or any information storage or retrieval system,
without prior permission in writing from the publishers.

Bloomsbury Publishing Plc does not have any control over, or responsibility for, any
third-party websites referred to or in this book. All internet addresses given in this book were
correct at the time of going to press. The author and publisher regret any inconvenience caused if
addresses have changed or sites have ceased to exist, but
can accept no responsibility for any such changes.

A catalogue record for this book is available from the British Library.

Library of Congress Cataloging-in-Publication Data
Names: Chapman, James, 1968- author.
Title: Contemporary British television drama / James Chapman.
Description: London ; New York : Bloomsbury Academic, 2020. | Includes
bibliographical references and index. |
Identifiers: LCCN 2020003290 | ISBN 9781780765228
(hardback) | ISBN 9781780765235 (paperback) | ISBN 9781350152496 (pdf) |
ISBN 9781350152502 (epub)
Subjects: LCSH: Television series–Great Britain–History and criticism. |
Television series–Social aspects–Great Britain. | Television
programs–Great Britain–History–21st century.
Classification: LCC PN1992.3.G7 C47 2020 | DDC 791.4502/809410905–dc23
LC record available at https://lccn.loc.gov/2020003290

ISBN: HB: 978-1-7807-6522-8
        PB: 978-1-7807-6523-5
        ePDF: 978-1-3501-5249-6
        ePUB: 978-1-3501-5250-2

Typeset by Integra Software Services Pvt. Ltd.
Printed and bound in Great Britain

To find out more about our authors and books visit www.bloomsbury.com
and sign up for our newsletters

For my Llewella … forever

Contents

Acknowledgements   viii

Abbreviations   x

Introduction   1

1   *Spooks*   11

2   *Foyle's War*   33

3   *Hustle*   51

4   *Life on Mars*   65

5   *Ashes to Ashes*   83

6   *Downton Abbey*   99

7   *Sherlock*   115

8   *Broadchurch*   135

Notes   155

Bibliography   176

Index   182

Acknowledgements

I have approached this book in a spirit of joie de vivre: as a minor diversion between bigger and more ambitious research projects. I thought it would be fun to write about some recent British television dramas that I have found particularly engaging on both a personal and an intellectual level. However, this sort of academic indulgence has been made possible only by the fact that I am fortunate to work in an environment where I have the freedom to be able to pursue my own interests without the pressure that every research output should be directed towards the REF. I should like to record my appreciation for the collegiality of 'Team Film' at the University of Leicester – Guy Barefoot, Claire Jenkins, Gozde Naiboglu, Lin Feng and Jenny Stewart – and to acknowledge formally the Academic Study Leave Committee of the College of Social Sciences, Arts and Humanities which approved the period of sabbatical leave during which this book was written.

Authors need publishers as well as time for reflection and writing, and I have been fortunate to enjoy a long association with Philippa Brewster and the team at I.B. Tauris who have published eight of my previous books and who contracted this before the company's merger with Bloomsbury. Philippa has encouraged me to follow my own interests and has supported my efforts to demonstrate that it is possible to take popular film and television seriously without theorizing them into abstraction. Anna Coatman and Maddy Hamey-Thomas both had inputs into the project as list editors for visual culture. At Bloomsbury, Rebecca Barden and Anna Coatman (again) have seen the book through to publication.

My ideas and arguments have taken shape through discussions with other scholars at various conferences, seminars and workshops. In particular, I would like to acknowledge my appreciation of the work of Jonathan Bignell, Lez Cooke, Christine Geraghty, John Hill, Tobias Hochscherf and Stephen Lacey, who have all made major contributions to shaping the field of television studies: their influence extends far beyond the endnotes and bibliography.

I am also grateful to the two readers of the manuscript for their supportive comments about the timeliness of the book and their constructive feedback which has significantly improved the introduction and last chapter. Needless to say, however, all flaws, omissions and flights of interpretational fancy are my responsibility alone.

While some of the material included in this book has appeared in previous guises, it has been significantly revised for publication here. Chapter 2 is an updated version of an essay that first appeared as 'Policing the People's War: *Foyle's War* and British Television Drama', in *Repicturing the Second World War: Representations in Film and Television*, edited by Michael Paris (Basingstoke: Palgrave Macmillan, 2007), pp. 26–38. An earlier – and cruder – version of Chapter 4 appeared as an article entitled 'Not "Another Bloody Cop Show": *Life on Mars* and British Television Drama', *Film International*, 7: 2 (2009), pp. 6–19. And Chapter 6 is an expanded version of a piece originally published as '*Downton Abbey*: Reinventing British Costume Drama', in *British Television Drama*, edited by Jonathan Bignell and Stephen Lacey (Basingstoke: Palgrave Macmillan, 2nd edn, 2014), pp. 131–42.

Contemporary British Television Drama is dedicated, with all my love, to my wife Llewella, my strongest supporter and kindest critic, who not only went above and beyond the call of marital duty in enduring *Downton Abbey* but also demonstrated that she can pick a googly when she saw *Broadchurch* for the first time.

Abbreviations

ABC	Associated British Corporation
ABC	Australian Broadcasting Corporation
BAFTA	British Academy of Film and Television Arts
BAME	Black Asian Minority Ethnic
BBC	British Broadcasting Corporation
DVD	Digital Versatile Disc
HD	High Definition
ITA	Independent Television Authority
ITC	Incorporated Television Company
ITV	Independent Television
PBS	Public Broadcasting Service
S4C	Sianel Pedwar Cymru (Channel 4 Wales)

Introduction

[In] very broad industry terms, I think at that point, shall we say seven years ago [*c.* 2001], I think that show [*Spooks*] really made series TV in the UK exciting again, because, I think, as a nation, a lot of our work is defined by playwrights and theatre, which is fantastic in many ways, but I think they made TV series start to feel sexy, start to feel quite American, in the good ways – that kind of pace, [the] wit of the story-telling, the clear definition of a genre, and I think at that point we needed that.

Julie Gardner[1]

In the early 2000s the landscape of television drama in Britain was transformed by a cycle of high-end drama series – including, but not limited to, *Spooks*, *Hustle*, *Life on Mars*, *Ashes to Ashes* and *Sherlock* – that collectively marked the emergence of a new style of television fiction. These series, which were all popular with the viewing public, represented a convergence between, on the one hand, genres with a rich historical and cultural legacy on British television, such as the spy drama and the police/crime series, and, on the other hand, the professional practices and production values of what has come to be known in television scholarship as 'American Quality Television' (or 'AQTV').[2] This book analyses what might be called 'British Quality Television' through case studies of eight major dramas – including also *Foyle's War*, *Downton Abbey* and *Broadchurch* in addition to those mentioned above – produced for the main terrestrial broadcasters since the turn of the millennium.

Most histories of British television identify the 1960s as the 'golden age' of television drama: in particular this was a period characterized by the cultural ascendancy of the single play – exemplified by anthology series such as ABC's *Armchair Theatre* and the BBC's *The Wednesday Play* – and by the early work of progressive writers such as David Mercer (*A Suitable Case for Treatment*),

Dennis Potter (*Stand Up, Nigel Barton*) and Nell Dunn (*Up the Junction*), whose social realist plays did much to define the critical and formal paradigms of British television drama. The 'popular' was represented by adventure and telefantasy series such as ABC's *The Avengers* and the BBC's *Doctor Who* which, however, tended to be regarded as low-brow fare which were less culturally significant than the more socially and formally progressive single plays. This distinction between the 'serious' and the 'popular' has informed much television scholarship, which has continued to privilege authored drama and social realism at the expense of popular genres and fantasy. John Caughie notes how the canon of British television drama has been shaped by developments in 'serious' drama:

> It is symptomatic of its cultural and professional prestige that these exceptions seem to occur most frequently in 'serious' television drama. *Armchair Theatre, The Wednesday Play*, single plays like *Cathy Come Home*, serials like *The Singing Detective*, and the tentative emergence of a canon around a few writers, producers, and directors (Dennis Potter, Ken Loach, Tony Garnett; even, from early history, Rudolph Cartier) begin to constitute a crest-line of television marked out by monuments.[3]

More recently, there has been a welcome trend within television scholarship to accept that the popular genre series which comprise the bulk of drama production – the police and detective series, the medical drama, the soap opera – are worthy of critical attention as representative products of a popular culture that speaks to and about its audiences. Nevertheless, the idea that the best – meaning the most culturally and formally progressive – drama is represented by social realism persists in the critical discourses of British television. In 2010, for example, Jimmy McGovern, writer of *Boys from the Blackstuff, Cracker* and *The Street*, criticized the modern broadcasters' preference for 'drama that doesn't matter' – he mentioned in particular the revival of *Doctor Who* and ITV's costume drama *Downton Abbey* – and asserted the need for urgent contemporary subject matter: 'The only way to tell stories on TV is to convince people that what they are seeing is actually happening now and is real ... I just can't handle the tongue-in-cheek approach, the kind of thing you see on *Dr Who*.'[4]

The persistence of this discourse has had the effect of marginalizing other kinds of drama in British television studies. The tendency to privilege 'authored' drama in academic publishing is exemplified by the 'Television Series' published by Manchester University Press which includes (uniformly excellent) studies of Tony Garnett, Troy Kennedy Martin, Trevor Griffits, Alan Clarke, Alan Bennett, Lynda La Plante, Jack Rosenthal and Jimmy McGovern.[5] In contrast, studies of popular drama have often focused on 'cult' texts that are defined by their difference from the norm: *Doctor Who* – resurrected by the BBC to great popular and critical acclaim in 2005 – has been the chief beneficiary of what (following Matt Hills) may be termed 'scholar fandom'. This still leaves a significant hinterland of television that is not authored drama in the traditional sense but might not be deemed cult. *Life on Mars* is the one case study in this book that possibly qualifies as a cult text: it is also the only one that (so far) has been the subject of a book-length academic study.[6] Indeed, it might seem surprising that there has hitherto been very little scholarly interest in series such as *Spooks* and *Hustle* (even – relatively speaking – on *Life on Mars* given that it is now over a decade since the series concluded) in contrast to the extensive critical literature on American Quality Television exemplified by series such as *The Sopranos, The West Wing, Desperate Housewives, Lost, Boardwalk Empire, The Wire, Mad Men* and *Breaking Bad*. Indeed, one of the aims of this book is to argue that contemporary British drama is of equal narrative and formal interest as American Quality Television and is just as deserving of attention.

The early twenty-first century was a challenging period for British television drama. On one level drama was struggling to maintain its place at the forefront of the schedules: audiences even for soap operas – traditionally the most popular form of drama with viewers – were declining. Hence, ITV's *Coronation Street* and the BBC's *EastEnders*, which once had commanded audiences near the 20 million mark, now regularly drew only around half that many viewers. This can be explained in part by the transition from a three- or four-channel broadcasting landscape to a multi-channel environment with new cable, satellite and digital channels emerging and in part by the rise of alternative formats, in particular the popularity of so-called 'Reality TV', exemplified by soap-styled shows such as Channel 4's *Big Brother* and ITV's *I'm a Celebrity, Get Me Out of Here*. At the same time, British television faced a major challenge from imported American drama which some critics regarded as superior to the home-grown product. In 2002, for example, Mark

Thompson, the newly appointed chief executive of Channel 4, wrote in the press: 'When you're looking for ambitious, complex and above all modern TV, you find yourself watching not British, but American pieces: *Six Feet Under*, say, or *24*. There are exceptions but the idea that British television is teeming with that kind of creative risk is a joke.'[7] This was echoed by Andrew Billen, television critic of *The Guardian*, who argued that the reasons for the popularity of American drama were not just its production values and slick visual style but also the superior quality of its writing. In contrast, the authored drama, which had once been a strength of British television, had been eroded by changes in production practices: 'As filmed drama became the norm, directors assumed control and the great age of writers such as Dennis Potter, Alan Sillitoe, Alan Porter, Mike Leigh and Don Taylor slipped away … Classic serials aside, there has been no comparable renaissance in British drama and so no leap in audience expectations.'[8]

From around 2002 there were signs that British drama was adopting some of the style and practices of American Quality Television. For Julie Gardner, the head of drama at BBC Wales between 2003 and 2009, it was the success of the spy drama *Spooks* that made British television 'start to feel quite American'. This is echoed by television critic Mark Duguid: '*Life on Mars* exemplified a new development in the 2000s, the arrival of "high-concept" drama on UK screens. The likes of paranoid MI5 drama *Spooks* (BBC, 2002–), elaborate con-artist showcase *Hustle* (BBC, 2004–) and modern exorcist thriller *Apparitions* (BBC, 2008) imported a practice already common on US screens, grabbing audience attention with a concise, original and often fantastical premise.'[9] The term 'high-concept' is one used in the film and television industries in reference to a basic premise that is easy to understand – and therefore makes a good 'pitch' to studio or network executives – in contrast to 'low-concept' which might not have such a straightforward or well-defined premise. Robin Nelson defines 'high-concept' – and the associated term 'high-end' drama – thus:

> I take the primary definition of 'high end' from the industry to indicate big budgets, along with a 'prime-time' position in the schedule of a major channel … The industry term 'high concept' partly informs my sense of 'high end' but, where in the UK this might be inflected towards a social realist drama with a social purpose or an adaptation of a classic novel (Austen,

Eliot, Dickens) with high-art connotations, in the USA it might indicate the philosophical direction of *Star Trek*.[10]

Most of the case studies included in this book fit this understanding of 'high-concept' drama: *Spooks* (spies combat terrorism), *Hustle* (confidence tricksters pulling the 'long con'), *Life on Mars* (modern cop finds himself in the 1970s) and *Sherlock* (a modern rendering of Sherlock Holmes). Others exemplify more traditional genres but were still produced with 'high-end' production values and were screened in primetime by one of the major broadcasters: *Foyle's War* (police detective on the home front during the Second World War), *Downton Abbey* (aristocratic costume drama) and *Broadchurch* (a police procedural drama which marked the re-emergence of the fixed-length serial).

There were several contexts for the emergence of British Quality Television. At an institutional level the Broadcasting Act of 1990 had fundamentally altered the landscape of British television production. As well as changing the process for the renewal of franchises for the ITV network – a change which in the long term has seen the reduction of the number of franchise holders culminating in the merger of the 'big two' Granada and Carlton to form ITV plc in 2003 – the Broadcasting Act also mandated that the BBC and ITV must contract a certain quota of their programme content from outside producers. This created the conditions for the emergence of more independent companies producing drama content such as Celtic Films (which made a series of successful television films adapted from the *Sharpe* novels of Bernard Cornwell in the 1990s), Greenlit Productions (*Midsommer Murders, Foyle's War*), Kudos Film and Television Productions (*Spooks, Hustle, Life on Mars, Ashes to Ashes*), Carnival Films (*Hotel Babylon, Whitechapel, Downton Abbey*), Hartswood Films (*Jekyll, Sherlock, The Guilty*) and Left Bank Productions (*Wallander, Strike Force*). It is significant that several of the most popular British dramas of the 2000s – including *Spooks, Foyle's War, Hustle, Life on Mars, Downton Abbey* and *Sherlock* – originated with independent producers who pitched them to the major broadcasters rather than being 'in house' productions that originated with the broadcasters themselves.[11]

Stephen Garrett, the founder of Kudos, which produced *Spooks, Hustle* and *Life on Mars*, explained that these series 'are all funded in the old-world way': the broadcaster agrees a price (known as the tariff) with the producer to cover most of the production costs with the producer providing the remainder themselves and recouping from DVD sales and overseas sales.[12] For the broadcaster this is a means of protecting its investment at a time of ever-rising production costs: a high-end drama such as *Spooks* reportedly cost £900,000 per one-hour episode in contrast to the £250,000 of a series such as the medical drama *Casualty* which exemplifies the 'cheap and cheerful domestic dramas that form the bedrock of the TV schedule'. A symptom of the costs of high-end drama production is that most British series in this category are now commissioned in reduced quantities. The first series of *Spooks* was just six episodes (this rose to ten and later eight for subsequent series), *Hustle* and *Life on Mars* had six and eight episodes per series respectively, while *Foyle's War* and *Sherlock* comprised feature-length episodes commissioned in series of four or three. This practice has divided opinion. For Paul Abbott, writer of *Clocking Off*, *State of Play* and *Shameless*, it was an indication of the conservatism and risk-averse nature of British television: 'We should have 26-parters ... We are kind of addicted to a really damaging level of safety valve now.'[13] But television historian Lez Cooke points out that this practice is a means of maintaining quality at a time of increasing production costs: 'While British television drama cannot compete with the budgets and scale of American television drama, the undoubted quality of recent British television drama is a result of original ideas being concentrated into fewer episodes and series, not played out until they are exhausted.'[14]

Another context for the changing nature of television drama in the early twenty-first century is technological change in the industry. In particular, the advent of digital cameras and editing facilities has revolutionized the 'look' of television drama. Following the eclipse of live studio drama in the 1960s, there were essentially two modes of drama production: either to shoot on film, which was more expensive but which gave the product a more glossy finish, or to shoot on videotape which was cheaper but grainier. However, the difference in quality and grain between film and videotape has largely disappeared since the emergence of digital cameras in the late 1990s. Drama continued to be originated on film in the early 2000s – *Spooks*, *Foyle's War*, *Hustle*, *Life on Mars* and *Ashes to Ashes*, for example, were all shot on film (Super 16) but were transferred to digital formats for editing and post-production – but by 2010 digital had become the norm: *Downton Abbey*, *Sherlock* and *Broadchurch* were all shot using digital video formats. A consequence of these technological changes is that contemporary television drama has a much more 'cinematic' feel, while the adoption of digital technologies for post-production has allowed innovations in storytelling such as the technique known as 'ramping' (which accelerates the background movement to indicate a passage of time without recourse to a dissolve or fade) and the elliptical editing demonstrated in series such as *Spooks*, *Hustle* and *Sherlock*. This period also coincided with the arrival of high definition (HD) television with its much sharper image resolution: *Hustle*, for example, switched to HD from its fourth series in 2007, *Ashes to Ashes* from its third series in 2010, while *Sherlock*, *Downton Abbey* and *Broadchurch* were in HD from the start.

Other changes can be seen at the level of professional practice. One of these has been the adoption of the American practice of a 'showrunner' – a term used to describe a creative producer who is often also the primary writer of a series in preference to the more traditional practice of having a team of writers who work under the general guidance and oversight of a script editor. Examples include Joss Whedon (*Buffy the Vampire Slayer*), David Chase (*The Sopranos*), Aaron Sorkin (*The West Wing*) and David Simon (*The Wire*). In Britain the practice had historical precedents – for example, Brian Clemens and Albert Fennell had performed this sort of role for later episodes of *The Avengers* during the 1960s even if the term 'showrunner' had no currency at the time – but it became more commonplace in the 2000s with producer-writers such as Anthony Horowitz (*Foyle's War*), Russell T. Davies (*Doctor Who*), Steven Moffat (*Doctor Who*, *Sherlock*), Matthew Graham and Ashley Pharoah (*Life on Mars*, *Ashes to Ashes*), Julian Fellowes (*Downton Abbey*) and Chris Chibnall (*Broadchurch*) all imposing their *imprimatur* upon the content and style of their dramas. Ben Stephenson, head of BBC Drama Commissioning in 2014, saw this practice as instrumental to their success: 'If you look at all the shows really that have been successful in the US [*sic*] – whether it's Julian Fellowes with *Downton Abbey* or Heidi Thomas with *Call the Midwife* or Steven and Mark Gatiss with *Sherlock* – they are all driven, in the main, by one writer.'[15]

A word of explanation is necessary for the case studies I have selected for this book. To some extent they reveal my own cultural interests and personal preferences: I make no bones of the fact that some of these series have been among my favourite dramas of the new millennium. There is a preponderance of crime and action-oriented shows, although this also reflects the genre profile of television drama and the popularity of those genres. That said I believe that an objective case can be made for the inclusion of each. *Spooks* and *Hustle*, for example, did much to define British Quality Television with their glossy production values and their formal innovations in narrative and storytelling. *Life on Mars* and its sequel *Ashes to Ashes* were transformative examples of a staple genre of British drama (the police series), and *Life on Mars* in particular became something of a cult series: I have included a separate chapter on *Ashes to Ashes* as I argue that it deserves to be considered in its own right though the two series really represent two parts of the same continuing narrative. *Sherlock* selects itself as the series that attracted the highest drama audiences for the new millennium other than soap operas as well as representing the fullest extent of the new 'cinematic' aesthetic.[16] However, it is important to recognize that not all recent dramas necessarily fit the *Spooks–Hustle–Sherlock* paradigm. As in all periods of television history, narrative and formal innovation is balanced by the persistence of residual forms, hence the inclusion of the costume dramas *Foyle's War* and *Downton Abbey* (*Foyle's War* is also a variant of the detective series) which were just as successful as *Spooks* and *Sherlock*. And I have concluded with *Broadchurch*, which seems to me to suggest possible new directions that shift away from the high-concept model and the ascendancy of fast-paced, elliptical narrative.

It is significant that most of the series included herein have also been successful exports. There is still a history to be written of the export of British television ever since the Incorporated Television Programme Company (ITPC) sold *The Adventures of Robin Hood* to the American CBS network in 1955. The absence of such a history is surprising given that British television has often been more successful than British cinema in the international market – including the Holy Grail of the United States. Television has – and continues to be – a vehicle for both the economic and cultural export of Britishness: to this extent producers such as Kudos are the modern-day successors to ITC which produced series such as *Danger Man*, *The Saint*, *The Baron* and *Man in a Suitcase* in the 1960s. Indeed, the ever-increasing production costs of high-end drama make international sales an economic imperative – especially for Britain where there is no real equivalent of the domestic syndication market that has existed in the United States since the 1950s. *Sherlock* and *Downton Abbey* have been the most successful British drama exports of recent years – the latter drew record audiences for a drama series for the Public Broadcasting Service (PBS) in the United States – while *Life on Mars* has been remade for American, Spanish and Russian domestic television.

There are of course other examples I could have included that would all make equally good case studies: *State of Play, Blackpool, Shameless, The Street, Hotel Babylon, Cranford, Lark Rise to Candleford, Luther, The Hour, Call the Midwife, Ripper Street, Peaky Blinders, Happy Valley, Poldark* and *The Bodyguard* all in their different ways demonstrate the range and quality of contemporary British television drama. In particular, the emergence of women showrunners such as Heidi Thomas (*Call the Midwife*) and Sally Wainwright (*Happy Valley*) is surely a subject for further research. I have not included *Doctor Who* for the simple reason that I have written about it elsewhere and there has in any event been a veritable tidal wave of both popular and scholarly publications on the series since its successful revival in 2005. I have also restricted myself to the terrestrial broadcasters which are responsible for the bulk of original drama production in Britain. This is not to deny the importance of non-terrestrial drama – Sky Atlantic in particular has begun to invest in high-end dramas such as *The Tunnel* (the English-language version of the successful Danish police procedural *The Bridge*) and Netflix has successfully branched into British-themed historical drama with *The Crown* – but for the time being it continues to be primetime terrestrial drama which draws the biggest audiences in the United Kingdom. In 2016 the combined audience share for the BBC and ITV (across all channels) was 53.5 per cent with BBC1 drawing 22 per cent of the audience and ITV1 14.7 per cent. In contrast, the highest share for a satellite or cable broadcaster was British Sky Broadcasting with 8.3 per cent followed by the UKTV Group (5.4 per cent), which in any event shows only repeats, and the AMC Network UK (1.4 per cent).[17]

Each of the case studies seeks to place the series in their institutional and ideological contexts of production, to analyse their formal and narrative components, to consider their place in wider taxonomies of genre and to consider their critical and popular reception. In the absence of archival sources for recent television series, I have drawn instead upon the production and reception discourses of the series as exemplified by published interviews, press packs and DVD extras and commentaries: the latter – especially when they involve writers and producers – can be a useful source for understanding the cultural dynamics of drama production provided one bears in mind that they represent what might be termed the 'official' discourses of the series. I have not provided detailed plot summaries of individual episodes as these would clutter up the text and I am assuming that readers will wish to view (or re-view) the series for themselves: in any event plot descriptions are easily available online for those who want to know (for example) which episode of *Spooks* features death by deep-fat fryer (1.2) or which episode of *Life on Mars* begins with a parody of *Camberwick Green* (2.5). As per my previous books on popular television drama, *Saints and Avengers* and *Swashbucklers*, I have sought to balance my own analyses of the series with an account of their critical reception. Contemporary reviews are too often neglected in television studies or are drawn upon selectively in order to provide evidence for the writer's own theoretical or critical interpretation. Nevertheless, it seems to me that an analysis of reviews and other press or online commentary is revealing about the cultural and critical contexts in which television drama is discussed. Sometimes it highlights that the issues deemed significant about a drama at the time are not necessarily those which preoccupy academic critics: a good case in point is *Ashes to Ashes* where newspaper reviewers were less interested in the question of gender representation than subsequent academic commentaries.

And, needless to say, my case studies serve as no more than an introduction to the series concerned which are all rewarding texts for further discussion. There are already some welcome signs that recent British drama is starting to emerge from the shadow of American Quality Television. In particular, there is a growing scholarship on the British police drama, which has sought to place series such as *Life on Mars* in their historical and cultural contexts. But the scholarship is partial and fragmentary, and as yet there has been no book-length study of these millennial dramas. *Contemporary British Television Drama* may have the first word on some of these dramas: it will surely not be the last.

Spooks

Spooks (2002–11) is the series that marked the emergence of British Quality Television. First broadcast in May 2002, *Spooks* would run for ten years and notch up a total of eighty-six one-hour episodes.[1] It was a critical and popular success, winning awards for Best Drama Series from BAFTA (2003) and the Royal Television Society (2003) and regularly attracting audiences over 7 million. The BBC's head of Drama Commissioning Ben Stephenson called it a 'groundbreaking series ... [which] redefined drama on the channel for a new generation'.[2] *Spooks* marked the breakthrough for Kudos Productions, which would emerge as one of the major independent drama producers over the next decade. *Spooks* was not only visually stylish but also topical. Its tales of terror plots, conspiracies and counter-espionage caught the public mood in the wake of the 11 September 2001 terrorist attacks on New York and Washington, DC. The success of *Spooks* (the title is a British colloquialism for spies) may be attributed in part to its timing: it appeared at precisely the right moment to tap into the *Zeitgeist*. To this extent *Spooks* can be read as a vehicle for examining contemporary social anxieties around issues such as terrorism, state surveillance, the protection of civil liberties and the relationship between the security services and the government.

The production of *Spooks* demonstrates the new political and cultural economies of the British television industry in the early twenty-first century. Kudos Film and Television Productions, founded in 1992, was one of the new independent producers set up following the Broadcasting Act of 1990. Kudos now describes itself as 'the UK's most successful and original producer of popular award-winning quality scripted film and television ... responsible for era-defining hits *Spooks*, *Hustle*, and *Life on Mars*'.[3] However, it did not start out quite so auspiciously. In the 1990s Kudos produced programmes across a range of genres – including an angling magazine (*Screaming Reels* for Channel 4), cookery programmes (*Nigel Slater's Real Food* for Channel 4, *Roald Dahl's Revolting Recipes* for BBC1), presenter-led documentary (*Desperately Seeking Something* for Channel 4) and children's fantasy (*The Magician's House* for CBBC) – and only established itself in the field of drama with *Psychos* (1999), a six-part series for Channel 4 set on the psychiatric ward of a Glasgow hospital. *Spooks* was intended to be different from other 'precinct-based dramas' such as the police or hospital series. Kudos Chief Executive Stephen Garrett suggested that a series about the Security Service – popularly known as MI5 – would be 'a bit like a cop show only bigger'. Garrett also averred that the decision to make a spy drama was informed by the association of the genre with British film and fiction: 'There is something quintessentially British about espionage. Because of Bond and because of [John] Le Carré's work, the world associates Brits with spying; we are perceived as having a genuine talent for duplicity, deception and telling lies. It's something we should be incredibly proud of!'[4]

Even so the commissioning of *Spooks* was not a straightforward process. Kudos had initially offered the series to Channel 4 which turned it down on the grounds that the spy series had come to be regarded as a moribund genre following the end of the Cold War. The spy series had emerged as a major television genre in the 1960s with a cycle of British-made spy adventure series including *Danger Man*, *The Avengers*, *The Prisoner*, *Man in a Suitcase*, *The Champions* and *Department S*. David Buxton has characterized these series – and their American counterparts such as *The Man from U.N.C.L.E.*, *I Spy*, *Get Smart* and *Mission: Impossible* – as 'pop' series on account of their fantastical content and their privileging of visual style in contrast to the psychological realism of what Buxton terms the 'human nature' series.[5] The 'pop' series flourished during the 1960s when it was perfectly attuned to the period's obsession with style over content and the preference for irony. It reached its height with *The Avengers*, a witty, sophisticated series that quickly abandoned its original realist mode and became increasingly fantastical and parodic over its nine years and six seasons. While the 'pop' series persisted beyond the 1960s – exemplified by *The New Avengers* in the 1970s, *C.A.T.S. Eyes* in the 1980s and *Bugs* in the 1990s – the dominant trend in spy drama in the 1970s and 1980s was towards the more realistic mode of series such as *Callan*, *The Sandbaggers*, *Mr Palfrey of Westminster* and the BBC's acclaimed triptych of John le Carré adaptations: *Tinker, Tailor, Soldier, Spy*, *Smiley's People* and *A Perfect Spy*. These series were all characterized by their psychological realism, believable characters and a pervading sense of moral and ideological ambiguity. In the 1980s the spy drama provided particularly fertile ground for writers of 'quality' drama including Stephen Poliakoff (*Soft Targets*) and Troy Kennedy Martin, who scripted both the 'heritage' spy adventure series *Reilly: Ace of Spies* and the exemplary paranoid conspiracy serial *Edge of Darkness*. Yet by the end of the decade there was a sense that the spy drama had run out of cultural energy. The last major spy series before *Spooks* – ITV's expensively produced mini-series of Len Deighton's best-selling trilogy *Game, Set and Match* – had failed miserably in the ratings. This may explain why the spy drama was largely absent from British television screens throughout the 1990s. Instead, the representation of television spies turned to comedy, exemplified by *The Piglet Files*, a workplace sitcom about MI5, and *Sleepers*, a comedy-drama about two deep-cover Soviet agents forgotten after the end of the Cold War.[6]

Spooks therefore represented something of a risk for Kudos and the BBC insofar as it marked the return of a genre that had seemingly died with the end of the Cold War. Indeed, there is some anecdotal evidence that the television industry did not expect it to be a success. According to Julie Gardner, the future head of BBC Drama Commissioning,

> I was working for ITV when *Spooks* was about to air and there was this brilliant conversation where I said 'Oh my God, that's such a good idea, I'd love to do a spy show, Christ, we should've thought of that.' The person I was talking to said 'It will be terrible; it's for the BBC, it will be so wordy, it will all be about the Cold War and oh God, it will just be so wordy and dull.' Maybe … And then episode one [*sic*] saw a head in a chip-fat-fryer … Okay, it's not wordy, then, it's not 1950s Cold War, we're not doing 'state of the nation'.[7]

The production of *Spooks* also benefitted (if benefitted is an appropriate term in this context) from external events. The series had been commissioned before the events of 11 September 2001 when terrorists acting on behalf of the Al-Qaeda organization hijacked three passenger airliners and deliberately crashed them into the twin towers of the World Trade Center in New York and the Pentagon building in Washington: a fourth hijacked plane – believed to have been targeting the White House – crashed when passengers attempted to regain control. David Wolstencroft, credited as the series' creator, averred that 9/11 'sidewinded' *Spooks* insofar as it 'perversely made it as relevant as can be'.[8] The first series of *Spooks* began shooting in November 2001: scripts were hurriedly rewritten to take account of the 'War on Terror'. In this sense *Spooks* could not have been more timely or more topical.

Spooks had impressive production credentials: it is evident that from the outset it was conceived as a high-end flagship drama. At a cost of £900,000 per episode, it was squarely in the upper-cost bracket of British drama production.[9] David Wolstencroft, who had written *Psychos*, collaborated in the development of the series with playwright Howard Brenton, returning to television for the first time in fifteen years. Brenton was brought on board for his 'radical' and 'provocative' outlook: his previous work included *The Churchill Play* and *The Romans in Britain*, which had both dealt with the suppression of civil liberties – a theme that would also inform *Spooks*. The original cast was a combination of experienced actors – Peter Firth as spymaster Harry Pearce and Jenny Agutter as duplicitous Tessa Phillips – and emerging new talents Matthew Macfadyen, Keeley Hawes and David Oyelowo as the team of case officers who comprised the fictitious 'Section D' of MI5. Firth would remain a constant presence from the first episode to the last while the rest of the cast would regularly be refreshed. The series also attracted a string of 'name' guest stars – including Anthony Head, Tim Piggott-Smith, Robert Hardy, Ian McDiarmid, Martine McCutcheon, Andy Serkis, Richard Johnson and Alice Krige – while Hugh Laurie (as 'old school' MI6 Section Chief Jools Siviter), Tim McInnerny (as Joint Intelligence Committee Chairman Oliver Mace) and Gemma Jones (as intelligence analyst Connie James) all had recurring roles.

The success of *Spooks* in resurrecting the television spy drama may be attributed to several factors. On a formal level, *Spooks* represented a number of innovations in British television fiction. From the outset the decision was made not to include any onscreen credits: viewers wanting to know cast or production details were therefore obliged to look online (or – it might be suggested more cynically – to purchase the licensed book publications).[10] The 'house style' of *Spooks* was established during the first season by directors Bharat Nalluri, Rob Bailey and Andy Wilson. It was characterized by its fast pacing and elliptical editing, employing devices such as split-screen narration and the technique of 'ramping' which accelerates background motion in order to indicate a time-shift instead of a fade or dissolve. It would seem that the innovations in shooting style were to some extent developed on set rather than planned in advance: while early episodes tend to favour a mounted camera, the first season sees a shift towards a hand-held camera that is both more mobile and more intimate. The use of split-screen narration – generally held to have been influenced by the American action-thriller series 24, which began a year before Spooks in 2001, though it had been employed long before that in feature films such as The Thomas Crown Affair (1968) – was only decided upon during post-production. The narration in Spooks is restless and the camera rarely stays still: conversation scenes, for example, are shot with the camera circling around the characters in a 360° arc rather than using the standard technique of shot/reverse shot. The narration of Spooks reflects the motifs of spying and surveillance: characters are often filmed as if from concealed positions (a feature of Sidney J. Furie's 1965 film of The Ipcress File), events are depicted through grainy CCTV-style footage and each episode ends on a freeze frame. At times the series makes conscious visual references: a meeting between MI5 and CIA officers at the London Aquarium (episode 2.4), for example, is nothing if not an homage to the famous sequence in Alfred Hitchcock's Sabotage (1936).

The production strategy of Spooks was to modernize the television spy drama for the twenty-first century: to this extent it sets out to differentiate itself from serials such as Tinker, Tailor, Soldier, Spy and Smiley's People on every level. In contrast to the middle-aged, white, male world of John le Carré's 'Circus', the agents in Spooks are characterized as young, attractive, multicultural and mixed gender. The three male leads of Spooks – Tom Quinn (Matthew Macfadyen), Adam Carter (Rupert Penry-Jones) and Lucas North (Richard Armitage) – are all handsome and heroic in the mould of Ian Fleming's fictional secret agent James Bond rather than le Carré's anonymous and ordinary George Smiley (so memorably incarnated by Alec Guinness in the two BBC serials). The unproblematic inclusion of women as part of the team – regular characters included Zoë Reynolds (Keeley Hawes) in series 1–3, Fiona Carter (Olga Sosnovska) in series 3–4, Jo Portman (Miranda Raison) in series 4–8, Ros Myers (Hermione Norris) in series 5–8, Beth Bailey (Sophia Myles) in series 9 and Erin Watts (Lara Pulver) in series 10 – suggests that sexism in the Security

Service is a thing of the past: this contrasts markedly with the first episode of ITV's *The Sandbaggers* in 1979 where the entry of a woman into the cosy male world is the focus of considerable gender anxiety. Similarly, the inclusion of characters from minority ethnic backgrounds – including Danny Hunter (David Oyelowo) in series 1–3, Zafar Younis (Raza Jaffrey) in series 3–6 and Tariq Masood (Shazad Latif) in series 8–10 – was clearly intended to represent the modern, multicultural face of Blairite Britain. The casting of *Spooks* therefore positioned the series in relation to the BBC's strategy for representing cultural diversity. The BBC Annual Report for 2008–09, for example, began with the statement: 'The UK is an incredibly diverse place, and we aim to reflect this diversity at national, regional and local levels.'[11]

Spooks also differentiates itself from its predecessors in its production design and its visual style. The clubland world of the 'Circus' with its old-fashioned trappings of leather armchairs and wood-panelled offices is reserved in *Spooks* for 'old school' spies such as the upper-class throwback Jools Siviter: instead, MI5 operates from a high-tech facility known as 'The Grid' characterized by its sleek modernism. (As the production team was unable to film at the real MI5 building Thames House on Millbank, it used instead the Freemasons' Hall: it seems more than a little ironic that the headquarters of the United Grand Lodge of England should feature as the bastion of the secret state.) The glossy, high-contrast style of *Spooks* identifies it as an heir – visually at least – to the 'pop' aesthetic of 1960s spy adventure series such as *Danger Man* and *The Avengers*. And also like *The Avengers*, which had presented an image of Britain (or rather England) combining tradition and modernity (vintage cars, stately homes and elegant gentleman's tailoring co exist with computers, robots and avant-garde fashions), *Spooks* combines traditional visual signifiers of London such as the Royal Opera House and the Houses of Parliament with the modern face of the city represented by newer landmarks such as the Millennium Bridge and the Thames Flood Barrier. This visual strategy also characterizes other post-millennial British television dramas – including *Doctor Who*, *Hustle* and *Sherlock* – and can be seen as part of a strategy to project a tourist-friendly image of modern Britain for both domestic and overseas consumption.

The promotional discourses of *Spooks* – exemplified by press releases and interviews with the producers, writers and cast members – were at pains to emphasize its relevance and topicality. According to Gareth Neame, then head of Independent Drama Commissioning for the BBC: 'In a world where the role of the intelligence services and secret agents is being thrown into greater relief, *Spooks* is a timely new drama from a first-class creative team and a superb cast. MI5 are in the news every day – they're in the front line in the war against terrorism. But until now, how they go about it has been hidden.'[12] The existence of MI5 – the organization responsible for domestic intelligence gathering and counter-espionage more formally known as the Security Service – had only been officially acknowledged since the early 1990s: in 1991 the identity of the Director-General of MI5 (Dame Stella Rimington) had been revealed for the first time, and in 1997 the agency launched its first public recruitment campaign. According to Christopher Andrew's authorized history – published to mark the centenary of MI5 in 2009 – Rimington felt that one of her main achievements as Director-General was 'the demystification of the Service and the creation of a more informed public and media perception'.[13] *Spooks* has sometimes been seen as part of this process. The first episode even includes a public relations officer welcoming a group of journalists to MI5 headquarters and explaining its role: 'Officially we're the Security Service. Unofficially we prefer MI5 or simply just Five. Our main function: to protect Britain's national security.' The press pack for the first series named former MI5 officer Nick Day as a 'research consultant'. However, David Shayler, an MI5 whistle-blower who had been prosecuted under the Official Secrets Act in 2000 for revealing that the service had spied on Labour politicians, claimed that 'I was the original consultant for the programme when Kudos, the producer, first came up with the idea two years ago. I even came up with the title *Spooks* – as a joke.'[14]

Spooks marks a particularly significant moment in the history of the spy drama insofar as it represents a point of convergence between the two modes that hitherto characterized the genre. In his book *Cover Stories*, a history of British literary spy fiction, Michael Denning differentiates 'between those that we might call magical thrillers, where there is a clear contest between Good and Evil with a virtuous hero defeating an alien and evil villain, and those that we might call existential thrillers, which play on a dialectic of good and evil overdetermined by moral dilemmas'.[15] The 'magical' thriller is characterized by narratives of action and adventure and a public-school ethos of spying as a game: it is exemplified by characters such as John Buchan's Richard Hannay, Sapper's Bulldog Drummond and Ian Fleming's James Bond. In contrast, the 'existential' thriller is concerned with psychology rather than action and tends to use the activity of spying as a means of exploring social and political anxieties: it is exemplified by the work of Graham Greene, Eric Ambler, John le Carré and Len Deighton. Similar lineages or taxonomies can be identified in television spy drama: *The Avengers* is the pre-eminent 'magical' thriller while *Callan* and the John le Carré adaptations exemplify the existential thriller, with a series like *Danger Man* straddling the two. *Spooks* also set out to combine aspects of both: this was a conscious strategy that informed the production discourse of the series. David Wolstencroft averred that he sought to position *Spooks* in relation to both traditions: 'I thought there was a completely new place to put it, which was between the le Carré type, sinister public-schoolboy old school [*sic*], and the fantasist Bond-type things.'[16] Matthew Macfadyen similarly described his character of Tom Quinn as being 'in the middle somewhere between George Smiley and James Bond'.[17]

A characteristic of much contemporary television drama is its awareness of its own fictionality: *Spooks* is no exception. This is especially so in the series' early period. 'It wasn't like this in George's day,' a character remarks in the first episode: a further indication that *Spooks* set out to differentiate itself from the world of *Tinker, Tailor, Soldier, Spy* (though, in fact, George Smiley's 'Circus' was MI6 rather than MI5). When Zoë goes undercover in a video rental store in order to befriend a Serbian terrorist known to be a film aficionado, it is an opportunity to comment on the nature of the spy genre: 'I'm not a fan of spy stories. They always make espionage seem so exciting. If you ask me, it's probably the opposite' (2.1). And the last episode of series two begins with a hit man called Karharias watching *The Third Man* on television. Nancy Banks-Smith, television critic of *The Guardian*, understood the reference: 'A man in a mask ordered Karharias to assassinate someone and immediately shot him. Now, this may seem counterproductive, but in *The Third Man*, you remember, Harry Lime only pretended to be dead... And now Tom, when he is declared missing believed drowned, will also become one of the living dead.'[18]

While the melodramatic plot devices of *Spooks* – assassinations, bomb plots, the theft of nuclear weapons, even attempted coups by the military and the intelligence community itself – belong to the realm of the sensational adventure thriller, in certain other respects the series draws upon themes and motifs from the existential mode of the thriller. The nature of identity and the self, for example, is a recurring theme. A subplot running throughout series one concerns Tom's relationship with his girlfriend Ellie and her young daughter Maisie who do not know he is a spy and think he is an IT analyst called Matthew Archer. Tom's 'Matthew Archer' identity is kept in a box containing (fake) documents and personal effects. The struggle of separating his real and fictional identities puts a strain on Tom's relationship with Ellie ('I can't do this much longer … I just want to keep things simple'). When he reveals the truth, Ellie's response ('Who are you?') explicitly problematizes the question of identity. At one point Tom even remarks, 'I don't know who I am any more'. Another theme of the existential thriller is the sense of disillusion and despair. A particular characteristic of *Spooks* is that it counters assertions of patriotism and duty ('I've told you I do a job serving my country. Is that such a bad thing?') with a degree of scepticism about those values. This is demonstrated forcefully in the first series when MI5 officer Peter Salter (Anthony Head) – a 'legend' of the Service – comes to identify with the anti-capitalist group he has been tasked to infiltrate. Salter has become disillusioned with modern society: 'When the Soviet Union was cracked, we thought, yeah, we've got something. My father died for it. Democracy. Now there's nothing. It's all gone. It's dead. No-one believes in anything any more' (1.4).

Another theme borrowed from the John le Carré–Len Deighton school of spy fiction is that of treachery and deceit. It seems that barely a season of *Spooks* would pass without the revelation of a mole or traitor within the Security Service. Ruth Evershed (Nicola Walker), a recruit from GCHQ (Government Communications Headquarters), is originally a mole for another government department: the character remained and became an unconsummated love interest for 'Section D' chief Harry Pearce. In series six Ros Myers is 'turned' by a secretive international organization known as 'Yalta': the character is afterwards rehabilitated and promoted to section chief. At the end of series seven Connie James – an intelligence analyst whose name was possibly a reference to Connie Sachs in *Tinker, Tailor, Soldier, Spy* – is revealed as a mole for the Russian Federal Security Bureau (successor to the KGB). And at the end of series nine it turns out that Lucas North – whose release from a Russian prison and return to duty had been negotiated by Harry at the beginning of series seven – is not Lucas North at all but a mercenary called John Bateman who has assumed North's identity. The frequency of moles and traitors in

Spooks irresistibly brings to mind not only fictional traitors such as le Carré's Bill Haydon (*Tinker, Tailor, Soldier, Spy*) but also their real-life models: Donald Maclean, Guy Burgess, Kim Philby, John Cairncross and Anthony Blunt.[19]

On a narrative level *Spooks* marks a shift away from the secret war and power plays between nation-states that characterized much Cold War spy fiction and repositions the genre in relation to the ideological landscape of the 'War on Terror'. Or as David Wolstencroft put it: 'Espionage these days is more about preventing atrocity than nation against nation.'[20] The origin of *Spooks* coincided precisely with the moment when the Security Service identified the primary terrorist threat to the United Kingdom as being Islamic extremism rather than Irish nationalists ('the old enemy', as Harry refers to them in episode 1.6). *Spooks*, however, dramatizes threats and conspiracies from across the full range of the political and ideological spectrum: these include – but are not limited to – radical American anti-abortionists (1.1), the British Far Right (1.2), Kurdish separatists (1.3), anti-capitalist activists (1.4), dissident members of the IRA (1.6), a Serbian war criminal (2.1), British-born Islamic fundamentalists (2.2), cyber terrorists (2.3), the Russian Mafia (2.4), a disaffected British army officer plotting a coup (2.8), a Colombian drugs cartel (2.9), a renegade ex-CIA agent (2.10), Far Right Zionists (3.4), the Turkish Mafia (3.6), Iraqi Ba'ath loyalists (3.10), eco-terrorists (4.1–4.2), Al-Qaeda (5.3), Mossad (5.8) and even a radical Christian group (5.8). It would seem therefore that the strategy of embracing diversity in *Spooks* also extended to its representation of enemies of the state. The sheer range of terror plots – some, it must be said, less plausible than others – meant that *Spooks* could not be accused of singling out any particular political or ethnic group as the 'enemy'.[21] That said one particular episode did provoke controversy. Episode 2.2 focuses on the threat posed by the radicalization of young Muslim men in a Birmingham mosque: the climax has a sixteen-year-old blowing himself up with a 'martyr's belt'. The Muslim Council of Britain complained that the episode 'pandered to grossly offensive and Islamophobic caricatures of imams, Muslim students and mosques' and 'served to reinforce many negative stereotypes of British Muslims'.[22] Following the episode's broadcast it was reported that the Birmingham Central Mosque was vandalized with graffiti declaring: 'Suicide bombers inside – kill the bombers.' The press also reported an assault on a Muslim student in Birmingham who was allegedly told by his attackers: 'You have been spooked.'[23] The Broadcasting Standards Commission rejected the charge that the episode encouraged Islamophobia, pointing out that it also featured sympathetic Muslim characters, although it acknowledged the 'concern felt by many British Muslims at the excessive influence on the tiny minority advocating violence in the name of Islam'.[24]

Spooks was no stranger to controversy. It had established a reputation for edginess in only its second episode. This focused on the undercover investigation of a British Far Right group responsible for orchestrating a campaign of racial violence. The episode attracted much notoriety for killing off the character of MI5 trainee Helen Flynn (Lisa Faulkner). Helen's death is shocking not only because of its manner – her head is shoved into a deep-fat fryer by the villain Osborne (Kevin McNally) – but also because the character had seemingly been created as a point of identification for viewers who would expect her to develop throughout the series. The incident prompted 334 complaints to the BBC, although Stephen Garrett justified it on dramatic grounds: 'It ambushed the audience by doing what television almost never does... Now when viewers sit down to watch future episodes of *Spooks* they are in no doubt whatsoever that absolutely anything can happen. No one is safe. And that, it seemed to us, was an unusually compelling proposition for a television drama.'[25] Nor was Helen the only casualty in *Spooks*: others who would die in the line of duty in later seasons included Danny Hunter (executed as a hostage by Iraqi nationalists at the end of series three), Fiona Carter (shot dead by her vengeance-crazed ex-husband), Zafar Younis (tortured and murdered by an Al-Qaeda group in Afghanistan), Adam Carter (blown up by a car bomb at the start of series seven), Jo Portman (accidentally shot by Ros Myers during a terrorist siege) and Ros herself (killed in an explosion while trying to save the Home Secretary).

Political scientist Christian Erickson has argued that series such as *Spooks* and *24* need to be positioned in relation to 'the political dynamics of the George W. Bush and Tony Blair/Gordon Brown administrations' counterterrorist and counterinsurgency policies, as they reflect debates about the extent of the threat and the required response that takes place in the "real", and further, that they 'should be understood as fictionalised reflections of the debates about proper counterterrorist and counterinsurgency policies shaped by nearly seven years of global "war(s) on terror," internal security mobilisation, and the invasion and occupation in Afghanistan and Iraq'.[26] *Spooks* is perhaps even more finely attuned to the ideological and political climate in Britain than Erickson suggests. The first two series of *Spooks* – broadcast in the spring/early summer of 2002 and 2003 respectively – adhere more or less to a stateist ideology. While there are hints of rivalry with the 'sister service' MI6 (the Secret Intelligence Service responsible for overseas operations) and while the relationship with the American 'cousins' is represented as occasionally problematic – although Tom nevertheless enjoys his own 'special relationship' with the CIA London liaison Christine Gale (Megan Dodds) in series two – the overall ideology of these early episodes is generally pro-state in the sense that the role of the Security Service is the 'defence of the realm' against domestic and foreign terrorist threats. Episode 1.2 even goes so far as implicitly to endorse state violence when Helen's murderer, who has escaped arrest on a technicality, is shot dead by a motorcycle-riding hit man. What amounts to state-sanctioned murder without recourse to due process of law is ideologically justified in the narrative context of the episode in that the villain Osborne is a thoroughly vile character: not only is he an instigator of racist violence, he is directly responsible for at least two deaths and is a wife-beater to boot. His assassination – implicitly by the Security Service – is presented as ideologically unproblematic.

However, from the third series of *Spooks*, broadcast in the autumn of 2004, there is evidence of a realignment in its politics. While the diverse range of terrorist threats remains, there is a shift of narrative emphasis from the Security Service as protector of the state to the idea of the Security Service as a bulwark against the expansion and abuse of state power. Episode 3.1, for example, centres on a politically motivated attempt by the Joint Intelligence Committee (JIC) to take control of MI5 – occasioned by Tom Quinn apparently going 'rogue' at the end of series two – and explores the question of political influence over the intelligence services. Harry has to defend the independence of MI5 against interference by Machiavellian JIC Chairman Oliver Mace: 'You want to reduce us to some firm of decorators only to be wheeled out when you want some kind of whitewash.' It is difficult not to read this as an allusion to the role of the real JIC in allegedly pressuring the intelligence services to provide evidence of the existence of Weapons of Mass Destructions (WMDs) by Iraq – what later came to be dubbed the 'dodgy dossier' – in order to provide ideological legitimation for Britain's participation in the US-led invasion of Iraq in 2003. Howard Brenton, who wrote the episode, confirmed this reading:

> What was on my mind was the dossier and how MI6 had appeared to have been put under enormous political pressure. It had occurred to me that in reality the JIC had become more and more powerful and I wanted to reflect that ... There is a culture at the present within government of loose cannons who are not elected but who are immensely influential and seem to despise ministers who sit around the Cabinet table. They are shadowy, unelected voices, who spend their time whispering in the ear of the prime minister.[27]

Later episodes draw quite clear parallels with the mistreatment of prisoners at Guantánamo Bay and Abu Ghraib (3.9) and the practice of 'extraordinary rendition' in which terror suspects are transported overseas for interrogation (4.7). In this period, Section D finds itself occupied as much in countering the machinations of ambitious politicians such as Oliver Mace – deposed when it is revealed he was responsible for the illegal torture of terror suspects – and National Security Co-Ordinator Juliet Shaw (Anna Chancellor).

How can we explain this ideological shift in the series? It needs to be borne in mind that the longer-than usual gap between the second and third seasons of *Spooks* coincided with a major crisis for the BBC in its relations with the government. On 29 May 2003 Radio 4's flagship current affairs programme *Today* had featured a report by investigative journalist Andrew Gilligan alleging that the government of Tony Blair had 'sexed up' the Iraqi WMD dossier: the report – and the subsequent suicide of a senior United Nations weapons inspector Dr David Kelly who was 'outed' as the source – led to a judicial enquiry under Lord Hutton which severely censured the BBC and brought about the resignations of both the Chairman of Governors Gavyn Davies and the Director-General Greg Dyke. The Hutton Report was greeted with incredulity by the British media – by the time of its publication in January 2004 it had become apparent in the aftermath of the Iraq War that Saddam Hussein had not after all possessed any WMDs – and was accused of being a whitewash of the government's role in doctoring intelligence. The shadow of the Hutton Report hangs over series three of *Spooks*, where scripts were amended to include more reference to government cover-ups and political pressure on the intelligence services. Brenton confirmed that he had been influenced by the case of David Kelly: he averred that the character of Professor Forest (Ian McDiarmid) in episode 3.2 – an academic whose career and reputation are ruined as part of an elaborate deception plot – was based on Kelly: 'We did want to have a theme of a very decent man who is put under enormous pressure and whose weakness is his own vanity.'[28]

The most extreme manifestation of the abuse of political power in *Spooks* came in the two-part opening story of series five in 2006. Against a background of political and social unrest occasioned by a fuel shortage and a series of terrorist attacks on oil depots, Section D uncovers a conspiracy by a cabal of right-wing politicians, civil servants, businessmen and media tycoons to overthrow the government and declare a state of national emergency. The conspirators argue that the United Kingdom has become ungovernable and that the institutions of democratic government are not equipped to deal with the threat posed by modern terrorism: 'Britain needs a new kind of leadership ... I wonder why we fetishize democracy so much.' They propose to introduce martial law including detention of terrorist suspects without trial and even summary execution. In opposing the conspiracy the Security Service is presented as protecting civil liberties against the extreme authoritarian tendencies of a political cabal. As Harry remarks: 'Britain will be run by an unelected committee with the silhouette of a hangman behind it.' It transpires that the conspirators themselves have engineered terrorist incidents – including a car bomb near the Houses of Parliament that nearly kills the Home Secretary and the attempted kidnapping of the Prime Minister's son in order to ensure his compliance – and that their policy of detention really amounts to rounding up their political opponents. While the idea of a conspiracy involving senior officers of MI6 and the Cabinet Secretary may seem somewhat far-fetched, the storyline nevertheless tapped into real political anxieties. Series five of *Spooks* was produced in the aftermath of the 7 July 2005 bombings in London – suicide attacks on the city's public transport network carried out by a group of radicalized British Muslims – and the subsequent controversy surrounding the Terrorism Act of 2006. This had introduced wide-ranging new anti-terror laws including new offences of encouraging and training for terrorism, although the most controversial clause – to allow detention of terror suspects for up to ninety days without charge – was blocked following a revolt by Labour backbenchers who voted with the Opposition against the legislation. The political justification offered by government ministers in support of the legislation – Home Secretary Charles Clarke expressed his frustration 'over our failure, my failure, to actually get over to all of our parliamentarians the scale of the issues involved' – at times sounded like only a watered-down version of the rhetoric of the conspirators in *Spooks*.[29]

It could be argued that the ideological trajectory of *Spooks* had seen it transformed from a sensational, if not entirely implausible, spy series to an extreme manifestation of the paranoid conspiracy thriller. In the process the role of the Security Service had shifted from an authoritarian 'defence of the realm' discourse to a liberal bulwark against totalitarianism and the suppression of civil liberties. Later series of *Spooks* gradually shifted back towards an ideological middle ground: the tension running throughout the series between the need for a robust security apparatus on the one hand and the protection of civil liberties on the other was displaced by the re-emergence of more traditional geopolitical and nation-state threats to Britain's security. Series six (2007), which features a serialized 'story arc' in the style of *24*, concerns Iran's attempt to acquire a nuclear weapon. The tension occasionally evident in the Anglo-American security relationship in previous seasons of *Spooks* comes to the fore in this series: the British government attempts to barter a new peace deal in the Middle East which involves providing technology for Iran to develop a non-military nuclear power programme but finds its good intentions sabotaged by a combination of a renegade faction in the CIA and a shadowy organization known as 'Yalta' (a reference to the Yalta Agreement of 1945) whose members include disenfranchised members of various security agencies and whose purpose is to counter what it sees as the harmful consequences of US foreign policy. From series seven (2008), *Spooks* returned to more familiar ideological terrain as the main threat to British security became a resurgent Russia. This was consistent with the deterioration of Anglo-Russian relations from around 2006 when Russia alleged that the British Secret Intelligence Service was funding human rights and other non-governmental organizations in Russia. Following the assassination of ex-KGB officer Alexander Litvinenko in London – widely believed to have been carried out by Russia's Federal Security Bureau (FSB) – MI5 described Russia as a 'very real threat' to national security and declared publicly that 'Russia is a country which is under suspicion of committing murder on British streets and it must be assumed that having done it they will do it again.'[30] Hence, the later series of *Spooks* feature Chechen terrorists carrying out bomb attacks in London (7.1), Russia engaged in cyber terrorism against Britain (7.2) and the revelation that Connie James is an FSB mole (7.8). The secret war escalates when Harry shoots and kills the FSB chief in London (7.2) in retaliation for his involvement in Adam Carter's death and the subsequent kidnapping of Harry by the FSB at the end of series seven. The story arc of series eight (2009) centres around an old Cold War operation known as 'Sugarhorse', while series ten (2010) concerns a plot by dissident factions on both sides to force Britain and Russia into open war.

The critical reception of *Spooks* was largely positive: most reviewers welcomed it as superior entertainment that deserved comparison with the best imported US dramas such as *The West Wing* and *24*. All critics commented on its topicality and slick production values, although there were differing opinions about its status as quality drama. On the one hand, there were those who felt it should not be taken too seriously: it was 'high class hokum' and 'shiny and insubstantial'.[31] Matthew Sweet (*The Independent*) called it 'a daft cop series' and asked rhetorically: 'Why do the silliest things on television come in the most serious wrappers?'[32] And Robert Shrimsley (*The Financial Times*) wrote at the end of series two that '*Spooks* is a prime example of that surprisingly rare species – high quality tosh. These are programmes which the viewer realises have stretched credibility well beyond breaking point but which rattle along at such a sharp pace as to remain hugely enjoyable.'[33] On the other hand, there were others who felt that *Spooks* exhibited a degree of intelligence and sophistication in its writing that raised it above the level of a formulaic genre series. One review in *The Guardian* called it 'a total rarity: a polished British action series that's neither tame nor predictable, and arrives complete with its own shadowy, cynical air of moral ambiguity'.[34] *The Times* found it 'a smart, well-made, human series, which manages to enthral as well as thrill. Its development of characters is excellent, too, as you would expect with people involved such as David Wolstencroft and Howard Brenton'.[35] And for James Walton (*Daily Telegraph*) it was 'unashamedly intelligent, never underestimates its viewers and provides us with the ever-reliable pleasure of being taken behind the political scenes'.[36] Furthermore, the favourable opinion persisted beyond the series' early years. Mark Lawson, writing in 2008, averred that '*Spooks* is one of the highest achievements of popular drama. This week's episode – twisting, shocking, breathlessly gripping – was typical of the smart writing, affecting performances and atmospheric direction maintained over seven seasons'.[37]

Other reviewers found *Spooks* to be more than just superior entertainment and saw it as a reflection of the *Zeitgeist*. Early in its history, *Time Out* suggested that '*Spooks* could well become essential post-September 11 viewing'.[38] The fourth series (2005) began with a two-part story about a terrorist bomb campaign in London – filmed before but broadcast after the suicide bomb attacks on the London transport network on 7 July 2005 – that prompted one critic to remark that '*Spooks* does have the handy – if not always happy – knack of being topical'.[39] Leigh Holward (*The Guardian*) similarly observed that series seven included 'a number of very near the knuckle episodes' – these included the attempted bombing of a Remembrance Day ceremony in London (7.1) and an attempt to bring about the collapse of the banking system (7.5) – and remarked: 'Catching the BBC News straight after felt like I was still watching a drama'.[40] And at the end of the last series Benji Wilson (*The Telegraph*) wrote: 'Events of the last decade have reduced the distance between the laughably implausible and the horribly real to a very thin line. *Spooks*' brilliance has been to tiptoe along that line from start to finish. It was first aired six months after 9/11, and ever since then a combination of actual events, political rhetoric and pandemic paranoia has lent it just enough credibility to survive'.[41]

Spooks had a more mixed reception within the intelligence community. On one level the series, especially in its early years, was credited with raising public awareness of MI5 and its role: it was reported that visits to the MI5 website soared following the broadcast of early episodes and that applications to join the service doubled. MI5 initially enjoyed the publicity, while at the same time pointing out that *Spooks* was 'unrealistic and far-fetched' and gave a wholly inaccurate impression of the organization and its work. The Security Service felt that the series might encourage the 'wrong sort' of recruits who were attracted by the glamour and adventure of *Spooks* rather than the mundane reality of intelligence work.[42] However, it was later reported that the death toll of characters in *Spooks* was having a deterrent effect on recruitment to MI5, especially among women, with a 'security source' quoted as saying: 'We want to attract more females but the *Spooks* programme may be having a bad effect because of the way some of the female characters have been killed off'.[43]

Real former 'spooks' lined up to ridicule the series. David Shayler, perhaps smarting from being edged out of the consultant's role, now sought to distance himself from it:

> I also advised Kudos that their proposed plotlines of violent anti-abortionists and international rightwing extremists were the stuff of liberal-left fantasy rather than any reflection of the real and vital work MI5 does in protection of our security and our democracy ... It lamely rehearses every cliche in the book, while introducing dangerous misconceptions about MI5 ... Despite all its claims, *Spooks* is just another routine drama, more Saturday teatime kids' stuff than the late-night sophistication of *Sopranos* or *24*. If the producers of the programme think they are offering verisimilitude then they've been had.[44]

Among the misconceptions promoted by the series was that MI5 officers had powers of arrest and routinely carried firearms. Shayler also suggested that *Spooks* was entirely fanciful in its portrayal of officers' lifestyles ('It is never explained in *Spooks* how officers living in central London can afford such lavish designer labels and cosmopolitan lifestyles on a salary 10% higher than a civil servant of equivalent grade') and misrepresented the working culture of the Security Service ('All the young male characters wear open-necked shirts. They wouldn't get far in the real MI5 where a tie – and a sober one at that – is *de rigeur*. I was once pulled up in my annual report for ties said to be "too loud"'). And at the start of the final season of *Spooks*, John le Carré weighed into the debate with a summary dismissal of the entire series: 'I don't watch *Spooks*. It's crap. I'm sorry. I have been in that world for almost half a century and once in it you get a notion of what constrains you and what doesn't ... The idea that people just go around shooting and killing people and so on is crazy.'[45]

There are mixed accounts of the decision to end *Spooks* after ten years – a long run by modern standards for any television drama. The *Daily Mail* – a mass-market newspaper ideologically hostile to the BBC – claimed that 'spy drama *Spooks* is being axed by the BBC. This autumn's series – the tenth – will be its last, the broadcaster confirmed yesterday'.[46] It blamed the decision on falling ratings for the final series and on the freezing of the licence fee by the Conservative–Liberal Democrat coalition government formed following the general election of 2010. The BBC for its part, however, said that 'it was producer Kudos' suggestion to end *Spooks*.'[47] This was confirmed by Jane

Featherstone: 'I feel very sad about it. It was a very difficult decision to make. But we didn't want to get to the point where the BBC said we don't really want another one, we wanted to kill it off in its prime.'[48] Whether *Spooks* was in fact killed off in its prime is a moot point. The audience ratings, which had peaked at 7.5 million early in the series' history, had fallen to an average of 5.4 million for the last series in 2011. This was attributed in the media to the last series of *Spooks* being moved from its usual Monday-evening slot to Sunday evenings during the autumn when it was in competition with ITV's ratings heavyweight *Downton Abbey* – a curious scheduling decision that is difficult to explain. However, the fact was that audiences for *Spooks* had been in steady decline since 2007, suggesting that it was not the *Downton Abbey* factor that was responsible for its demise but rather the gradual erosion that eventually takes its toll of all long-running series.[49] It should also be taken into account that the lifetime of *Spooks* had seen significant changes in viewing habits – including the advent of the online catch-up service BBC iPlayer at the end of 2007 – which made the 'overnight' viewing figures a rather less useful barometer of a programme's popularity than they had once been.

The success of *Spooks* – which was sold to international markets including the United States (where it was entitled *MI-5* as the word 'spook' is a racially offensive term), Canada, Australia, New Zealand, France, Germany, the Netherlands, Sweden, Denmark, Finland, the Czech Republic, Hungary, India and Brazil – would prompt Kudos to reorient its production strategy towards glossy, expensively produced high-end dramas such as *Hustle*, *Life on Mars*, *Ashes to Ashes*, *The Hour*, *Death in Paradise* and *The Tunnel*. It would also venture into feature film production with the romantic comedy *Miss Pettigrew Lives for a Day* (2008), a remake of Graham Greene's *Brighton Rock* (2010) and the comedy drama *Salmon Fishing in the Yemen* (2011). There had been talk for some years of a feature film of *Spooks*: this finally emerged as *Spooks: The Greater Good* in 2015. The production of the spin-off feature film was not a new idea: in the 1970s there had been films of the spy drama *Callan* (1974) and the police series *The Sweeney* – *Sweeney!* (1976) and *Sweeney 2* (1978), while more recent decades had seen big-budget Hollywood reinventions of 1960s adventure series including films of *Mission: Impossible* (1996) and its sequels, *The Avengers* (1997) and *The Saint* (1998). *Spooks: The Greater Good* was written by Jonathan Brackley and Sam Vincent, who had steered the last two seasons of the television series, and directed by Bharat Nalluri, who directed the first and last episodes of *Spooks*. The feature film budget allowed a broader canvas than the television series – it was shot on location in Berlin, Moscow, London and the Isle of Man with the studio sequences at Pinewood Studios – while the film's promotional strategy attempted to position it in relation to contemporary spy films ('*Mission: Impossible* meets *Jason Bourne*') rather than emphasizing its television origins.

Any feature film spin-off of a popular television series is invariably caught between the desire to maintain faith with audiences of the original and the imperative of appealing to a wider cinema-going public who may not necessarily be familiar with the television series. So it was with *Spooks: The Greater Good*. On the one hand, the film maintains continuity with the television series through the presence of Peter Firth as Harry Pearce and other returning cast members including Hugh Simon (data analyst Malcolm Wynn-Jones who left in series eight), Tim McInnerny (as a rehabilitated Oliver Mace now in the role of Director-General of MI5) and Lara Pulver (Erin Watts) – although the latter is murdered by a terrorist cell early in the film, a reminder of the series' legacy of killing off cast members at regular intervals. On the other hand, the film introduces a new action-lead in the form of Kit Harington, star of the internationally successful fantasy adventure series *Game of Thrones*, as Will Holloway, a 'loose cannon' recommissioned by MI5. The film's narrative is consistent with the fictional universe of *Spooks*: MI5 loses terrorist prisoner Qasim during a handover which turns out to have been engineered by the ambitious Deputy Director-General Geraldine Maltby (Jennifer Ehle) in order to discredit the current regime and ensure her own promotion. At the same time it also reflects the narratives of the Jason Bourne films as the disgraced Harry fakes his own suicide and goes 'rogue' in order to expose the conspiracy.

The US entertainment industry bible *Variety* felt that the film worked neither as an extension of the television series nor as a standalone feature in its own right and predicted that it would struggle to find a cinema audience:

> A strained, superfluous spinoff from a globally popular, now-defunct BBC spy drama that was itself something of a nostalgia exercise, Bharat Nalluri's chrome-colored thriller plays less as an organic extension of the series' universe than an all-purpose piece nominally tailored to fit the *Spooks* franchise ... Nearly four years after the show's exit from TV screens, existing

fans may deem this workmanlike return too late; for any uninitiated viewers, seeking a British take on 'Bourne' territory, it's almost certainly too late.[50]

This prediction turned out to be correct: *Spooks: The Greater Good* grossed a disappointing £4.7 million at the United Kingdom box office and seems to have disappeared without trace in America. The formula of a spy drama that combined elements of both the 'magical' and the 'existential' thriller traditions proved less successful for cinema than it had for television. On the one hand, *Spooks: The Greater Good* was too parochially British in its content to compete on equal terms with international spy adventure films such as *Mission Impossible: Rogue Nation, The Man from U.N.C.L.E* or the James Bond spectacular *Spectre* that were all released in 2015. Nor did it have any real 'names' for the box office: even Harington was only a television star. On the other hand, it lacked the credibility and intelligence of more serious spy fare such as Thomas Alfredson's film of *Tinker, Tailor, Soldier, Spy* (2011). What the film demonstrates, ultimately, is that the qualities that make a popular television drama do not necessarily translate successfully into the cinema.

Foyle's War

While *Spooks* led the way in the emergence of the new style of British Quality Television in the early 2000s, the different but equally successful *Foyle's War* (2002–15) exemplifies the persistence of residual forms.[1] *Foyle's War* was not in the *Spooks* style of high-concept, visually stylish contemporary drama: instead, it represents what might be described as a more old-fashioned mode of drama characterized by literate writing, slow pacing and understated acting. *Foyle's War* can be seen as a hybrid of two long-established and highly popular genres: the costume drama and the detective series. On the one hand, it belongs to a lineage of historical dramas focusing on the British home front during the Second World War: others included *A Family at War, Danger UXB, We'll Meet Again, No Bananas* and *Land Girls*. On the other hand, it also exemplifies the police/detective series with 'heritage' characteristics: a genre that also includes *Inspector Morse* – and its spin-offs *Lewis* and *Endeavour* – *The Ruth Rendell Mysteries, Midsomer Murders* and *Grantchester*. It was evidently a successful formula: *Foyle's War* regularly drew audiences over 8 million in the competitive Sunday-evening primetime slot. Its first series in 2002 won BAFTA's Lew Grade Audience Award and its second in 2003 was nominated for BAFTA's Best Television Drama Series.[2]

Foyle's War was conceived as a replacement for the ITV network's flagship detective series *Inspector Morse*, which had run for thirteen years between 1987 and 2000. *Inspector Morse* was based on a series of cerebral detective novels by Colin Dexter but latterly featured original scripts by writers including Anthony Minghella and Julian Mitchell. *Inspector Morse* was innovative in several respects. While it was a contemporary detective series, it adopted many of the characteristics of the period or 'heritage' drama including its leisurely pacing and highly pictorialist photography: it was particularly notable for its lovingly photographed locations in and around the dreaming spires of Oxford. Producer Kenny McBain's insistence on shooting on film and the adoption of feature-length episodes (thirty-three in total) differentiated it from other episodic police series. *Inspector Morse* was more 'cinematic' in style than other contemporary police dramas such as *The Bill* or *Rockcliffe's Babies*. Audiences warmed to the crusty, irritable, beer-loving, crossword-solving Chief Inspector Morse (John Thaw) and his down-to-earth Geordie sidekick Sergeant Lewis (Kevin Whately). *Inspector Morse* attracted audiences of 15 million and was sold to many overseas broadcasters where its production values and heritage trappings marked it as 'quality' British drama.[3]

Ever since the regular production of *Inspector Morse* ceased in 1993 – a number of one-off specials appeared more or less annually until the character's eventual demise in 'The Remorseful Day' in 2000 – the ITV network had been looking for a replacement that would match its success. *The Ruth Rendell Mysteries* (starring George Baker as the bucolic Chief Inspector Wexford) and *Midsomer Murders* (with John Nettles as Chief Inspector Barnaby residing in a perennially sunny English county with a staggeringly high murder rate) both enjoyed long runs without ever quite matching the critical acclaim of *Inspector Morse*, while the two attempts at dramatizing Ian Rankin's *Rebus* novels – initially with a miscast John Hannah, then with a more plausible Ken Stott – were both misfires. *Foyle's War* was one of many ideas pitched to ITV Network Centre as a possible *Inspector Morse* replacement: others included *The Last Detective*, starring Peter Davison and based on the 'Dangerous Davies' novels by Leslie Thomas, which ran for four series between 2003 and 2007, and *Lloyd and Hall*, starring Philip Glenister and Michelle Collins and based on the books by Jill McGown, which did not progress beyond a pilot episode. Nick Elliott, ITV's Controller of Programmes, evidently saw *Foyle's War* in the same tradition as *Inspector Morse* when he said that it was 'definitely not a war series. The war will provide the background colour for the series, in the same way Oxford did for *Inspector Morse*.'[4] A two-hour pilot episode was commissioned in 2001 from Greenlit Productions, an independent production company set up in 1998 by Jill Green, scripted by Green's husband, Anthony Horowitz, who had also devised *Midsomer Murders* and the BBC's short-lived telefantasy series *Crime Traveller*. A full series of four episodes was commissioned on the strength of the pilot, and the success of the first series meant that further

episodes were soon ordered.[5] It is evident that from the outset *Foyle's War* was
seen as a potentially long-running series: Horowitz mapped out a narrative arc
that would take the eponymous detective from 1940 until the end of the war
in 1945.[6]

Foyle's War was adroitly packaged to appeal to both the audience for detective
series and the audience for period dramas. The influence of *Inspector Morse*
is evident in the characterization of Detective Superintendent Christopher
Foyle (Michael Kitchen), a lonely widower with a son in the Royal Air Force
and a fondness for single malt whisky and fly fishing. Horowitz revealed that
he named the protagonist after the chairman of Foyles bookshop in Charing
Cross Road, where he carried out much of his research:

> I spent so much time looking at books in the history department of Foyles
> that I had the idea of altering the name of the series from *Ransome's War*, as
> I had originally intended, to *Foyle's War*, which straightaway struck me as
> much better. Not only does 'Foyle' have more of a historical resonance, but it
> fits the character much better, too. On top of that, he foils crime, doesn't he?[7]

In common with recent trends in detective fiction, including the Morse
and Rebus novels, *Foyle's War* affords more space to characterization than
'golden age' police detectives such as Freeman Wills Crofts's Inspector French,
Ngaio Marsh's Inspector Alleyn or Josephine Tey's Inspector Grant, who as
protagonists were virtually cyphers with little real personality of their own.
(For many years it was a convention of English crime fiction that while
amateur sleuths could be eccentric and highly individualistic, police detectives
were almost invariably a dull and methodical bunch.) Reviewers were warm
in their praise for Michael Kitchen's subtle and nuanced performance as Foyle,
described as one of 'calmly anguished decency' and as being 'undemonstrative
yet commanding'.[8]

All the major genre conventions of the detective series are present in
Foyle's War. Foyle himself is a detective of the old school: he is tenacious and
determined, and he achieves his results through methodical investigation
and intellectual effort. (*Foyle's War* does include some more action-oriented
sequences including a car chase in 'Among the Few' and armed robbery in
'The Funk Hole', although Foyle himself is usually an onlooker rather than
a participant in these scenes.) Foyle is notably sympathetic towards social

outsiders: he expresses compassion for a man persecuted for his homosexuality ('Among the Few') – this was a criminal offence at the time – and opposes a colour bar following the arrival of Black US troops later in the war ('Killing Time'). He has the requisite 'team' of assistants: Detective Sergeant Paul Milner (Anthony Howell) – a policeman before the war who joined the army but has been invalided out after losing a leg during the Norway campaign – and his driver Samantha Stewart (Honeysuckle Weeks). Again consistent with the modern television police series, *Foyle's War* features narrative arcs for the supporting characters: early episodes explore Milner's sense of embitterment over the disastrous Norway campaign ('The White Feather') and a recurring theme of the first half of the series is the pressure on his marriage as his wife cannot come to terms with his injury. 'Bleak Midwinter' is the obligatory episode in which Milner is suspected of murdering his wife. Samantha, or 'Sam' as she prefers, who has transferred to the police from the Motorised Transport Corps, represents modern, mobile wartime femininity: she is keen to 'do her bit' for the war effort, much to the chagrin of her father, a vicar who disapproves of the social changes brought about during the war ('It's my opinion that any sort of morality has been shot to pieces by this dreadful war').

At the same time, *Foyle's War* also draws upon the conventions of the historical drama series. There had been a cycle of popular Second World War-themed series during the 1970s, including *Colditz*, *A Family at War*, *We'll Meet Again*, *Enemy at the Door* and *Secret Army*. The genre was less visible over the next two decades, although there were important developments in the 1980s when the wartime drama focused on the experiences of women, whether incarcerated in a Japanese internment camp (BBC1's *Tenko*) or as agents of the Special Operations Executive (*Wish Me Luck*). *Tenko* might be seen as an early instance of a genre hybrid in that it could be seen both as a war drama and as a women-in-prison drama – a genre that came to prominence with the imported Australian series *Prisoner Cell Block H* and the home-grown equivalent *Bad Girls*. Similarly, the epic American mini-series *The Winds of War*, based on the massive novel by Herman Wouk, was part-war story and part-soap opera. The BBC's only major wartime drama of the 1990s was *No Bananas*, although its time-travelling wartime sitcom *Goodnight, Sweetheart* also proved extremely popular. One explanation for the success of *Foyle's War* is simply that – rather like *Spooks* in a different sort of way – the time was ripe for the revival of a genre that had been dormant for some time. Indeed, ITV followed *Foyle's War* with a number of other Second World War-themed series over the next few years including *P.O.W.* and *Island at War*.

The production discourse of *Foyle's War* – consistent with quality historical drama in general – was at pains to assert its authenticity. In the words of its executive producer Jill Green: 'We're really proud of the way they combine complex and meaty storylines with real historical detail from the war.'[9] *Foyle's War* demonstrates the meticulous attention to period in its historical references and *mise-en-scène* that characterizes the British historical drama: only a pedant would argue that Foyle's son Andrew flies the wrong mark of Spitfire for the Battle of Britain or that the GPO Film Unit did not become the Crown Film Unit until January 1941. (The pedants did complain of course – usually in the letters pages of the *Daily Telegraph* – although by and large *Foyle's War* was able to avoid the perils of anachronism that sometimes marr historical drama: Hastings was reportedly chosen as the location rather than London because the historic parts of the town had fewer visible television aerials.) Some stories make direct reference to actual wartime events. 'Casualties of War' includes a subplot about the development of the 'bouncing bomb' used in the Ruhr dams raid of May 1943 – a well-known event thanks to the perennially popular film *The Dam Busters* (1955) – while 'All Clear' refers to the Slapton Sands tragedy of April 1944 when a training exercise in preparation for D-Day was intercepted by German E-boats resulting in the deaths of 750 American servicemen (an event that was kept out of the news at the time). Actual historical individuals are absent from *Foyle's War*, although the character of Mr Jameson (Bill Patterson) in 'Enemy Fire' is clearly based on the pioneering plastic surgeon Archibald McIndoe.

Foyle's War would offer a decidedly 'revisionist' account of the historical experience of the Second World War. The dominant popular narrative of the war – disseminated through countless films beginning during the war itself such as *Fires Were Started* and *Millions Like Us* and persisting in many later popular histories and television series – is one of national unity and social cohesion: everyone working together in the common cause. It is a narrative that privileges 'the spirit of the Blitz' as a metaphor for British stoicism and endurance under bombardment – again present in wartime propaganda films such as *London Can Take It!* and *Christmas Under Fire* – and which was popularized in Winston Churchill's oft-quoted 'their Finest Hour' speech of 18 June 1940. While this view has been nuanced by historians such as Angus Calder and Paul Addison, who have drawn attention to the social and political tensions within the wartime consensus, the dominant popular narrative of the Second World War nevertheless remains that of 'the people's war'. *Foyle's War*, however, focusing as it does on the investigation of wartime crimes, challenges the idea of wartime Britain as a united and socially cohesive nation. As one reviewer, Thomas Sutcliffe (*The Independent*), observed at the end of the second series:

> What's interesting about *Foyle's War*, though (given that it's a mainstream ITV1 drama and not a David Hare play), is that it necessarily has to chip away at the national myth of solidarity if its detective is to have any crime to investigate. In most episodes, the drama is about those who aren't pulling together, but are prepared to do anything to pull ahead, whether it's looting bombed houses or running black-market frauds. It's an unusually watchable form of historical revisionism.[10]

Foyle's War dramatizes another side of the people's war – one characterized by 'larceny, breaking and entering, civil offences – and murder'.[11] Indeed, murder seems to have been particularly rife in wartime Hastings, although other crimes featured in the series include the wartime offences of black marketeering and sedition as well as more commonplace criminal behaviour such as theft, robbery and blackmail. A recurring theme of the early episodes of *Foyle's War*, especially, is the incidental references to the range of new criminal offences created under the Defence Regulations. When Foyle complains about 'twenty-six rewrites to the police war instructions' ('Among the Few') and the shortage of manpower affecting the force ('The German Woman'), he is expressing grievances felt by the British police during the war which found itself having to investigate more crimes with fewer officers.

It has been argued that the principal attraction of detective stories is that 'they make order out of chaos on our behalf; they bring moral certainty to the messiness of life'.[12] To some extent this is true of *Foyle's War*, but at the same time the series is characterized by an acute awareness of the moral dilemmas and political complications that arise from policing in wartime. This moral maze is evident from the very first episode. In 'The German Woman', Foyle investigates the particularly brutal murder of an 'alien' for which there is no shortage of suspects. Foyle maintains that the victim's nationality is of no consequence and that her murderer must be brought to book: this is not a view shared by the local people, especially after the village pub is hit by a bomb and a girl is killed ('One more dead German – who gives a damn?'). Greta Beaumont's privileged social position – she is married to a local magistrate who has used his influence to save her from internment as an enemy alien – is contrasted with the plight of another alien, an elderly Jewish music teacher called Krämer who is interned under the Defence Regulations and whose wife dies in prison. In the event the murderer turns out to be the boyfriend of Beaumont's daughter who had been conducting an affair with his future stepmother-in-law. He believes he is immune from prosecution due to the national importance of his work for the Admiralty: Foyle arrests him anyway in the full knowledge that he will probably hang for the crime. During the course of the investigation, Foyle learns that the dead woman's brother is in the *Abwehr* (German military intelligence) and that the panel that cleared her despite evidence of this possible threat to national security was chaired by Foyle's superior officer Assistant Commissioner Summers – the first (and by no means last) suggestion in the series of corruption and conspiracy in high places.

The revisionist strategy of *Foyle's War* is most evident in episodes that question – and to an extent sometimes even subvert – the popular narrative of Britain's 'Finest Hour'. 'Fifty Ships', for example, includes a subplot about a group of firemen who loot bombed houses for valuables – a narrative that entirely subverts the heroic image of firemen promoted in Humphrey Jennings's celebrated wartime tribute *Fires Were Started* (1943). In 'A War of Nerves' it turns out that an army of the members of bomb disposal unit – the unsung heroes of the Blitz whose work was dramatized in the late 1970s television series *Danger UXB* – have also been helping themselves to loot. In 'The Funk Hole' a policeman traumatized by the death of his children when a bomb hit their school kills the councillor who had forgotten to order the school's evacuation. (This episode bears some similarity to the feature film *Green for Danger* [1946], which concerns murder in a military hospital: the local postman dies on the operating table but turns out to have been killed by a nurse whose mother had died in an air raid and blamed the postman who had led the rescue team that failed to reach her in time.) *Foyle's War* even dares to suggest that not all of 'the Few' were unsullied heroes. In 'Eagle Day', for example, Foyle investigates the murder of a lecherous group captain shot by the father of a WAAF (Women's Auxiliary Air Force) who has committed suicide after he raped her. And in 'Among the Few' a Battle of Britain fighter pilot murders a girl who threatens to expose him as a homosexual: on this occasion justice takes its natural course when he is killed in action on his next sortie.

Horowitz explained the revisionism of *Foyle's War* in these terms: 'We tell true stories of what went on during the war and we are still finding new things to say.'[13] While nothing in the series was especially new to historians, some of the incidents it dramatizes might not have been familiar to the general public. In 'A Lesson for Murder', for example, Foyle's investigation leads him to a mysterious warehouse hidden away in the country and guarded by armed troops. It turns out that the warehouse is a storage facility for masses of coffins, prepared secretly in anticipation of the Blitz. As the foreman tells Foyle:

> They're preparin'. They know what's comin'. The Luftwaffe. The most powerful air force in the world. Ay, there's been a few bombs down in the south east, but that was just a taster. Soon they'll target London and there's gonna be more bodies than you can imagine. And they're gonna need coffins. Someone has to make 'em. Nobody's to know. They're worried about morale. And with good reason. You seen enough?

The 'myth' of the Blitz has become such an accepted part of the popular narrative of the war – from the GPO Film Unit's *London Can Take It!* to Channel 4's sixty-fifth anniversary drama-documentary *Blitz: London's Firestorm*, which both suggest that bombing did not seriously undermine civilian morale – that it is now overlooked that the government at the time expected the damage and casualties to be far worse. The mass production of coffins in anticipation is a fact written out of most 'Finest Hour' histories.

'The French Drop' is another example of the revisionist strategy of *Foyle's War*. This episode concerns the early history of the Special Operations Executive (SOE), the secret organization tasked with 'setting Europe ablaze'. The standard history of SOE is one of heroic agents, particularly women such as Odette Churchill and Violet Szabo whose stories were celebrated in

British cinema in the 1950s: *Odette* and *Carve Her Name with Pride*. However, there is another, less familiar history of SOE that reveals its early days to have been dogged by costly mistakes caused by a combination of incompetence, bureaucracy and petty institutional rivalries with MI6 (the Secret Intelligence Service). In 'The French Drop' Foyle investigates the apparent suicide of an SOE agent: it turns out that the agent was killed due to the incompetence of his superiors – on his first mission to France he was parachuted into a minefield – and the body (which turns out to be another person) is SOE's attempt to cover up their own mistake. Foyle is faced with the dilemma of whether to reveal the truth to the dead agent's father – who happens to be a senior officer in MI6 who regards SOE as 'a bunch of upstarts and amateurs wasting precious time and resources' – although on this occasion he is persuaded to keep his silence by SOE's 'Miss Pierce' (Ellie Haddington): 'Until now we've been fighting the war by conventional methods and we're losing, Mr Foyle. But I swear to you that one day we will make a difference.'

The historical revisionism of *Foyle's War* takes on a distinctly liberal ideological orientation. The extent to which the series' politics may be ascribed solely to the agency of Horowitz is difficult to say, although as its creator and principal writer – Horowitz wrote twenty-six of the twenty-eight episodes of *Foyle's War* – it seems reasonable to assume that its content would reflect his own preoccupations. As the series develops, it demonstrates its liberal-left politics in its generally negative representation of corporate capitalism and in its sympathy for dissidents and outsiders. Vested interests and officialdom are never to be trusted. In 'War Games', for example, Foyle investigates the activities of a company called Empire and European Foods, which has violated the Trading with the Enemy Act by making an agreement through neutral Switzerland to supply Germany with margarine after the war regardless of the outcome: its director Sir Reginald Walker asserts that 'business is bigger than war'. When it emerges that Walker's son Simon is a closet Nazi (he has a swastika and other Nazi paraphernalia hidden in the wine cellar), the episode is making a clear equation between capitalism and Fascism. Corporate profiteering also features in 'A War of Nerves', where the unscrupulous Talbot brothers, shipyard owners, have embezzled money from the government for bogus contracts and murder a member of a bomb disposal squad who discovers their secret. And 'The Funk Hole' centres on a country house hotel that serves as 'a hiding place for people with more money than conscience who want to buy their way out of the war'. The suggestion that the rich are able to lead a comfortable and pampered existence through the black market again demonstrates how *Foyle's War* seeks to highlight the persistence of social and economic inequality during the 'people's war'.

The representation of political dissidents in *Foyle's War* provides further evidence of its ideological liberalism. 'A Lesson in Murder' begins with the death in police custody of a conscientious objector who is found hanged in his cell. Foyle soon discovers that the prisoner had been abused by a custody sergeant, who had turned a hose on the naked victim. It turns out that the chairman of the committee hearing submissions from conscientious objectors is taking bribes to let people off military service: he murders a child evacuee to avoid being found out and is shot dead by his wife when she discovers what he has done. In 'A War of Nerves' Foyle is assigned to investigate the People's Convention, a real left-wing group that called for friendship with the Soviet Union and enjoyed some support among the industrial working classes. There is a subtle but significant ideological difference between Foyle's view of the Convention ('a left-wing group of intellectuals') and that of Assistant Commissioner Rose ('a group of communist agitators') which suggests that Foyle is more sympathetic to their views – or at least to their right to hold their views. It turns out that the police have planted evidence in order to try to arrest the Convention's leader for sedition.

However, this sympathy towards dissidents does not extend to Fascists. 'The White Feather' concerns a group known as the Friday Club, a society of Fascists and anti-Semites led by the charismatic Guy Spencer. Spencer is clearly modelled on Sir Oswald Mosley, leader of the British Union of Fascists who was interned in 1940. Mosley argued that Britain had been dragged into the war against Germany by Jewish interests: Guy Spencer similarly claims that the war is a Zionist conspiracy 'to overthrow Christianity and conquer the world'. In making Spencer's supporters members of the establishment – they include an MP and prominent socialites – the episode is referring quite directly to the existence of pro-German sympathies among the British upper classes during the 1930s and even during the war itself. Mosley was married to socialite Diana Mitford, whose sister Unity was a professed admirer of Hitler, while there have long been unsubstantiated rumours that the Duke of

Windsor was a Nazi sympathizer. The episode is set in May 1940 at the time of the Dunkirk evacuation and ends with Foyle listening to the famous radio broadcast about the 'little ships' by J. B. Priestley. In associating Foyle with the voice of 'friendly socialism', the episode is at pains to distance its protagonist from the views of Spencer/Mosley.[14]

Nowhere are the revisionist politics of *Foyle's War* better demonstrated than in 'Fifty Ships', which offers a distinctly jaundiced view of the 'special relationship' between Britain and the United States. Howard Paige is a ruthless, boorish American millionaire who also happens to be a leading pro-Anglophile with political influence. Paige is visiting Britain in September 1940 on a special diplomatic mission for the US government (still officially neutral at the time). He comes to Foyle's attention when he is implicated in the murder of a local drunkard. Richard Hunter was a broken man, a former engineering student cheated out of royalties for a synchromesh gear exchange that he invented but which Paige patented. When Hunter confronts Paige and asks him for money in order to send his son to university, Paige shoots and kills him. The murder is witnessed by a German spy who has been landed by U-boat but who is arrested the following morning when he tries to order a pint of beer at nine o'clock in the morning. The irony here is that the German, Meyer, proves to be a much more honourable character than Paige, the erstwhile ally: Meyer – knowing that he will be hanged as a spy – nevertheless tells the authorities of the murder he has witnessed. On this occasion, the murderer is allowed to go free. As Paige's British government minder explains:

> We need the Americans, Mr Foyle, they're the best friends we have. If we can't persuade them to provide us with arms, food, ammunition and all the rest of it, we will not survive … Whatever else he may be, Paige has been a great supporter of our country. The American Allies of England have made a huge difference. They've managed to broker a deal that will almost certainly be the start of many more. They've created a lifeline that could last the entire war.

The deal that Paige has negotiated is the transfer of fifty US destroyers to the Royal Navy in return for the long-term lease of British naval bases in the Caribbean – another example of how *Foyle's War* anchors its plots in the real historical context of the Second World War (though in fact the destroyer deal was brokered by the British Ambassador in Washington, Lord Lothian).

Although Foyle is adamant that justice has merely been deferred, the smirk on Paige's face as he leaves suggests that he knows he has, literally, got away with murder.

From the outset *Foyle's War* was a popular success. Its first episode was watched by 8.9 million viewers and its audience reached a high of just over 10 million for 'Eagle Day'. The critical reception was more lukewarm: there were no outright negative reviews but the consensus seemed to be that it was a fairly traditional sort of drama. 'I caught up a little late with *Foyle's War* after someone enthused about Michael Kitchen's performance', wrote Tom Sutcliffe (*The Independent*): he described it as an 'old school detective series' which was 'a little too dependent on whodunnit clichés'.[15] For John Preston (*Sunday Telegraph*) it was 'yet another period detective drama' that had been 'subtly assembled and richly layered with emotional nuance' but where 'there were also a great many formulaic elements'.[16] Jonathan Meades (*The Times*) admired Kitchen, whose performance was 'an unalloyed display of high art' comparable to 'a virtuoso musician' but one that was 'conducted within the depressingly broad confines of yet another detective series'.[17] A consistent criticism of *Foyle's War* was its slow narrative pace. This had never been much of a problem for *Inspector Morse* but by the time of *Foyle's War* there was evidently an expectation of more urgency in storytelling. Paul Hoggart (*The Times*) disliked what he saw as 'the longueurs of *Foyle's War*... After two slow hours of it, I was crawling up the walls, yearning for a touch of subtlety or depth'.[18] Simon Edge (*Daily Express*) felt that 'Invasion' was a 'cripplingly slow episode' and joked that 'the murder took nearly as long to happen as it did for the Americans to enter the war'.[19] And the *Radio Times* suggested that 'Bad Blood' 'played out at a pace that only a tortoise waking from hibernation would find racy'.[20]

A few reviewers addressed its credentials as history. James Walton (*Daily Telegraph*) felt that 'ITV has finally come up with something promising' – in reference to the network's 'long quest for the new Morse' – and suggested that the wartime setting of *Foyle's War* 'isn't merely a nostalgic backdrop. Instead, it becomes a clever way of adding both moral complexity and dramatic depth'.[21] But Peter Paterson (*Daily Mail*), perhaps reflecting the newspaper's editorial line, railed against the intrusion of modern political correctness into *Foyle's War*, averring that it was 'arrogant to think 21st century patterns of behaviour can be applied retrospectively to those far-off times. It's no good pretending prejudices against homosexuals or the Irish – the two issues raised – were taboos to our grandfathers as much as ourselves'.[22] John C. Murray in the Melbourne newspaper *The Age* (*Foyle's War* was shown on the ABC network in Australia) called it 'a pastiche of unevenly paced plots straight out of the Agatha Christie songbook... Its admirable recreations of the visual and social surfaces of Britain in 1940 provide some moments of keen dramatic tension and others teetering on the ludicrous, with the whole enterprise smothered in an almost parodic air of bourgeois English decency'.[23]

The reception of *Foyle's War* highlights a difference between critical culture on the one hand and popular taste on the other. Most critics seem to have been rather grudging in their acceptance of *Foyle's War*: they recognized it as 'quality' drama but in a sense it was the wrong sort of quality to become too excited about. Hence, the consensus was that it was well written and well acted but that it was a little too conventional in its content and form. But audiences evidently loved it: *Foyle's War* performed consistently well in terms of ratings (it generally drew more viewers than *Spooks*) and regularly attracted a 25–30 per cent share of the audience. In the absence of any empirical research into its audiences, any explanation for the popularity of *Foyle's War* is necessarily speculative. But it might be that a factor in its success was its hybrid nature straddling the detective series and the historical drama. Here I advance the (entirely unscientific and wholly anecdotal) viewing sample of my own parents. My father likes detective series: he enjoys *Life on Mars* and *Sherlock* as well as repeats of *Inspector Morse*, *The Adventures of Sherlock Holmes* and *Agatha Christie's Poirot* on ITV3. He is not a particular fan of costume drama: he does not watch *Downton Abbey* (which he refers to as a 'soap' – my father loathes soap operas). He regards the Holmes and Poirot series as detective shows first and foremost rather than as costume dramas. In contrast, my mother is not a devotee of police or detective series – she has no interest in Holmes or Poirot – but she enjoys costume dramas, especially *Downton Abbey* and *Call the Midwife*. *Foyle's War* is one of the few series they have watched together: the one enjoying it as a detective series, the other being more interested in its period detail and historic *mise-en-scène*.

Foyle's War did so consistently well in the ratings that it came as something of a surprise when the series was abruptly cancelled in 2007. The reasons for the decision are far from clear, although most accounts suggest that it was ITV's Director of Programmes, Simon Shaps, who was responsible.[24] Horowitz suggested the cancellation was partly an economic decision but that it also arose in part from a sense that the series was thought to appeal to the wrong demographic: 'Part of the reason was financial. *Foyle's War* is undoubtedly an expensive series to make. But senior executives also had their eye on their favourite chimera – the "yoof audience". This was certainly a mistake. As far as I can tell, our viewers are not exclusively old.'[25] With his carefully planned narrative arc for the series scuppered by the network's decision, Horowitz was obliged to miss out most of 1944, dropping planned stories connected to the Warsaw Uprising, D-Day and flying bombs, in order to conclude the series on VE-Day ('All Clear'). Yet no sooner had the last episode been broadcast than discussions began about the possible return of *Foyle's War* – prompted by the fact that the last episode secured a 28 per cent audience share with an 'overnight' audience of 7.1 million. Shaps's decision to cancel the series was overturned by his successor, Peter Fincham, who recommissioned it in 2008.[26] In the event there would be a further three series of *Foyle's War*, comprising nine episodes in total, broadcast between 2010 and 2015.

Horowitz decided to continue the narrative of *Foyle's War* into the post-war period rather than returning to fill in the 'missing' cases from the war. The formula was not changed fundamentally: *Foyle's War* continued to find 'new' or 'unknown' (to the general public at least) incidents to provide the topical background for murder mysteries. Indeed, the post-war episodes are often more directly rooted in specific aspects of the historical experience than the wartime episodes. 'The Russia House' concerns the plight of 'White Russians' who seek to avoid repatriation to the Soviet Union at the end of the war: the episode is critical of the British government's 'betrayal' on the altar of geopolitical expediency. 'The Hide' deals with a different group of political dissidents: Englishmen who fought alongside the Nazis as part of a group known as the British Free Corps (a real unit of the Waffen SS comprising several dozen British and Commonwealth prisoners of war who joined the Nazis). And 'Killing Time' addresses social prejudice rather than political duplicity as Foyle investigates a murder case involving the mother of a mixed-race baby fathered by a Black American GI who is the chief suspect when her new boyfriend is killed. The sixth series ends with Foyle retiring

from the police force and setting off for America to 'tie up some loose ends' –
understood as a reference back to his promise to bring Howard Paige to justice
at the end of 'Fifty Ships'.

The last six episodes of *Foyle's War* in 2013 and 2015 opened up a new
direction for the series by repositioning it within the political and ideological
contexts of the early Cold War period. The series' production discourse
presented this as a means of refreshing the formula. According to Horowitz:

> We were completely reinvigorated by the changes. Just when we might have
> found ourselves slipping into a formula, we had to confront a whole new set
> of rules. This was the atomic age. The country had woken up, quite late, to a
> new enemy in Stalin's Russia. Peace had proved itself to be a disappointment.
> The streets were grey, the atmosphere steely. We tend to look at the Home
> Front as being slightly rose-tinted. The new world of Foyle's (Cold) War was
> anything but.[27]

Foyle is recruited to MI5 and investigates cases such as a Soviet spy ring
operating in Britain ('The Eternity Ring') and the attempted assassination of
MI5 officer Hilda Pierce ('Elise'). As one might expect given the politics of
the wartime episodes, however, *Foyle's War* is far from a straightforward anti-
communist narrative. Instead, it works as a sort of period John le Carré in
which the Cold War background is used to explore the moral and ideological
complexities of the post-war period. The sentiment that the war has been
won but the peace might be lost pervades these episodes. They present a
political landscape in which the 'enemy' is no longer so easy to identify. The
geopolitical realignment of the immediate post-war period is the subject of
'Snowflake' in which a former SS officer is protected by MI5 for providing
them with intelligence about the Soviets: this might be read as a metaphor of
the political rehabilitation of (West) Germany after the war as former enemies
became allies in the new Cold War landscape. 'The Cage' concerns Foyle's
investigation into the death in custody of several Soviet prisoners: the plot
bears some parallel with the true-life case of Robin 'Twin Eye' Stephens who
was tried (and acquitted) for the mistreatment of German prisoners after the
war. Like the wartime episodes, actual historical incidents are used for topical
background, including the Nuremberg war crimes trials ('High Castle') and
the armed campaign against the British occupation of Palestine ('Trespass').

The transformation of *Foyle's War* into a period spy drama demonstrates the fluidity between detective and spy fiction. The work of spy writers such as John le Carré, Anthony Price and Ted Allbeury straddles the genres insofar as the plot structure of their novels is often based on investigation and deduction in contrast to the action-based narratives of the sensational thriller school. Reviewers generally felt that the post-war stories had successfully refreshed *Foyle's War*. Gerard O'Donovan (*Daily Telegraph*) averred that 'this felt more like a series at the height of its powers rather than an invitation to bid farewell to dear old Christopher Foyle, that most decent and understated wartime copper who latterly morphed so successfully into MI5's only reliable chap in the Cold War's early days'. He went on:

> The series had a renewed vigour of late. For many – myself included –Foyle's bleak Cold War escapades rekindled a flagging interest. Creator Anthony Horowitz's decision to root the postwar stories in real life cases brought new grit and relevance, exploring the early nuclear arms race and resurgent anti-semitism in recent episodes. This episode juggled wartime and postwar eras, echoing a scandal in which young British agents were sent to certain death in occupied Europe by a Special Operations Executive unwilling to admit its network had been compromised, while a subplot involving spivs and police corruption kept bringing us back to 1946.[28]

In America, where *Foyle's War* was shown by the free-to-air Public Broadcasting Service (PBS), the Cold War episodes seem to have been more successful than the wartime stories. Mike Hale (*New York Times*) felt that it was 'one of the best cop shows on television ... This grayer, chillier *Foyle's War* may not suit everyone, but it's admirable, and a bit remarkable, that Mr Horowitz has moved the series forward in a way that makes historical and dramatic sense.'[29] *Foyle's War* found a particular champion in Mary McNamara of the *Los Angeles Times*, who called it 'one of television's masterpieces'.[30] On another occasion, McNamara averred that it was 'one of the best shows of the century ... *Foyle's War* is the Mona Lisa of television: small, quiet, utterly hypnotic and mysteriously perfect'.[31]

Foyle's War eventually came to an end in 2015: its second cancellation was evidently rather more consensual than the first. Horowitz said: 'It had to come to an end sometime. We went from 1940 all the way to 1947 – and I told countless stories about the war. I felt that there were no more true stories to tell about that period, I'd sort of covered pretty much every angle.'[32] Audiences had slipped from an average of 7.7 million for the seventh series in 2013 to 5.8 million for the eighth series in 2015 (though this still represented around a 20 per cent audience share). Nevertheless, *Foyle's War* had succeeded in providing the *Inspector Morse* replacement that ITV had wanted – it matched the ratings for *Lewis*, the official sequel to *Inspector Morse*, which ran from 2006 to 2015 – and in the process had demonstrated that the heritage detective drama still had a place even in the era of the new high-concept style of television fiction exemplified by *Spooks*, *Hustle* and *Life on Mars*.

3

Hustle

Hustle (2004–12) – a glossy, contemporary drama focusing on a group of 'good' con artists – was very much a stable mate of *Spooks*.[1] It was produced by Kudos Film and Television Productions for the BBC, and several of the same production team – including Bharat Nalluri (credited as 'executive director' of *Hustle*), writer Matthew Graham and executive producers Jane Featherstone and Simon Crawford Collins – had also worked on *Spooks*. Kudos brought in Tony Jordan, co-creator of the BBC's flagship weekday soap opera *EastEnders*, to develop Nalluri's original idea into a workable format. *Hustle* ran for eight series (forty-eight episodes) over nine years and consistently averaged around 6 million viewers. On the face of it, *Hustle* was the antithesis of serious television drama: there is no pretence of social or even psychological realism in the series, where each episode shows the gang setting up an unsuspecting 'mark' and pulling off an elaborately planned and executed confidence trick. At the same time, however, *Hustle* was emphatically 'high-concept' drama: high production values, intricate plotting, a glossy visual style and a formula that remained unchanged over its eight series.

The production ecology of *Hustle* differed from *Spooks* in a number of key respects. Although successful in terms of international sales, *Spooks* never really made much impact in the United States where it was shown on the cable network A&E – perhaps because it was saddled with the meaningless (for American audiences at least) title of *MI: 5*. In contrast, there is much evidence to suggest that from the outset *Hustle* gravitated towards America. The casting of Robert Vaughn as the veteran 'grifter' Albert Stroller brought a name familiar to American viewers: Vaughn had appeared in films including *The Magnificent Seven* and *Bullitt* and was best known for playing Napoleon Solo in 1960s secret agent series *The Man from U.N.C.L.E.* From its third series in 2006, *Hustle* was

produced in association with the American cable network AMC, a division
of Rainbow Media, a twenty-four-hour movie channel which also broadcast
some original drama content. According to AMC Vice-President Ron Sorcher:
'*Hustle* is the epitome of cinematic cool, a tribute to the great heist and caper
films of the past, which fits perfectly within our slot of original programs.'[2] The
co-production model was becoming increasingly common at the time: ITV's
Hornblower (1998–2003) had been produced in association with the A&E
network, and *Torchwood: Miracle Day* in 2011 – the last series of the *Doctor
Who* spin-off *Torchwood* – was a co-production between the BBC and cable
channel Starz. The extent of the additional funding provided by the American
partner is not clear – if it followed the model of other co-productions between
British broadcasters and US cable networks, it is likely that the BBC was still
the largest contributor – though it allowed the fourth series to include locations
in Los Angeles and Las Vegas.

The production discourse of *Hustle* sought to position it as a 'high-concept'
drama: to this extent it looked to promote the series' quality as entertainment
and – significantly given its subject matter could have laid it open to accusations
of glamourizing crime – it disavowed any suggestion of serious intent. In fact,
rarely has there been a television drama that was at such pains to assert that
it was not meant to be taken seriously. According to Tony Jordan: 'We are not
trying to preach to you or show you how wonderful the emergency services
are. We're just going to entertain you. Sod the gritty realism. We're going to
make you grin.'[3] The publicity materials made much of the fact that *Hustle* was
from the same stable as *Spooks*, although in fact there are significant differences
between the two series. *Spooks*, at the beginning at least, had tried to suggest
that it was based in some kind of reality but there was no such pretence with
Hustle. In the same interview Jordan averred that he did not meet any real con
artists while writing the scripts: 'They are not that easy to find. The only way
that I could meet a real-life 21st century long con player was to visit the HQ of
one of the banks or the CEO of Enron. They are all within the establishment
these days.'[4]

Neither the content nor the genre conventions of *Hustle* were particularly
original. The tradition of the 'caper' or heist movie extends back to Jules
Dassin's classic *Rififi* (1955) but really emerged in the 1960s with a cycle of
films including *Ocean's 11*, *Topkapi*, *Gambit*, *The Thomas Crown Affair* and

The Italian Job. A television series entitled *The Rogues* ran for one season on the American NBC network in 1964–65: it starred David Niven, Charles Boyer and Gig Young as three con artists who would selectively set up a 'mark' provided the intended target was wealthy and unscrupulous. The moral imperative that the victim of the con should in some sense 'deserve' to be conned would be carried forward into *Hustle*. The genre was lent a degree of cultural respectability by *The Sting* (1973), which won the Academy Award for Best Picture, and *The Grifters* (1990). *Hustle* acknowledges both those films by describing its con artists as 'grifters', while references to *The Sting* recur throughout the series from the very first episode when one of the team is introduced as 'Mr Redford' (Robert Redford starred in *The Sting* alongside Paul Newman). The film acknowledged as the model for *Hustle* was *Ocean's Eleven* (2001), director Steven Soderbergh's stylish remake of the original 'Rat Pack' film of 1960 in which a group of crooks and conmen led by Danny Ocean (George Clooney) succeed in robbing three Las Vegas casinos simultaneously: unlike the original film – starring Frank Sinatra and his 'Rat Pack' cronies Dean Martin, Peter Lawford and Sammy Davis Jr – the gang in the remake get away with the loot (in 1960 the Hollywood Production Code was still strong enough to insist that 'crime does not pay': hence, the stolen cash ends up being accidentally cremated in a funeral parlour). According to Jane Featherstone: '*Ocean's Eleven* was on around the time Bharat and I first spoke, and I think it helped to inspire us, but really we took our inspiration from a whole catalogue of movies and books – we wanted to make something that had the energy, verve, style and pure entertainment value of those sorts of films.'[5]

The content and style of *Hustle* therefore invite comparison with the long tradition of 'caper' movies in Hollywood and British cinema. It might also be related to television series such as *Mission: Impossible* and *The A-Team*. *Mission: Impossible* (1966–73) had featured a secret task force assigned to undertake special assignments that usually involved bringing off some form of elaborately conceived deception: each episode focused on the planning and execution of the mission and would typically involve something going wrong that required the group to adapt their plan and improvise a solution. *The A-Team* (1983–87) featured a disavowed US Army special forces unit who put their military skills to use as mercenaries: a specific link to *Hustle* was that Robert Vaughn played General Stockwell in later episodes. *Mission: Impossible* and (less successfully) *The A-Team* were both turned into feature films, in 1996 and 2008, with *Mission: Impossible* becoming a successful franchise extending for over twenty years. There is a general link between *Hustle* and these two series in the motif of the tight-knit team who all bring their specialist skills to bear in planning and carrying out an elaborate confidence trick against an unsuspecting target. Michael Stone – aka 'Mickey Bricks' (Adrian Lester) – is the group's leader and chief strategist: he is the equivalent of Peter Graves's Jim Phelps in *Mission: Impossible* and George Peppard's Hannibal Smith in *The A-Team*. As in *Mission: Impossible* and *The A-Team*, all the members of the group in *Hustle* have their specific roles: Albert (Vaughn) is the 'roper' who identifies potential marks and draws them in, Stacey (Jaime Murray) is the 'lure' who uses her glamour and sexuality to ensnare victims and Ash (Robert Glenister) is the 'fixer' responsible for finding the locations and props necessary to make the con look convincing. There are quite close parallels between the characters of Stacey and Cinnamon Carter (Barbara Bain) and between Ash and technical expert Barney (Greg Morris) in *Mission: Impossible*, while Danny Blue (Marc Warren) – usually the one to draw the short straw for the more humiliating and embarrassing situations – is the series' equivalent of 'Howling Mad' Murdock (Dwight Schultz) in *The A-Team*. Adrian Lester was absent for the fourth series in 2007 – this was explained by suggesting that Danny has gone to Australia to sell the Sydney Opera House – but returned for later series. Warren and Murray left at the end of series four: their roles were taken by Matt Di Angelo and Kelly Adams as brother-and-sister con artists Sean and Emma Kennedy.

Hustle is the very definition of a generic or formula drama: the basic narrative of each episode is essentially the same with the main variations being the identity of the 'mark' and the method of the con. In this context it is useful to adapt Umberto Eco's famous structuralist analysis of Ian Fleming's James Bond novels to an analysis of *Hustle*. Eco compared the Bond stories to a game of chess in which the characters all make pre-determined 'moves': hence, Bond is assigned to a mission by 'M', head of the British Secret Service; Bond travels to an overseas destination where he meets allies and the girl (who is usually in the service of the villain); Bond gives first check to the villain, or the villain gives first check to Bond; Bond seduces the girl and in so doing detaches her from the villain's service; Bond and the girl are captured by the villain; the villain lectures Bond on the nature of power and tortures him in some cruel and ingenious way, but Bond escapes (often with the girl's help) and vanquishes the villain. 'The reader's pleasure consists of finding himself immersed in a game of which he knows the pieces and the rules – and perhaps the outcome – drawing pleasure simply from the minimal variations by which the victor realises his objective,' Eco writes. 'The novels of Fleming,' he went on, 'exploit in exemplary measure that element of foregone play which is typical of the escape machine geared to the entertainment of the masses.'[6]

So it is with *Hustle*. Each episode follows the team as they plan and execute a 'long con' – an elaborately plotted deception directed against a particular 'mark' with the aim of relieving them of money or valuables. Each member of the team plays out their assigned role and like the characters in the Bond novels acts in a pre determined way. There are references throughout to the nature and ethics of 'grifting' – a repeated mantra of the series is that 'you can't cheat an honest man' – and a focus on the methods and techniques of the con artist. Among the repeated motifs are the 'angel scam' (conning the victim into investing in a non-existent feature film) and 'the wire' (a variation of the con in *The Sting* in which the team convinces their mark that they are able to delay the flow of information – for example into a bank or the Stock Exchange – which allows them to profit from advance knowledge of currency fluctuations or share prices). Other favourite cons include selling fake artwork and collectibles (rare stamps, comic books) and property scams (such as selling the London Eye and the 'Hollywood' sign). Each episode would also feature a number of 'short cons' which the team carry out on unsuspecting members of the public: these often involve distraction and pick-pocketing to procure the necessary IDs to gain access to locations necessary for the 'long con' (an office in a particular building for example). At some point it would usually appear either that the con has been discovered or that something else has gone wrong: but it then transpires that the contingency has been anticipated and a flashback reveals certain plot points that had been withheld. This narrative device had been used in *The Sting* and *Ocean's Eleven*: it is integral to the formula of *Hustle* whose writers had to devise increasingly imaginative situations as the series went on. In this sense each episode of *Hustle* is itself a sort of confidence trick played on the spectator, whose pleasure arises in large measure from trying to second-guess the writers as to what the 'twist' will be.

One episode may suffice to demonstrate both the narrative formula of *Hustle* and the limited extent of variation that it allows. 'Albert's Challenge' (3.2) – like *Spooks* episodes of *Hustle* do not have individual titles but titles have been assigned on the BBC's website – is a text-book exercise in how to play both the long con and the short con: it differs from most other episodes in the identity of the mark. An undercurrent throughout the first two series of *Hustle* is the tension between Mickey and Danny, who challenges Mickey's automatic right to be leader of the group. At a loose end as they wait for confirmation that their latest mark has taken the bait, the tension spills over into an argument. Albert suggests deciding the issue once and for all through something known as 'Henderson's Challenge' – a reference to an American grifter in New York in the 1920s. Mickey and Danny are to be dropped off in the centre of London at 12 noon with nothing (not even any clothes) and whoever has acquired the most in cash and valuables by six o'clock will be deemed the winner. Danny – a highly accomplished short con artist – enacts a number of scams including 'the badger' (which involves him pimping Stacey who pretends to be a prostitute) and selling a fake river cruise to unsuspecting tourists. Mickey – acknowledged as a master of the long con – reasons that he cannot beat Danny at his own game so opts to put all his eggs in one basket by setting up just one mark ('I've got one I've had in mind for a while'). Danny, who by the middle of the afternoon has 'earned' several thousand pounds, is suspicious that Mickey seems to be too relaxed: he follows Mickey and – working out that Mickey is carrying out an art con (selling a fake collectible stamp) – tries to scupper Mickey's con by buying the fake himself from the forger. It turns out of course that Danny himself is the mark that Mickey has been setting up and has himself fallen for the con ('The sweetest con of all is to con another grifter'). The lesson has been learnt and Mickey and Danny have resolved their differences. Albert draws the moral: 'You must recognize each other's strengths and not be threatened by them.' Yet there is still another twist: a flashback reveals that Albert had made a wager with Stacey and Ash that he could get Mickey and Danny naked in the centre of London and it turns out that he invented the whole idea of 'Henderson's Challenge' just in order to achieve this.

Other aspects of the *Hustle* formula are to be found in its formal conventions. *Hustle* is shot in a similar 'house style' to *Spooks* – several of the directors worked on both series – and employs the full range of elliptical storytelling devices including ramping, time-lapse photography and split-screen. But it takes narrational sophistication further with a number of formal innovations. *Hustle* frequently breaks the so-called 'fourth wall' by having characters (usually Mickey) address the audience directly: these moments range from a subtle wink or smile towards the camera as the con takes shape to a monologue that offers a commentary on the action so far. The device has the effect of detaching the actors from their characters and reminding the audience that they are playing out roles. The breaking of the fourth wall is a device associated with the experimental theatre of Berthold Brecht, but it has been relatively rare in popular television (as opposed to 'authored' dramas such as those of Dennis Potter): the American detective/romantic comedy series *Moonlighting* and – to a lesser extent – the BBC's *Lovejoy* are among the popular dramas that have employed this technique. This is not to suggest that *Hustle* should be claimed as Brechtian television in the manner of something like Potter's *Pennies from Heaven* or *The Singing Detective*: but what it does demonstrate, perhaps, is how the high-concept drama incorporates some aspects of more progressive forms into its own conventions. Another non-naturalistic technique employed extensively in *Hustle* is what for want of a better term has been called 'stop time': moments where some of the scene appears 'frozen' in time but where some characters are still able to move and talk. This technique was used from the very first episode where the team explains the nature of the con artist's work while their mark is frozen in the act of pouring coffee: 'You see the first rule of the con ... Is you can't cheat an honest man ... The only way this thing works is if you want something for nothing ... So we give you nothing for something.'

Another device that *Hustle* employs is the inclusion of fantasy sequences – especially song-and-dance numbers – which again might draw comparison with the work of Dennis Potter: *Pennies from Heaven* and *The Singing Detective* both included such fantasy moments. In *Hustle* these usually take the form of a pastiche of particular cinematic modes and styles related to the nature of the con: hence, a movie investment scam involves the cast performing a song-and-dance number in the style of a classic Hollywood musical (1.2), while a 'silent movie' sequence of flickering black-and-white images is used when Danny and Stacey pull off an old con trick from the 1920s that involves selling a dog to a bartender (1.4). A later episode trades upon Kelly Adams's resemblance to pop star Kylie Minogue by having her perform Kylie's 'Can't Get You Out of My Head' in order to close a con against a mark who wants to hire the singer for a private party (6.1). Such inserts again demonstrate how *Hustle* employs non-naturalistic devices to highlight its own artifice. To this end it represents a significant shift away from the classic realist conventions of more conventional dramas. Sometimes the fantasy sequences are integrated into the narrative. 'A Bollywood Dream' (3.4) involves the team working the 'angel scam', this time against Kulvinder Samar, an amoral businessman who runs a series of sweatshops producing counterfeit clothes who mistreats his employees (it is a convention of *Hustle* that the mark should be a thoroughly deplorable individual: this can be seen as a strategy of ideological legitimation for a series in which the protagonists are themselves criminals). Samar rumbles the con but then suffers short-term memory loss following a car crash. The team realizes this gives them a unique opportunity of playing the same con on the same mark again, but Samar is now a changed man as a consequence of the accident who is horrified when he sees the conditions in his factory and resolves to give his wealth to charity. His visit to the set of the fake Bollywood movie (Samar had wanted to be an actor as a young man but his ambitions were thwarted by his father) is the cue for a Bollywood-style performance number in which Samar reveals that he has seen through the scam again and the team decides that as his personality has changed so completely they cannot go through with the con. As Mickey remarks: 'We're about to break our code and con a good man ... We walk away.'

It will be clear that *Hustle* is a highly self-referential text: it takes every opportunity to flaunt its awareness of its own status as fiction. This is also apparent in the series' constant allusions to popular film and television. This is not unique to *Hustle* of course – it had been a regular feature of *Moonlighting* and had become a stock-in-trade of American telefantasy series such as *Buffy the Vampire Slayer* and *The New Adventures of Robin Hood* – but it is especially prominent in *Hustle*. In particular, the series refers to caper and con-artist films: examples include the gang resurrecting the old con trick known as 'the wire' ('The last time I saw that was in *The Sting*') (1.6) and Mickey getting into a film-recording studio by pretending to be the producer of *Ocean's Thirteen* (3.4). The series employs in-jokes which assume knowledge of popular culture on the part of audiences. For example, the casting of Richard Chamberlain as a guest star in one episode prompts references to Dr Kildaire (3.3) – Chamberlain had starred in the popular medical drama series of *Dr Kildaire* in the 1960s – while the final episode acknowledges Robert Vaughn's presence when Danny, returning to help the gang pull off their last big con before they retire, suggests forming a new group and calling themselves 'the magnificent seven' (8.6).

While such allusions may be seen as little more than audience-pleasing moments for those viewers who 'get' the references, however, *Hustle* is rather more sophisticated in its mobilization of popular film and television than most other 'postmodern' television series. It may be argued that allusions – especially to cinema – are integrated into the narrative fabric of the series. Take the very first episode as an example. Mickey, newly released from prison, is getting his old crew back together to pull off 'one last con' when they are interrupted by Danny, who tries to blag his way into the gang. Mickey asks Danny if he has seen *The Sting*: Danny replies that he has not. Mickey initially shows Danny the door but later accepts him, although as yet he does not trust him. Danny is picked up by the police and is offered a deal if he will testify against the others (Mickey is under police surveillance: it has been established that it 'is a matter of personal pride to every fraud investigator in the country to be the one who nails him'). As the gang is about to pull off the con, their hotel room is raided by police officers: in the ensuing commotion Mickey is shot and apparently killed by DI De Palma. De Palma then repeats his offer to Danny to let him off if he provides evidence against the rest of the gang: at this point Danny demonstrates his true colours through his loyalty to the gang ('I ain't no grass'). It then turns out that De Palma is not a policeman after all but another con artist who has taken the place of the real detective (whose ID has been stolen and changed) in order to test Danny. Mickey's shooting has been faked, just as the ending of *The Sting* has the conmen apparently shot and killed by the Feds. The whole deception arises from the fact that Danny has not seen *The Sting* and therefore does not recognize the set-up.

Hustle is the perfect exemplar of what, following David Buxton, may be termed the 'pop series'. For Buxton the 'pop series' – exemplified by 1960s adventure series such as *Danger Man, The Prisoner, The Avengers* and *The Man from U.N.C.L.E.* – is characterized by its glossy surface, the prominence it affords to the trappings of consumerism and its complete disavowal of psychological realism in its plotting and characterization: it differs from what

he describes as the 'human nature series' – a term that encompasses different
genres including the Western (*Gunsmoke*, *Bonanza*), the law-and-order police
series (*The Untouchables*, *The FBI*) and even science fiction (*Star Trek*) – which
privileges 'realistic' content and character behaviour. Buxton suggests that the
pop series was a product of the ideological and cultural conditions of the 1960s:

> The moment of pop has come and gone. It is impossible to recreate the
> excitement provoked by the emergence of a modern consumer society,
> the seduction exercised by pleasingly designed objects, the overwhelming
> presence of a greater aesthetic sensibility. But pop has passed into our
> common-sense expectations of the worlds of advertising, fashion, music
> and television and foreshadowed many of the characteristics of the present
> 'postmodern' vision of the world.[7]

It seems to me, however, that an argument can be made for the persistence
of the pop series beyond the 1960s: in particular, the productions of Kudos –
Spooks and *Hustle* (and perhaps to a lesser extent *Ashes to Ashes*) – exemplify
the pop style and aesthetic. The first series of *Hustle* does demonstrate some
residual aspects of the human nature series in the subplot of Mickey's wife
seeking a divorce and some comments on the loneliness of the con artist
('If you want to be a grifter, don't have anything in your life you can't walk
away from in a second'), but these traces of psychological realism have all but
disappeared by the start of the second series. Indeed, Adrian Lester – hitherto
known as a stage rather than a television actor – gave the series' retreat from
psychological realism as his reason for taking a sabbatical during the fourth
series saying that it had 'just got a little bit too "light"'.[8]

Yet beneath the lightness of *Hustle* it might be that there is evidence of
an ideological import of sorts. In his analysis of the contemporaneous series
drama *Hotel Babylon* (2006–09) – produced by Carnival Films for the BBC
and sharing a number of the same stylistic features as *Hustle* – Stephen Harper
argues that it uses the generic formula of the hotel drama in order to 'address
"social issues" within a broadly liberal perspective'.[9] The same might be said of
Hustle. The protagonists may themselves be crooks but they are 'good' crooks
in contrast to their marks who are characterized in wholly negative terms:
unscrupulous businessmen, greedy bankers, corrupt judges, bent policemen,
gangsters, people traffickers, arms dealers, cheating politicians, property
developers, fraudsters and about every other favourite stock villain of popular

drama. Many of the targets are outright villains: an unscrupulous casino owner who has Albert viciously beaten up for cheating at cards (1.2), a ruthless porn baron (4.2) or a Turkish businessman who has murdered his way to the top (8.8). Others are con artists themselves who do not follow the same moral code as the grafters: the owner of a nursing home who swindles the residents out of their property (4.3) or the charity hostess who keeps most of the money raised through her charitable events to spend on herself (4.4). This can be seen as a strategy by which Hustle establishes moral and ideological legitimation for the gang: all the villains deserve to be conned. In this sense *Hustle* is a highly manipulative series: it 'cons' the audience into accepting a black-and-white morality while dazzling us with its glossy aesthetic and narrational tricks that serve to distract our attention from questioning the ambivalence of our identification with a gang of crooks.

The underlying ideology of *Hustle* might be understood in terms of the contrast between good capitalism and bad capitalism. All the marks are wealthy (it is a matter of principle for the gang that they never con anyone who cannot afford it) but they are also greedy: their wealth has been acquired through either sharp practice or outright criminality. They also tend to be associated with vested interests and the establishment. The representation of corporate capitalism as parasitic and exploitative has been a familiar theme of popular fiction and *Hustle* is no exception: scratch a wealthy man (or woman) to find a crook. Perhaps the closest that the series ever comes to social comment is in the first episode of series five where Mickey returns to London to find the gang has disbanded following the credit crunch of 2008: 'Wherever you look, there's misery. The recession is affecting ordinary people. The rich keep getting richer.' In contrast, Mickey and his gang are on the side of the 'little people': they represent a modern variation on the Robin Hood myth insofar as they rob from the rich – and occasionally help the poor. When Ash masquerades as a cleaner to gain access to an office building, for example, he is sympathetic to the plight of the underpaid workers and ensures that they also benefit from the proceeds of the con (5.4). *Hustle* suggests that its protagonists possess an underlying sense of morality – expressed in terms of something known as 'the grifters' code' – that makes them more honourable than their victims. It is a point of honour that they never set out to con anyone who does not deserve it. And to reinforce the gang's credentials as 'good' con artists there are episodes in which they act not for personal gain but rather from a philanthropic impulse: a property con to save a community centre from closure (3.8) or to con an unscrupulous football agent in order to bail out a local club that has gone bust (7.5).

All that said reviewers tended not to find any particular ideological import in *Hustle*: indeed, the series' disavowal of seriousness was evidently a plus factor for most critics who welcomed it in the terms the production discourse would have welcomed as a piece of fun entertainment. Jasper Rees (*The Times*) felt that it exhibited 'the snap and style of a series that has been cryogenically frozen since the 1960s and brought back to life … The wonderfully absurd result is a drama series that takes itself far less seriously than almost anything since *The Persuaders*'.[10] Gerard O'Donovan (*Daily Telegraph*) thought it was 'one exceptionally ambitious TV exercise … Nobody could argue that *Hustle* aspires to being anything other than escapist entertainment. As with *Spooks*, and a long line of glossy packages going all the way back to *The Avengers*, it gets its hooks into you through the glamour of the characters, not the plot'.[11] Jay Rayner (*The Guardian*) found it 'defiantly high-concept, tightly plotted, knowing stuff. In short, *Hustle* is a laugh, slick, glossy, and smart certainly, but a laugh all the same. Social realism it ain't'.[12] For James Walton (*Daily Telegraph*) the series' success was based on its pulling off a confidence trick on viewers: 'I think the main reason is that the programme goes about its work with such staggering and ultimately charming conviction that the audience become collaborators – or even marks – in the whole cheerfully slick confection.'[13] For Thomas Sutcliffe (*The Independent*): 'Such was the swagger and assurance that you probably didn't notice that the yarn it was spinning didn't make sense until it had taken your time and run off.'[14] The same point was echoed by Joe Joseph (*The Times*): '*Hustle* is an engaging, well-acted, snappily directed drama. It moves at a brisk enough pace for you not to notice (or, at least, not to mind too much) all the convenient coincidences and improbabilities until you reach the sting's denouement. *Hustle* is a tight hour of drama, sleekly edited, flatteringly lit, and stylishly executed.'[15] And Andrew Billen (*The Times*) suggested that '*Hustle* may be set in the present but it exists in a retro fantasy' and that it 'has an expect-the-unexpected predictability but is still slick tosh that chimes with a hoax-heavy climate.'[16]

There were a few dissenting voices. The critics who were less keen on *Hustle* tended to dismiss it as trivial and unsubstantial: this probably suggests the prevalence of a discourse of social and psychological realism that struggled to contextualize a series like *Hustle*. Fiona Sturges (*The Independent*) evidently felt that the idea was wearing thin as early as the second series: 'If *Hustle* didn't try so hard, you could perhaps love it more. It's largely due to the flashy editing that the series is looking dated just a year after it arrived on our screens.'[17] By its fifth series, the *Daily Telegraph* felt that it was 'definitely showing signs of wear'.[18] And for the *Metro*:

> The fact that *Hustle* has conned its way to a fourth series is a triumph of style over substance. With plots thinner than Nicole Richie and a bunch of characters cobbled together from crime drama clichés, this tale of supposedly loveable grifters, for all its glossy sheen, feels like a shabby rip-off ... *Hustle* wants to be *The Grifters* but it's so wide of the mark, it's criminal. [19]

In one particular respect, however, *Hustle* has been seen as a significant landmark in popular television. In casting Adrian Lester – a black British actor who had won acclaim for his performance as *Henry V* at the National Theatre in 2003 – *Hustle* was not setting out to make a statement about race: indeed, its own production discourse distanced it from social-issue drama at every opportunity. Nevertheless, it would be fair to say that even in the twenty-first century it is rare to have a mainstream popular drama in Britain with a black (or for that matter any non-white) actor in the leading role. British television has historically been colour blind: contemporary drama has only rarely reflected the social and ethnic diversity of British society following the mass immigration from the Commonwealth after the Second World War. Stephen Bourne, for example, has drawn attention to the marginalization of black characters – and the consequent lack of opportunities for black actors – in soaps and other television dramas.[20] There have been some exceptions of course: the 1960s adventure series *Department S* cast a black actor (Dennis Alba Peters) in an authority role as the secret service chief and more recently there have been important BAME (Black, Asian, Minority Ethnic) characters in *EastEnders* and medical dramas such as *Casualty* and *Holby City*. Nevertheless, it is still often the case that casting black actors is either a means of signposting a social problem drama or is merely a form of cultural tokenism. The issue of 'colour blind' casting arose in relation to the casting of a black actress (Sophie Okonedo) as Nancy in Sarah Phelps's adaptation of *Oliver Twist* for the BBC in 2007: the series' production discourse sought to 'justify' this historically on the grounds that there were thousands of black immigrants in the working-class areas of Victorian London, whereas BAME campaigners pointed out in response that as *Oliver Twist* was a work of fiction, the very idea that Okonedo's casting needed justification contributed to a racist discourse as it implied her ethnicity was more of a determinant for playing the role than her acting ability.[21]

However, *Hustle* might be seen to represent something different. An article in *Black Film Maker* suggested that *Hustle* (along with *55 Degrees North* which was broadcast on BBC1 in 2004) broke new ground by placing a black character at the centre of the narrative:

> The casting of Robert Vaughn is a real coup for the programme makers and helps to give *Hustle* its retro feel. The show can also boast having the coolest opening credits on British television. But what really makes *Hustle* stand out is Adrian Lester's ice cool portrayal of Mickey. The kind of thief who gains respect from police and criminals alike because he is the best in the business. Making him black gives the programme its added edge and, in a way, its mystery. You learn little about his past and you are never quite sure exactly what drives him on but watching Mickey at work is like watching a master craftsman, you feel it's a kind of privilege to simply see him strut his stuff even if you might be burned in the end.
>
> The show makes you feel that you are watching someone new and different and in a way you are. Lester plays a black character who is suave and sophisticated, a kind of criminal aristocrat who you feel, despite his recent release from prison, will somehow always manage to be one step ahead of the law. But also someone who has his own very own moral code, one that may seem odd to others but to Mickey nevertheless makes perfect sense. Lester's masterful portrayal of this prince amongst thieves has turned *Hustle* into a sure fire success.[22]

On one level it stands as an indictment of the institutional conservatism of British television that it took until 2004 for a black actor to be cast in the lead in a popular primetime drama. Yet on another level it is perhaps an indication that some progress has been made insofar as Lester's casting seems to have had nothing to do with his ethnicity: *Hustle* is literally colour blind insofar as race is not an issue. This can be seen in the fact that in the forty-two episodes of *Hustle* in which he appears, there is not a single reference to Mickey being black.

Life on Mars

'My name is Sam Tyler. I had an accident and I woke up in 1973. Am I mad, in a coma, or back in time? Whatever's happened it's like I've landed on a different planet. Now maybe if I can work out the reason, I can get home.' *Life on Mars* (2006–7) always had 'cult' written all over it. Take a staple genre of television drama, the police series, and add a twist by crossing it with the time-displacement narrative of American telefantasy series such as *Quantum Leap* and *Sliders*. Serve this with a heady dose of nostalgia for British popular culture of the 1970s, including its fashions, music and television. Hide away some tantalizing hints as to what it all means but leave the text open-ended like cult series such as *The Prisoner* and *Twin Peaks*. And leave audiences wanting more by limiting it to only sixteen episodes. It was evidently a successful formula: *Life on Mars* regularly drew weekday audiences around 7 million and won a host of television awards including two International Emmy Awards (2006 and 2008) – the television industry's equivalent of the Oscars – BAFTA's Pioneer Award (2006) and the Broadcasting Press Guild Award for Best Drama Series (2007).[1]

Life on Mars was the third major hit in row for Kudos Productions, following *Spooks* and *Hustle*. Like *Spooks*, however, *Life on Mars* had initially been regarded with scepticism in the television industry. It was conceived in the late 1990s by Matthew Graham, Tony Jordan and Ashley Pharoah who – according to what has now become established as the 'origin myth' of the series – went on an away-weekend to Blackpool to brainstorm ideas for new drama series.[2] They came up with an idea, initially entitled *Ford Granada* after one of the iconic car models of the 1970s, that was to have been a send-up of the styles and attitudes of the period. The project then spent several years in development at Channel 4 where it was reconfigured from a more light-hearted concept – possibly something in a similar tone to the BBC's Saturday-evening telefantasy series *Crime Traveller* – to a 'buddy' series in the mould of Thames Television's *The Sweeney* and the popular American import *Starsky and Hutch* focusing on the chalk-and-cheese relationship between progressive modern detective Sam Tyler and unreconstructed 1970s throwback Gene Hunt. The title was taken from a classic David Bowie song of 1973 to describe the sense of alienation felt by Sam upon finding himself in that year. However, the series was turned down by Channel 4 on the grounds that its premise was 'too silly ... a bit frivolous and a bit fanciful'.[3]

The commissioning of *Life on Mars* by BBC Wales in 2004 needs to be understood in an institutional and cultural context. As part of the renewal of its Royal Charter in 2007, the BBC had undertaken to produce more programme content outside London in what it referred to as its 'nations and regions' strategy. BBC Wales was mandated to produce content for the Welsh-language broadcaster S4C: it had also produced a limited amount of English-language drama for local consumption, but unlike other regional centres such as Bristol (*Casualty*), Belfast (*Ballykissangel*) and Glasgow (*Monarch of the Glen*) it had not produced any major network dramas. This all changed with the successful revival of the science fiction adventure series *Doctor Who* in 2005. Julie Gardner, then head of Drama at BBC Wales and the co-executive producer of *Doctor Who*, said that *Life on Mars* 'just hit the BBC at the right time ... We knew that we had a gap for a series. We knew, I don't know how, but instinctively we knew that it was worth a risk because it felt very bold'.[4] The BBC itself explicitly positioned *Life on Mars* in relation to its policy of regional diversification. Its Annual Report for 2006 declared: 'BBC Cymru Wales has been notably successful in supplying the network with memorable programming across a range of genres. Drama has been particularly strong, and includes some of the high points of BBC One, such as *Doctor Who* and *Life on Mars*.'[5] In fact, the Welsh connection of *Life on Mars* was tenuous to say the least: whereas *Doctor Who* was produced in house and in Cardiff, *Life on Mars* was made in Manchester by an independent producer. Nevertheless, the decision to base the series in Manchester rather than in London as initially envisaged is evidence of the extent to which *Life on Mars* was tied to a BBC initiative to promote regional drama production. In the event the 'northernness' *Life on Mars* would be one of its most distinctive features in representing the Britain of the 1970s.[6]

It is tempting to ascribe the success of *Life on Mars* to a form of television alchemy: that it was the outcome of a somehow perfect combination of concept, scripting, casting and performances. The production discourse of the series – as exemplified by the interviews with cast and crew on the DVD 'extras' – continuously asserted that everyone involved realized more or less from the outset *Life on Mars* was in some way 'special' or 'different'.[7] As with other successful television series there is a sense of the production team being particularly close-knit and enjoying working together. The two leads – John Simm as Sam Tyler and Philip Glenister as Gene Hunt – both drew acclaim for their powerful performances. While it would be disingenuous not to assign any significance to good writing and acting, however, the success of *Life on Mars* was no happy accident but rather should be seen as the outcome of a directed and highly programmatic strategy to produce a high-concept television drama. It is a sophisticated and multi-layered series that works on several different levels and makes significant demands upon the cultural competences of its viewers. Its success was due in no small measure to the producers' astute assessment of the tastes of television audiences. In particular, *Life on Mars* shows every indication of having been packaged for a specific audience demographic: thirty- and forty-something males with a nostalgia for macho 1970s cop shows like *The Sweeney*. At the same time, however, its appeal extended beyond that group: female viewers seem to have been drawn by the emotional drama of Sam's situation, as well as apparently regarding Glenister's Gene Hunt as an unlikely sex symbol.[8]

Life on Mars exemplified a strategy of product differentiation: a conscious attempt to do something different within the parameters of genre television. This idea was repeatedly asserted in the series' own production discourse. According to its co-creator and co-executive producer Matthew Graham: 'We'd all agreed what we didn't want to do. We'd all come off *City Central* and we all agreed that what we didn't want was another bloody cop show.'[9] Julie Gardner also indicated that it was the series' difference from the usual police formula that had interested her in the project:

> I started reading, and I can't remember what page it was, but I thought: 'Okay, it's a cop show, and it could turn into a kind of *Prime Suspect* thing, and his girlfriend has kind of been kidnapped; I can see where this is going and it's nicely written' – and then I turned the page, and it was like: 'Okay, it's

not that, now he's in the seventies!' ... I continued reading it and I absolutely loved it ... [It] felt like a great opportunity of, on one hand, doing a police show – and doing a police show in a very different kind of way – and it felt like doing a big concept show as well, that would say something about the world.[10]

Gardner's description of *Life on Mars* as 'a big concept show' aligns it with other high-concept dramas such as *Spooks* and *Hustle*, while her suggestion that it would 'say something about the world' indicates that it was seen as a serious drama with social and cultural ambitions beyond those of a more standard or ordinary drama.

The hybrid nature and narrative complexity of *Life on Mars* leave the series open to a wider-than-usual range of reading strategies. On one level it is a genre series: an example of the police/detective series that adheres to but at the same time also breaks some of the 'rules' of the genre. On another level it can be seen as a 1970s nostalgia show that associates it with other, non-drama formats such as the imported US sitcom *That Seventies Show* and BBC2's popular 'nostalgia-clip' show *I Love the 1970s*.[11] Furthermore, *Life on Mars* does not fit easily into the neat taxonomy of realist narrative or fantasy. Thus, on the one hand, it may be read as a realist text characterized by a strong degree of psychological realism and existential angst: in this reading the focus is on how Sam copes with his displacement and the central concern is whether he will recover from the trauma that has (apparently) put him in a coma. On the other hand, it also contains elements of telefantasy: in this reading the big questions are what is Sam doing in the 1970s and has he actually travelled back in time? Such is the narrative and formal complexity of *Life on Mars* that it cannot be reduced to any single interpretation: the series can be read as any or all of these things and its 'meaning' arises from the complex interaction between all those elements.

The basic situation of *Life on Mars* is set up at the beginning of its first episode. DCI (Detective Chief Inspector) Sam Tyler is introduced on a police raid to arrest Colin Raimes, a suspected murderer. During the subsequent interview, it turns out that Raimes has an alibi and so he has to be released. Sam's girlfriend Maya, another detective, believes that Raimes knows the identity of the real killer and trails him. She disappears: her bloodied shirt is found in a children's playground. Sam, driving from the crime scene in a distraught state, narrowly avoids a collision with another vehicle. He stops his car and gets out for some fresh air but is hit by another car and knocked unconscious. We hear the voices of paramedics ('Charge two hundred joules – stand clear') whom we assume are treating Sam at the scene, while Sam experiences flashbacks to a childhood scene. Sam then regains consciousness but finds himself on a patch of waste ground lying next to a much older car. He is dressed differently, a leather jacket and wide-collared shirt replacing his regulation suit. A uniformed policeman appears and asks what happened. Sam's warrant card identifies him as a detective inspector and documents in the car indicate that he is on transfer from C Division in Hyde to A Division of the Greater Manchester Police. A dazed and confused Sam makes his way to the police station where he meets his new boss DCI Gene Hunt and finds that he is now living in 1973. The remainder of the episode establishes what would become the narrative formula of *Life on Mars*: Sam and his new colleagues – antagonistic Detective Sergeant Ray Carling (Dean Andrews), dim-but-likeable Detective Constable Chris Skelton (Marshall Lancaster) and sympathetic WPC Annie Cartwright (Liz White) – investigate a crime during which Sam and Gene invariably clash over their different policing methods. While this goes on, Sam hears 'voices' – on the telephone, radio and television – which are inaudible to the others. He reasons that he is in a coma, that the voices are the medical staff treating him and that the world of 1973 in which he finds himself exists entirely in his own imagination, while his new colleagues, for their part, put his erratic behaviour down to his car accident, which as far as they are concerned happened while he was en route to his new division. In the first episode Sam investigates a crime with uncanny parallels to the murder he had been investigating before his accident and connects them as the work of a serial killer: it transpires that Colin Raimes – a child in 1973 – has witnessed the first murder.

One possible way of understanding *Life on Mars* is suggested by John Ellis's reading of the British fantasy film *A Matter of Life and Death* (1946), produced, written and directed by Michael Powell and Emeric Pressburger.[12] In that film, set during the last week of the Second World War in Europe, Squadron-Leader Peter Carter (David Niven) miraculously survives when he jumps out of his burning Lancaster bomber without a parachute and finds himself washed up on a beach. Shortly later he begins to experience hallucinations in which he is visited by a messenger from another world who tells him that his survival was a mistake and he should have died. Dr Reeves (Roger Livesey) diagnoses brain damage resulting in 'a series of highly organized hallucinations comparable to an experience of actual life'. Peter undergoes surgery to relieve the pressure on his brain: meanwhile in his imagination he is summoned to a heavenly tribunal where it has to plead his case to be allowed to live. Ellis offers a close textual reading of *A Matter of Life and Death* which argues that on a formal level the film works 'by exploiting the disjunctions between two discursive modes which propose rather different positions of intelligibility'.[13] It alternates between a 'documentary mode' (best exemplified in the opening sequence which gives 'a documentary-style tour of the universe' in Technicolor) and a 'fiction mode' (the romance that develops between Peter and love interest June – played by Kim Hunter). Elsewhere the film differentiates formally between its 'real' world (shot in colour, allowing space for emotionality, and open to social movement) and its 'other' world (shot in monochrome and characterized by a strongly hierarchical social order and a rigid legal system). Ellis contends that the formal system of *A Matter of Life and Death* 'is involved in the constant negotiation between the different subject-positions preferred by each discourse, and this work produces across the film a series of events which examine the nature of representation, resolutely refusing any equation between camera and eye, between image and real'.[14]

A similar reading may be offered of *Life on Mars*. The series revolves around the disjuncture between a discourse of rationality (Sam's insistence that he is from the future and is in a coma) and one of unreality (the world that he believes exists only in his imagination). Like Peter Carter, Sam experiences a series of highly organized hallucinations comparable to an experience of actual life. And just as Peter Carter faces the prospect of permanent brain damage if his operation fails, series 2 of *Life on Mars* suggests that Sam's coma has lasted so long due to the presence of a previously undiagnosed brain tumour which might kill him if it is not removed. Like *A Matter of Life and Death*, *Life on Mars* blurs the distinction between what is real and what is not. 'Real – unreal?' Sam muses to himself while looking at the distorted reflections of his face in a broken shaving mirror (episode 1.2). Sam's imaginary world seems so real to him that at times he starts to doubt his own sanity. At the end of episode one, for example, he resolves to take 'the definitive step I need to wake up' by jumping from the roof of the police building but starts to doubt himself when he feels that Annie, trying to pull him back from the edge, has sand on her hand because she caught it on a fire bucket ('Why would I invent that? Why would I bother with that bit of detail?').

There are further specific parallels between *Life on Mars* and *A Matter of Life and Death*. In both the boundary between the real and unreal worlds is porous: sounds and even characters bleed through from one to the other. Bowie's 'Life on Mars' – playing on the iPod in Sam's car in 2006 and heard again on a cassette when he arrives in 1973 – provides an aural bridge between the two worlds in a similar way to the repetitive musical theme of *A Matter of Life and Death*. At moments of crisis the division between the real and the imaginary threatens to collapse entirely. Sam constructs parallels between what happens in his imaginary world and his comatose state: when a gunman takes hostages in a newspaper office and threatens to shoot them at two o'clock, for example, Sam determines that he must save them by that hour or his life-support machine will be turned off (1.6). The conclusion of *Life on Mars* includes an even closer parallel with *A Matter of Life and Death*. In the film, while surgeons operate to relieve the pressure on his brain, Peter imagines himself on trial in a heavenly court: the same actor (Abraham Sofauer) plays both the judge presiding over the tribunal and the neurosurgeon. Similarly, in the last two episodes of *Life on Mars*, Sam is informed by DCI Frank Morgan (Ralph Brown) that he is part of an undercover operation (codenamed 'Operation MARS: Metropolitan Accountability and Reconciliation Strategy') investigating police misconduct: Frank Morgan is also the neurosurgeon operating to remove the tumour that is preventing Sam from regaining consciousness. (There is also another film reference here of course: Frank Morgan was the name of the actor who played both Professor Marvel and the Wizard in *The Wizard of Oz* [1939] – a film in which Dorothy, like Sam, imagines a fantasy world and realizes that what she wants most is to return home.)

There are other possible readings of the relationship between fantasy and reality in *Life on Mars*. One is that Sam really is in 1973 all along but is suffering from some form of mental trauma that has caused him to think he is from the future: in this case the 'voices' he hears are hallucinations. Evidence for this interpretation is that the sequences set in 2006 at the very beginning and end of the series are shot in a different style from those set in 1973: the opening of the first episode features 'silent' action that may perhaps be interpreted as a dream-like state, while in the last episode, when Sam (apparently) wakes from his coma, the present-day sequence has a somewhat unreal air about it. In the same episode the use of 'Somewhere over the Rainbow' on the soundtrack may also be read as indicating a fantasy world. (In *The Wizard of Oz*, Dorothy sings 'Somewhere over the Rainbow' when she is imagining a world far away from her home in Kansas. The recording of the song used in *Life on Mars* by Hawaiian musician Israel Kamabawiwoʻole is a more soulful interpretation than the sentimental version performed by Judy Garland in the film.) Another possible reading, suggested by the final episode, is that the conclusion of *Life on Mars* has Sam realize that he is a character in a television series. At the moment that Sam jumps from the roof of the police station in 2006 – mirroring the end of the first episode where he does not jump in 1973 – the soundtrack swells to a crescendo on Bowie's lyric: 'Take a look at the lawman beating up the wrong guy / O man, wonder if he'll ever know he's in a best-selling show?' A similar device had been used in Dennis Potter's serial *The Singing Detective* (1986) where, in the final episode, two minor characters discover they are fictional characters when they read the manuscript of *The Singing Detective* by crime novelist Philip Marlow.

Another reading of *Life on Mars* – and one that features prominently in the reception discourse of the series – is to understand it in relation to the history of the British television police series. Like *Spooks*, *Life on Mars* both sits within a specific generic taxonomy and at the same time is also a transformative example of that genre. The police series has been a staple of British television screens since the emergence of television as a mass-medium in the 1950s: hence, *Life on Mars* belongs to a tradition that also includes (but is not limited to) *Fabian of the Yard*, *Dixon of Dock Green*, *The Man from Interpol*, *Jacks and Knaves*, *Z Cars*, *Gideon's Way*, *No Hiding Place*, *Softly Softly*, *Special Branch*, *The Sweeney*, *Juliet Bravo*, *The Gentle Touch*, *Bergerac*, *The Bill*, *Dempsey and Makepeace*, *Bullman*, *Inspector Morse*, *Heartbeat*, *Hamish Macbeth*, *Prime Suspect*, *Cracker*, *Between the Lines*, *Blues and Twos*, *The Knock*, *Dalziel and Pascoe*, *Cops*, *The Commander*, *Silent Witness*, *The Vice*, *Waking the Dead*, *Liverpool One* and *New Tricks*. While all new genre series are informed by what has gone before, *Life on Mars* makes specific reference to its predecessors in the genre. Its Manchester setting may be seen as a link back to the 'northern realism' of the BBC's *Jacks and Knaves* (1962) and *Z Cars* (1962–78), both set in Liverpool, while the antagonistic 'buddy' pairing has been seen before in

ITV's *Dempsey and Makepeace* (1985–86) and the BBC's *Dalziel and Pascoe* (1996–2007). Other references are much more direct. When Sam advises Gene to go 'softly, softly', Gene replies 'I always preferred *Z Cars* myself' before breaking down a door (2.2). The most obvious reference point for *Life on Mars*, however, is *The Sweeney*, the tough law-and-order series focused on the Flying Squad ('Sweeney Todd' is rhyming slang for Flying Squad) starring John Thaw as the insubordinate, hard-drinking DI Jack Regan and Dennis Waterman as his sidekick DS George Carter. Most reviewers of *Life on Mars* saw Regan as the prototype for Gene Hunt. 'It's a shame that the late John Thaw isn't around to watch *Life on Mars*,' wrote Brian Viner (*The Independent*), 'partly because he grew up in those same Manchester mean streets, but mainly because Glenister plays Gene Hunt as an homage to Thaw's Jack Regan.'[15] In the first episode Hunt even 'quotes' a line from *The Sweeney* when he tells Sam 'don't ever waltz into my kingdom, acting king of the jungle' – a reference to the *Sweeney* episode 'Jigsaw' in which Carter's wife describes Regan as 'king of the jungle' and refers to him 'waltzing through his kingdom'.

On one level *Life on Mars* adheres to the themes and conventions of the police series. It features all the standard plots of the genre: murder, armed robbery, bombing, drug dealing, protection rackets, prostitution, kidnapping, football violence and hostage situations ('You are surrounded by armed bastards!' a gung-ho Gene tells the gunman in the last instance). There is even the obligatory episode in which Gene is suspected of committing a murder and has to prove his innocence (2.7). In this sense it would be fair to say that *Life on Mars* breaks no new ground in its content: topics such as racism (2.6), police corruption (2.1) and death in custody (1.7) had all featured in the long-running ITV series *The Bill* (1984–2010) before *Life on Mars*. Even *Dixon of Dock Green* had examined what happened when coppers go bad in a famous early episode 'The Rotten Apple'. To this extent *Life on Mars* sits firmly within the history of the British police series which has typically represented criminality as a social problem rather than as a simple matter of 'cops and robbers'. Nevertheless, *Life on Mars* was usually able to offer a fresh perspective on the familiar tropes and conventions of the genre. 'For a series critics foretold would run out of ideas before the end of its first season,' wrote Andrew Billen, '*Mars* continued in its second to find new things to say about racism, Asian immigration, Irish nationalism, heroin and wife-swapping.'[16]

The main theme of the police series throughout its history has been the representation of the police and policing: *Life on Mars* is no exception. To this extent the time displacement motif is really just a device to highlight how the methods of policing had changed between the 1970s and the early twenty-first century. If, as L. P. Hartley would have it, the past is a foreign country, it explains why Sam Tyler thinks he has 'landed on a different planet' when he arrives in 1973. He is shocked to discover that what he regards as basic procedures – such as reading suspects their rights upon arrest and tape-recording interviews – are not followed. In fact, these procedures did not become a legal requirement until the Police and Criminal Evidence Act of 1984. A running joke throughout the series is that Sam cannot remember the formal caution ('You have the right to remain silent...') and will keep reciting variations of it until one of the others (usually Gene) provides the vernacular alternative ('You're nicked!'). *Life on Mars* lays bare the social attitudes of the 1970s. Sam is appalled to find that his new colleagues demonstrate a degree of casual racism and sexism that would be unthinkable in the modern day. It has been suggested that the series' representation of the drinking culture in the police force (Gene takes his team to the Railway Arms every day at 'beer o'clock') is an accurate picture of the sort of behaviour commonplace at the time. Former Metropolitan Police Commissioner Sir John Stephens, for example, recalled his time in CID in the 1970s: 'We worked ridiculous hours, and then went drinking: hard drinking was still part of the culture... some senior officers deliberately encouraged drinking to see whether their subordinates could control themselves. Rules were then very loose.'[17]

A recurring theme of *Life on Mars* is the contrast between different modes of policing. On the one hand, Sam represents the face of modern, progressive policing. He follows procedures by the book, employs the latest investigative techniques such as psychological profiling and is insistent upon the methodical collection of evidence and the preservation of crime scenes. Gene, on the other hand, acts on instinct and is no stickler for the niceties of the law if it means he can get a 'result'. While Sam will attempt to reason with others, Gene's preferred method is a punch to the solar plexus. He is not averse to 'fitting up' a suspect if he believes it will serve the greater good. When confronted with a particularly grisly hammer murder and needing a quick arrest to placate the press, for instance, Gene has a straightforward solution: 'We pull in someone from the we-don't-like-you list, put their dabs on the hammer, charge 'em and we'll get it past the beak … There's loads of scum out there deserves another spell inside' (2.1). Gene sees his role as being to protect the public from 'scum' and he is not too particular how he goes about it: Sam is invariably aghast at what he sees as Gene's casual disregard for the law. For Gene the end justifies the means. The series makes it clear that his overriding concern is the preservation of law and order: 'This is *my* city. And it will be a safe place for my wife and my mum to walk around in.' This was consistent with the attitude of 1970s police series including *The Sweeney* which had a strong 'law-and-order' inflection and had been produced against the background of a perceived crime wave – especially in violent crimes such as armed robbery.

Life on Mars is careful not to side unequivocally with either 'old school' policing or modern methods. Neither Sam nor Gene is characterized as outright good cop/bad cop, and both are shown making mistakes. Most cases are solved through a combination of Sam's deductive reasoning and Gene's more instinctive approach. The series is critical of the casual sexism and racism of the 1970s but at the same time also has fun with the endemic political correctness of modern policing. The language used to describe prejudice is sent up when the detectives investigate a violent assault on an Asian shopkeeper:

Sam: I think we need to explore whether this attempted murder was a hate crime.

Gene: What, as opposed to one of those 'I really, really like you' sort of murders? (2.6)

And the series acknowledges that Gene's methods, unorthodox though they might be, are sometimes the more pragmatic. Episode 1.4 is a key example in this regard. Sam is shocked to discover that the police have 'an arrangement' with a local villain and nightclub owner called Stephen Warren. Gene explains that 'Mr Warren enjoys cordial relationships with the police. He keeps his streets spotlessly clean, no burglaries, no sex crimes, and he lets us know if any unsavory characters arrive in the city'. In return the police turn a blind eye to Warren's involvement in rent rackets and organized prostitution. Gene argues in favour of 'checks and balances' where the police reach an accommodation with bigger criminals to help control low-level crime. In the same episode it is also revealed that Gene has been taking 'back handers' for years. Warren is finally arrested when he oversteps the mark and orders the murder of an informant, but Gene's argument is vindicated to an extent when later in the series they have to contend with a crime wave as 'small fish try to climb to the top of the ladder' that has now been vacated following Warren's arrest (1.8).

A recurring theme of *Life on Mars* is the question of police accountability. Gene and his colleagues often act as if they are above the law, while Sam is adamant that their actions must be transparent and accountable:

Sam: If we can't police ourselves, how can the public support and trust us?
Gene: The public don't give a damn what we do as long as we get results!
       (1.7)

This exchange takes place during an episode concerning a death in custody in which a small-time drug dealer suffers a fatal heart attack after Ray feeds him cocaine in his cell. Sam wants to carry out a proper investigation; Gene prefers to cover up the incident and deal with it informally by demoting Ray to detective constable. In this regard the decision to set *Life on Mars* in the early 1970s is highly significant. This was a period when public trust in the police had been tarnished by revelations of corruption and malpractice. In 1972, for example, the Commissioner of the Metropolitan Police, Robert Mark, dismissed nearly 500 officers for corruption and set up a special unit to investigate complaints against the police.[18]

The historical period of *Life on Mars* is integral to the cultural and ideological project of the series. Undoubtedly, one of the reasons for the popular success of *Life on Mars* is its representation of the 1970s. The 1970s have long been considered 'the decade that taste forgot': the era of flares, wide lapels, glam rock and excessive facial hair.[19] Yet it is an inviolable rule of cultural history that all periods derided for their tastes and fashions are eventually reappraised: the 1970s are no exception. *Life on Mars* has been seen as part of a revival of cultural interest in the 1970s in the 'noughties' exemplified by nostalgia television (*I Love the 1970s*) and a wave of journalistic memoirs of growing up in the 1970s such as Andrew Collins's *Where Did It All Go Right? Growing Up Normal in the 1970s* (2003) and Harry Pearson's *Achtung Schweinehund! A Boy's Own Story of Imaginary Conflict* (2007). This nostalgia can be seen in the series' many references to the popular culture of the period, especially children's television programmes such as *Basil Brush* and *Camberwick Green*.

And the soundtrack of *Life on Mars* is a veritable 'sounds of the seventies': David Bowie, Paul McCartney and Wings, Blue Oyster Cult, Deep Purple, The Who, Roxy Music, T-Rex, Pink Floyd, Mott the Hoople, Wizzard, Sweet, Slade, Electric Light Orchestra, Thin Lizzy, Lindisfarne and (employed ironically) Roger Whittaker. One reading of *Life on Mars* is that it constructs the 1970s as an alternative to the present: the final episode concludes with Sam choosing to return to 1973 in preference to remaining in the present. However, as John Cook and Mary Irwin have rightly pointed out, *Life on Mars* 'is no "simple" nostalgia show. Its escapist seventies idyll is constantly problematised'.[20]

Even on a surface level it is very apparent that *Life on Mars* does not view the 1970s through the rose-tinted lens of nostalgia. This can be seen not only in its treatment of social problems such as racism and football hooliganism but also in its *mise-en-scène*. *Life on Mars* pictures 1970s Manchester as a bleak post-industrial environment of urban decline: it is shot mostly in dull, muted colours under what seem like perpetually overcast grey skies. Much of the action takes place around backstreets and terraced houses that hark back to the locations of British new wave films and early *Coronation Street*. The visual style of *Life on Mars* is consistent with the 'look' of films and television series of the period. In particular, the classic British gangster film *Get Carter* (1971) was a reference point for director Bharat Nalluri (who had also directed the first episodes of *Spooks* and *Hustle*) and director of photography Adam Suschitzky (whose grandfather Wolfgang Suschitzky photographed *Get Carter*) who between them largely determined the style of *Life on Mars*. There is a sense of Gene Hunt's Manchester, like Jack Carter's Newcastle, being a wild frontier town – a motif enhanced by Gene's habit of referring to himself as 'the sheriff' and his self-identification with the Hollywood Western exemplified by the poster of *High Noon* on his office wall.

Life on Mars does not parody or spoof the 1970s in the manner that a film such as *Austin Powers: International Man of Mystery* (1997) did for the 1960s: the culture and fashions of the period are reproduced authentically enough that modern viewers do indeed feel as if they have landed on a different planet. Yet at the same time the 1970s of *Life on Mars* is not so much the 'real' 1970s as the 1970s of popular memory. Nowhere is this more evident than in the series' mobilization of the popular culture of the period. *Life on Mars* employs popular cultural references as much more than just period dressing: they are integral to the politics of the series. The '*Camberwick Green* episode' (2.5) is a good case in point. This opens with a pastiche of the much-loved children's television show (presented as Sam's hallucination) in which a puppet version of Sam emerges from the magic box while a puppet version of Gene is 'kicking in a nonce' (pausing from kicking in said 'nonce' to wave to the camera). The intrusion of Gene's particular brand of law-enforcement into Sam's memory of his childhood television viewing is presented as transgressive: rogue coppers and 'nonces' do not belong in the safe world of children's television. It is also a means of representing Sam's mental trauma. Later, during a heated argument, Sam shouts at his dumbfounded colleague: 'You can attack me all you like, Gene Hunt, but stay out of *Camberwick Green*!'

Certainly, *Life on Mars* maintains a critical distance in its representation of the social attitudes of the 1970s. This is particularly evident in the attitudes towards gender and race. The character of WPC Annie Cartwright is used to problematize the issue of gender. Annie is the object of much sexist and misogynist banter: as a 'plonk' (someone deemed not very bright) she is never fully accepted by her male colleagues who assign her the menial tasks while making lurid comments about her breasts – treatment which she accepts as normal. To this extent *Life on Mars* seemingly inhabits a world in which second-wave feminism never happened. At the same time, however, the sexist attitudes on display in *Life on Mars* are treated ironically: 'There will never be a woman prime minister as long as I have a hole in my arse,' Gene declares confidently – six years before the election of Margaret Thatcher. It has been suggested that the outlook of *Life on Mars* towards sexism is similar to the so-called 'lads' mags' popular in the 1990s and 2000s such as *Loaded*, *Maxim* and *FHM* which catered for young(ish) adult males who appreciated pictures of scantily clad 'birds' but at the same time accepted women's rights. Ruth McElroy, for example, suggests that 'the series' writers share the conviction of lads' mags that sexism – and feminism – is a thing of the past, something to be recalled from the perspective of an improved, if sanitised, present'.[21]

Similarly, the racial politics of *Life on Mars* – or at least the racial politics represented by Gene and Ray – would seem to belong to the world of the now notorious 1970s sitcom *Love Thy Neighbour*. Bill Bryson recalled his horror at seeing this series for the first time in *Notes from a Small Island*: 'A sitcom came on called *My Neighbour is a Darkie*. I suppose that wasn't the actual title, but that was the gist of it – that there was something richly comic in the notion of having black people living next door ... It was hopelessly moronic.'[22] Again, *Life on Mars* is able to represent the racism of the 1970s in the knowledge that viewers would understand that racial epithets such as 'coon' and 'Paki' were fairly commonplace at the time: this sense of ironic distancing is perhaps best exemplified by Ray denying he is a racist ('I've got nothing personal against Gunga Dins'). Gene and his colleagues are selective racists: curiously, they are friendly with Nelson, the West Indian landlord of The Railway Arms, the backstreet pub they frequent. (Even Sam thinks a Rastafarian landlord is out of place as he asks incredulously: 'What part of my subconscious do *you* hail from?'). Episode 2.2 explores racism in the police force. Sam is delighted when he meets black policeman DC Glen Fletcher (Ray Emmet Brown) – whom he knows from the future as his mentor when Sam joined the police force – but is dismayed when Glen makes racist jokes against himself (of the 'I couldn't see you in the dark' variety – the sort of humour that characterized *Love Thy Neighbour*) in order to fit in and win acceptance from Gene and Ray. The idea of the black policeman having to act like an 'Uncle Tom' stereotype is cringe-worthy to modern eyes: but the point being made is that racial attitudes have moved on in the intervening years.

The production discourse of *Life on Mars* asserts that the character of DCI Gene Hunt was intended as an extreme parody of reactionary social attitudes: in one episode Sam calls him 'an overweight, over-the-hill, nicotine-stained borderline alcoholic homophobe with a superiority complex and an unhealthy obsession with male bonding' ('You make that sound like a bad thing', Gene retorts) (1.8). Whether this was necessarily understood by all viewers, however, is a moot point. Just as some viewers of *Till Death Us Do Part* in the 1960s championed working-class bigot Alf Garnett rather than understanding the character as a satire of reactionary social and racial politics, there is some anecdotal evidence to suggest that some viewers liked *Life on Mars* because it did not conform to the dictates of political correctness. In particular, Gene Hunt became something of a cult figure and his decidedly non-PC lines – 'This investigation is going at the speed of a spastic in a magnet factory'; 'The dealers round here are so scared we've got a better chance of getting Helen Keller to talk'; 'She's as nervous as a very small nun at a penguin shoot' – passed into folklore.[23] One of Gene's homophobic rants ('You great, soft, sissy, girly, nancy, French bender, Manchester United-supporting poof') prompted a complaint from the general secretary of the National Association of Schoolmasters and Union of Women Teachers that *Life on Mars* 'could have had a detrimental impact on young people's behaviour … If you've got abusive terms like "fairy boy", that is particularly worrying in a context where our evidence is showing that one of the factors which causes young people to commit suicide is the fact that in schools they are subject to homophobic bullying'.[24] As ever with such cases there is no hard evidence to substantiate the claim that the programme did indeed contribute to homophobia or bullying in the playground. The BBC responded that '[the] fictional character of DCI Hunt is an extreme, tongue-in-cheek take on a stereotypical 1970s bloke and the audience understand and revel in his abrasive and direct approach to his job and life in general'. It added that '*Life on Mars* is a post-watershed production, aimed at an adult audience'.[25]

Overall the critical and popular response to *Life on Mars* was overwhelmingly positive. The critical reception suggested that it was understood in the terms the production team had intended as more than just 'another bloody cop show'. This can be seen from reviews of the first series in the national press. Alison Graham, television editor of the *Radio Times*, described it as 'a genuinely innovative and imaginative take on an old genre'.[26] Mike Ward (*Daily Star*) concurred: 'If you reckon cop shows have run out of fresh ideas, take a look at BBC's new series *Life on Mars*. It might sound like a David Attenborough documentary set on a far-flung planet but this is actually one of the most inventive police dramas in years'.[27] For Sam Wollaston (*The Guardian*): '*Life on Mars* is more than just a jolly, tongue-in-cheek romp into the past. Once there, in 1973, we find ourselves immersed in a reasonably gripping police drama – yes, *The Sweeney*, perhaps, with better production values. But there's more to it than that too'.[28] Most reviewers found the premise of *Life on Mars* bold and original and acknowledged that it had been a significant risk on the part of the producers. According to John Preston (*Sunday Telegraph*):

> There's a very fine dividing line between a good idea and a rotten one, with everything hanging on the execution. You could, for example, take the bare

bones of *Life on Mars* and create something of surpassing awfulness … But it proves to work extremely well, in large part because it has the courage to play the concept with a steady hand and an almost straight face.[29]

Thomas Sutcliffe (*The Independent*) agreed: 'On paper, the idea of having a contemporary detective time-travel back into the Seventies gives off great gusts of desperation … A little surprising, then, to find that in practice the pony [*sic*] stands up amazingly well, even pulling some impressive pirouettes from time to time.'[30] A dissenting note was sounded by Victor Lewis-Smith (*Evening Standard*), who found 'little humorous potential' in the concept and felt that 'the series reworks the formats of so many earlier, better shows'. Lewis-Smith thought it 'ludicrous from the outset' and 'just could not take it seriously'.[31] However, this was a rare negative response in what was otherwise a very favourable critical reception.

Life on Mars was another successful export for the BBC: it was sold to New Zealand, Australia, Japan, Canada, Germany, Italy, the Netherlands, Norway, Sweden, Finland, Serbia, Greece and Israel among others. In the United States it was broadcast on the new BBC America channel. It also proved to be an exportable format in that it was remade for other television industries. This practice has been used extensively for light entertainment formats such as *Who Wants to Be a Millionaire?* and 'reality' shows such as *Big Brother* which are cheap to produce, but until recently has been less common for more expensive drama series. David E. Kelly produced an American version of *Life on Mars* for the ABC network in 2008.[32] This was followed in turn by a Spanish version (*La chica de ayer/Yesterday's Girl*) in 2009 and a Russian version (*The Dark Side of the Moon*) in 2012. The foreign-language versions were modified for local consumption: hence, the Spanish series is set in 1978 after the end of the Franco regime, while the Russian version is set in 1979 and reverses the character dynamic so that the modern policeman is the maverick who breaks the rules and finds himself constrained by the by-the-book bureaucratic procedures of the Communist era. To this extent *Life on Mars* was an early example of a trend that has seen successful drama series remade for different markets: the Danish-Swedish detective drama *The Bridge* (2011), for example, has been remade for the United States (*The Bridge*, 2013) and for Britain (*The Tunnel*, 2016), while there are both Swedish and British versions of *Wallander* adapted from the detective novels by Henning Mankell. Yet none of the other versions replicated the success of the original: the American *Life on Mars* was cancelled after one season, and neither the Spanish nor the Russian series seems to have been widely exported. *Life on Mars* was a genuine television original: a combination of high-concept and 'cult' drama that will remain forever one of the genuine landmarks of British television.

Ashes to Ashes

Ashes to Ashes (2008–10) is that rarity of television drama: a sequel that not only matched the popularity of the original but also succeeded in developing the successful formula in new directions rather than simply repeating it.[1] *Ashes to Ashes* was created by the same team of writers Matthew Graham and Ashley Pharoah, with Philip Glenister, Dean Andrews and Marshall Lancaster all reprising their roles from *Life on Mars* now joined by ex-*Spooks* star Keeley Hawes as Detective Inspector Alex Drake who takes the place of the time-displaced modern detective. *Ashes to Ashes* actually ran longer than *Life on Mars* (three series and twenty-four episodes) and maintained a similar audience share, averaging between 6 and 7 million viewers. Again the basic premise is summed up in the opening voice-over narration of each episode: 'My name is Alex Drake. I've been shot and that bullet has taken me back to 1981. I may be one second away from life or one second away from death. All I know is that I have to keep fighting – fight to live, fight to see my daughter, fight to get home.'[2]

The production discourse of *Ashes to Ashes* suggests that the decision to produce the series arose from what its makers regarded as the unfinished business of *Life on Mars*. It had been intended to make a third series of *Life on Mars* to wrap up the narrative with the idea that the characters were inhabiting a sort of limbo world for dead police officers: however, this was scotched when John Simm did not want to commit to another series and the writers were obliged to conclude the narrative differently. Ashley Pharoah told *Radio Times* that they were 'so loath ... to say goodbye to Gene Hunt and his Merry Men'.[3] It is clear that from the outset *Ashes to Ashes* was intended to be very much Gene Hunt's show. *Life on Mars* focused on Sam Tyler from both a psychological and a narrative point of view: Hunt had initially been the co-star, as it were.

However, the character had proved so popular with audiences, including both men and women, that it was a natural enough decision to build *Ashes to Ashes* around him. The decision to set *Ashes to Ashes* in the early 1980s rather than in the same period as *Life on Mars* was intended both to differentiate it from its predecessor and to explore how Gene would adapt to a different social-historical context. Jane Featherstone, executive producer for Kudos, said that 'we ... all realised that it could be brilliant to bring Gene into the eighties – a fascinating time of cultural, musical and political transition'.[4] Like *Foyle's War*, *Ashes to Ashes* would use the format of the police series to explore the wider social fabric of the period – more so, perhaps, than *Life on Mars* had done. A recurrent theme of *Ashes to Ashes* is Gene's realization that times are changing and that he is becoming an anachronism: 'They're sharpening the axe for coppers like me. But up until the last second, I will be out there, making a difference' (1.1). Matthew Graham likened Gene to 'an old, grizzled sheriff in a town that the railroad is approaching, like one of those westerns where the railway is coming and bringing modern ideas'.[5]

Stephen Lacey and Ruth McElroy contend that '*Ashes to Ashes* was more than simply a continuation of *Life on Mars* under a different title. Although the essential conceit of both shows was the same – that the narrative followed the attempts of a contemporary police detective, catapulted back in time by a serious accident, to return to their familiar world – much has changed'.[6] On the one hand, *Ashes to Ashes* inhabits the same fictional universe as *Life on Mars*: Gene, Ray and Chris have transferred to London and have been joined by WPC Sharon Granger (Montserrat Lombard). And it also represents a continuing narrative: indeed, *Ashes to Ashes* provides a resolution of sorts to the unanswered questions left hanging in *Life on Mars*. The end of *Life on Mars* had been open to different possible readings, but those possibilities are closed down by *Ashes to Ashes* which provides narrative closure for *Life on Mars* as well as for itself. This was due largely to the different production contexts: the open-endedness of *Life on Mars* was because Graham and Pharoah did not know whether it would be recommissioned, while they had greater certainty with *Ashes to Ashes* which was mapped out from the start as a three-series arc. On the other hand, *Ashes to Ashes* marks a departure from its predecessor insofar as it entirely reconfigures the central character relationship that provides its dramatic axis. In this context the decision to make the co-protagonist a woman places gender politics directly at the centre of *Ashes to Ashes* in a way that it had not been with the male 'buddy' narrative of *Life on Mars*. Hannah Hamad suggests that '*Ashes* is a markedly feminized relative to *Mars*, most obviously in that the protagonist and point of identification is a woman and in the relocation of the action from the masculinized North (Manchester) to the feminized South (London)'.[7] However, this 'feminization' of *Ashes to Ashes* would be a problematic issue for some commentators, as we shall see.

The first episode of *Ashes to Ashes* to a large extent mirrors the opening of *Life on Mars*, but with some important differences. Alex Drake is introduced as a police psychologist who is carrying out research into the experiences of officers who have suffered trauma: she is familiar with Sam Tyler's case as she has read transcripts of the tapes he made recounting his near-death experience. (Graham and Pharoah had started plotting *Ashes to Ashes* while writing the second series of *Life on Mars*: in the last episode of *Life on Mars* Sam mentions 'an officer who's collecting stuff for colleagues who've suffered trauma'). This immediately closes down readings of *Life on Mars* positing either that Sam did not wake from his coma or was in 1973 all along and imagined he was from the future: *Ashes to Ashes* makes sense only if Sam did indeed come out of his coma, however briefly, at the end of *Life on Mars* (Sam's case notes suggest that he died 'last April' following 'prolonged deep coma': this places his death in April 2007 – coinciding with the broadcast of the last episodes of *Life on Mars*). While driving her daughter to school, Alex receives an emergency call to attend a hostage situation. Arthur Layton, a psychologically disturbed criminal, is holding a tourist at gunpoint and has demanded that he speak to Alex: she does not recognize him but he appears to know her. The hostage is rescued but Layton escapes only to reappear shortly afterwards: he shoots Alex in the head at point-blank range. She experiences flashbacks to her childhood and sees the bullet in slow motion. Then she wakes up to the strains of Ultravox's 'Vienna' and finds herself on a pleasure boat on the River Thames: instead of her plain trouser suit and sensible flat shoes she is now wearing a short bright red mini-dress, a fake white fur coat and stiletto heels (clothes which imply a prostitute). Dazed and confused, she stumbles off the boat but is threatened by a drunken City trader who holds a knife to her throat: this is the cue for the screeching of tyres and the arrival of Gene, Ray and Chris in a red Audi Quattro.

So far the set-up of *Ashes to Ashes* has been a variation on the opening of *Life on Mars*, but with Gene's arrival on scene there is a marked change of mode. In *Life on Mars* the audience is as dumbfounded as Sam by what is happening: we see Gene through Sam's eyes and have no knowledge of who Gene is. In contrast, *Ashes to Ashes* plays on the audience's prior knowledge and expectations of the character: hitherto the episode has been building up to his appearance – and we have been expecting it. *Ashes to Ashes* does not disappoint us. Gene's entrance is played out as a parody of the style of the Hollywood action cinema of the 1980s exemplified by films such as *Top Gun* and *Lethal Weapon*: the use of slow motion and the heightened music mark this out as a 'star entrance' moment. The first shot of Gene is an anticipatory close-up of his snakeskin boots as he steps from the car – a reminder of Gene's identification with the role of the sheriff in the Hollywood Western – while a specific film reference can be found in the following long shot of Gene in the background framed between Alex's legs in the foreground: this is nothing if not a visual reference to the poster for the 1981 James Bond movie *For Your Eyes Only* (the poster is displayed on the wall of Gene's office). Gene's first line (to the man threatening Alex) conforms to our expectations while recalling an oft-quoted line from *Life on Mars*: 'Today, my friend, your diary entry will read: took a prozzie hostage and was shot by three armed bastards.' It is a highly stylized moment that simultaneously pays homage to Gene's 'star' presence while at the same time indicating that the style of *Ashes to Ashes* will be more parodic than its predecessor.

Ashes to Ashes therefore works from the premise that Alex knows she has been shot and that her mind has recreated the same fantasy world imagined by Sam Tyler which she knows from reading the transcripts of his tapes: 'Look at me! I am trained to get inside the criminal mind. And now I'm stuck in my own – with you!' She rationalizes that Gene and his colleagues are 'subconscious recessional forms', greets them with a breezy 'good morning, imaginary constructs' and places finger-quotation marks around 'Gene' when she talks to him to indicate that she knows he is not real. Alex experiences similar hallucinations as Sam: people speaking to her from television sets and messages on computer screens. She imagines that she sees her daughter Molly reflected in mirrors and screens. Just as Sam was haunted by the Test Card Girl, Alex is menaced throughout series one of *Ashes to Ashes* by the figure of the Pierrot clown from the music video for David Bowie's 'Ashes to Ashes'. And like Sam she interprets events in her imaginary world as metaphors for her comatose state: in the second series, for example, her alarm clock in 1982 is linked to her heart monitor in 2008. The idea that she might be 'one second from death' is at its most literal in the last episode of this series when she has to prevent an armed robbery: she understands this as a metaphor for her antibiotic medication being increased to 50 ml that will either 'kill or cure' the infection to her head wound. The life-or-death urgency of the situation is asserted in Alex's repeated line 'time's running out for me' and others such as 'the clock is ticking' (2.8).

The discursive modes of fantasy and reality are configured in different ways in *Ashes to Ashes*. In the first series Alex behaves in a similar fashion to Sam in *Life on Mars*: she believes there is a reason for her presence in 1981 and that is to prevent the death of her parents, liberal lawyers who were killed in a car-bomb explosion in October 1981. The first series follows an oedipal trajectory not entirely dissimilar to Sam encountering his own parents at the end of series one of *Life on Mars*. Alex clashes with her own mother over her treatment of her daughter (i.e. the young Alex) and is chastened by her mother's response ('I'd be ashamed if she grew up to be like you'), although they are reconciled by the end of the series as Alex's mother decides to take a sabbatical from work to rebuild her relationship with the young Alex. However, Alex is unable to prevent her parents' death: it transpires that they were killed not as she thought by terrorists but by Alex's father who intended to kill his own family when he learnt of his wife's affair with their friend (and Alex's godfather) Evan. At this point the sinister Pierrot clown figure who has been a menacing presence throughout the first series removes his mask to reveal that he is Alex's father. Alex's real and imaginary worlds intersect when as a young girl she escapes from the car bomb and is rescued by none other than Gene who shields her from the truth and lets her believe it was a terrorist's bomb that killed her parents. In this sense the first series of *Ashes to Ashes* plays out a variation of the time-loop paradox used in other telefantasy series such as *Doctor Who* and *Crime Traveller*: Alex is unable to prevent her parents' death because in travelling back in time she has herself become a participant in those events. Yet she is rescued (in her own past) by a man whom she believes is merely an imaginary 'figment'.

In the previous chapter, I suggested that a reading of *Life on Mars* can be informed by John Ellis's analysis of the different discursive modes of knowledge and subjectivity in the film *A Matter of Life and Death*. This comparison to British cinema can be extended to *Ashes to Ashes*: the resolution of the series bears certain parallels with the British wartime film *The Halfway House* (1943). Directed by Basil Dearden for Ealing Studios, *The Halfway House* concerns a group of diverse travellers who converge at an inn (called the Halfway House) in Wales in 1943 where they are met by the innkeeper and his daughter. The characters – including a grieving couple who have lost their son, another couple in the middle of an acrimonious divorce, a black marketeer, an Irish nationalist and the conductor of a concert orchestra who has been told he has only months to live – are all in need of moral guidance: this is provided by the innkeeper and his daughter who offer each of them a solution. At the same time a number of visual and narrative clues – for example, someone notices that the innkeeper's daughter does not cast a shadow – reveal that the innkeeper and his daughter are not real: the inn was destroyed by a bomb a year ago and the travellers realize that they have been transported back in time and have another opportunity at their living their lives. *The Halfway House* was one of a number of allegorical dramas produced in Britain during the war – others included *Thunder Rock* and *They Came to a City* – and is 'both naturalistic and phantasmagorical' and a 'balance between the unreal and the desperately real'.[8]

While the parallel is not exact, there are nevertheless some rather striking similarities between *The Halfway House* and the last series of *Ashes to Ashes* which similarly combine the naturalistic and the phantasmagorical. This series marks a change of direction narratively in that the regular recurring characters are joined by DCI Jim Keats (Daniel Mays) who is antagonistic towards Gene but wants to befriend the others. Keats fuels Alex's increasing paranoia to the extent that she starts to suspect that Gene was responsible for Sam Tyler's death (Sam was supposed to have died in a 'jewellery blag' according to the account given by Gene). At the same time Alex and the others (apart from Gene) start to experience hallucinations of seeing stars while Alex is also haunted by nightmarish images of a young policeman with half his face shot off. In the final episode Alex follows a lead to Lancashire where she discovers a body in a policeman's uniform buried in a shallow grave: however, the warrant card identifies the body not as Sam Tyler, as she had expected, but as Gene Hunt. It turns out that Gene was shot and killed when he disturbed a robbery in the Coronation year of 1953. The others learn that they too are dead from videotapes given to them by Keats: Chris was shot during a hold-up, Shaz was stabbed by a car thief and Ray hanged himself in shame after 'bottling' joining the army and taking out his anger on a minor criminal whom he beat to death. The world they now inhabit is a limbo world for dead police officers – 'somewhere where we get sent to sort ourselves'. The motif of characters who do not realize they are dead has been used often enough in films such as *Castle Keep*, *The Sixth Sense* and *The Others*, although it seems to me that *The Halfway House* is a better parallel as, though the characters in the film are not dead, they have been transported to a place of temporal limbo where they are able to resolve their problems and come to terms with their lives. It becomes apparent in the last episode that the world of *Ashes to Ashes* (and therefore by extension the world of *Life on Mars*) is a state of limbo rather like the Halfway House Inn: the Railway Arms – which has 'magically' relocated from Manchester to London – fills that role. Gene, like the innkeeper in the film, adopts the role of a ferryman who helps the others come to terms with what happened to them so they can move on. At the end Gene elects to stay in the limbo world: the episode ends with a newly dead police officer arriving and demanding to know where his office and iPhone are: Gene's last words ('A word in your shell-like, pal?') provide a pleasing symmetry with the first episode of *Life on Mars*.[9]

The formal strategy of *Ashes to Ashes* largely follows the pattern established in *Life on Mars*. The 1980s are (re)imagined through the prism of popular culture: in particular, there are references to children's television (*Rainbow, Grange Hill, Jackanory, Blue Peter*) and light entertainment shows (*Larry Grayson's Generation Game, It's a Knockout*). *Life on Mars* had drawn upon popular memories of *The Sweeney* as a macho action series: the equivalent reference points for *Ashes to Ashes* are less specific but include *The Professionals* (Chris aspires to be Lewis Collins's character Bodie) as well as American imports such as *The A-Team* and *Miami Vice* (which both arrived a few years later than the 1981–83 time frame of *Ashes to Ashes*). The references are often parodic, such as the moment when Chris and Ray arrive to the rescue in slow motion to the strains of Vangelis's theme from the 1981 film *Chariots of Fire* (3.8). And like *Life on Mars*, *Ashes to Ashes* draws upon the popular music of the period. The pop music video was the new emerging media form of the early 1980s and is used extensively throughout *Ashes to Ashes*, again in a parodic mode. The best example – in its way the equivalent of the '*Camberwick Green* episode' of *Life on Mars* – is the near shot-for-shot reconstruction of the video for Billy Joel's hit single 'Uptown Girl' in which Gene 'performs' the role of Billy Joel with Alex as supermodel Chrissie Brinkley and the other male cops as the garage mechanics (3.2). The sequence has no narrative function (it is revealed to be Alex's dream) but can be understood as a way of suggesting that Alex's imaginary 1980s are derived from her girlhood memories of pop music. Otherwise *Ashes to Ashes* includes a more eclectic mixture of mainstream and indie pop than its predecessor: Ultravox, Adam and the Ants, Duran Duran, Human League, Blondie, Dexys Midnight Runners, The Jam, The Clash, The Specials, Thompson Twins, Spandau Ballet, Heaven 17, Tears for Fears, The Buzzcocks, Simple Minds, The Buggles, Echo and the Bunnymen, The Stranglers, The Cure and Frankie Goes to Hollywood. The musical soundscape can be understood both as a means of creating a sense of historical period and as an exercise in nostalgia for the (presumed) thirty-something audiences of *Ashes to Ashes*.

Ashes to Ashes differs visually from *Life on Mars*. In contrast to its predecessor, which had represented 1970s Manchester as a bleak environment shot in dull, muted colours, *Ashes to Ashes* sets out to capture the 'look' of the 1980s in all its gaudy excess. This is best exemplified in the change in Gene's 'motor' from a brown Ford Cortina in *Life on Mars* to a bright red Audi Quattro in *Ashes to Ashes*: the switch from a mass-produced British-made car – the Cortina was the most popular car in Britain in the 1970s – to a high-end German import not only symbolizes the transition in style and in technology that has taken place in the eight years between *Life on Mars* and the first series of *Ashes to Ashes* but also represents the emergence of the consumer-driven culture of the 1980s. (It might be stretching the point to suggest that the switch from a British- to a German-manufactured vehicle is a reflection of the decline of the British motor industry. Nevertheless at the end of the last episode of *Ashes to Ashes*, when his beloved Quattro has been shot to pieces by European gangsters, Gene is seen looking at a brochure for a Mercedes.) The excesses of the 1980s are also reflected in the fashions of *Ashes to Ashes*: Chris becoming a New Romantic (complete with eye make-up) is used for comedy, but Gene's smarter suits in contrast to his camel hair coat of *Life on Mars* can be seen as refashioning him in line with the 'look' of Thatcherite Britain.[10]

To some extent *Ashes to Ashes* is more directly rooted in the real historical landscape of the early 1980s than *Life on Mars* had been for the historical 1970s. There are frequent references to the government of Margaret Thatcher (or 'the Great Handbag' as Gene refers to her) and in particular to the redevelopment of the London Docklands (1.2) which came to symbolize Thatcherism's combination of economic regeneration and social dislocation. The second episode coincides with the Royal Wedding of Prince Charles and Lady Diana Spencer (29 July 1981) and the second series is set against the background of the Falklands War of 1982. And unlike *Life on Mars*, which in the main had not included real historical individuals (Marc Bolan is the one exception but even so he appears only very fleetingly: Sam recognizes the T-Rex frontman in a nightclub in episode 1.4), *Ashes to Ashes* occasionally does. Episode 1.8 is a key episode in this regard: it features the investigation into the Metropolitan Police by Lord Scarman (Geoffrey Palmer) in the wake of the Brixton riots of April 1981. The Scarman Report was highly critical of the institutionalized racism within the Metropolitan Police and concluded that a major cause of the riots had been the sense of alienation experienced by young black males who were often persecuted by the police on account of their ethnicity. In *Ashes to Ashes* Scarman makes an inspection of Gene's station on a day when the cells are full of protestors from a Gay Pride march, leading to the inevitable confrontation:

Scarman: The police harassment of homosexual and racial minorities is an endemic and ineradicable disease threatening the very survival of our society … I'll be keeping a beady eye on you, DCI Hunt.

Gene: Is that right? Well, you can take this home in your Harrods pipe and smoke it. In twenty years time, when the streets are awash with filth, and you're too frightened to leave your posh Belsize Park house after dark, don't come running to me, mate, because I'll be in Alicante, oiled up, skin sizzling in the midday sun like a burnt sausage … You can despise us, you can try and close us down, but you will never beat us, because we are *police officers*, we are brothers, we are un-bloody breakable!

Gene's impassioned speech prompts loud applause from his colleagues: the incident itself is a dramatic invention but it has some historical foundation in that the Police Federation was hostile towards Scarman and tried to block the implementation of some of his report's recommendations. It also marks a point at which *Ashes to Ashes* has come ideologically full circle from *Life on Mars* as it defends Gene's approach to policing against liberal reformers who are presented as removed from the realities of everyday policing.

The most significant difference between *Ashes to Ashes* and *Life on Mars*, however, is the greater prominence afforded to gender in the sequel. The decision to replace Sam Tyler with a woman fundamentally altered the gender politics of *Ashes to Ashes*. Alex Drake's presence in Gene Hunt's masculine world reconfigures the male 'buddy' narrative of *Life on Mars* into a male/female dynamic posited on a 'will they/won't they?' sexual tension that recalls other male/female detective pairings such as *The Avengers*, *Dempsey and Makepeace* (a mid-1980s British variation on *Starsky and Hutch* in which Hutch became a woman) and *Moonlighting*. The opening up of the possibility of a romantic relationship between Gene and Alex – their constant bickering clearly demonstrates that they are attracted to each other – was a production decision that recognized the significant following for Gene among female viewers. One female critic, Glenda Cooper, claimed to speak for 'millions of British women' when she averred that 'the only riddle [of *Life on Mars*] was why the hell did anyone think this was Tyler's show when a brief psychological profile, cursory examination of the evidence and old-fashioned gut instinct showed that there was only one man in the frame and that was DCI Gene Hunt.'[11] *Ashes to Ashes* acknowledges the ambivalence of women being attracted to Gene when Alex tells him over an intimate dinner: 'Even after forty years of feminism, there's still a sizeable number of intelligent women ... who'd give their eye teeth to be sitting here with you' (1.8). However, Alex's attraction to Gene is regarded as problematic by some other commentators. Helen Piper, for example, considers it a retrograde step that ultimately reinforces male control: 'Whereas *Life on Mars* had balanced the relative prominence of Tyler and Hunt within their dialectical friendship, patriarchal order is restored here. Drake is positioned as a potential love interest, destined to find that Hunt has more to teach her than she can have imagined, and this gives a rather different inflection to the thematic conflict over policing methods.'[12]

My reading of the Gene Hunt/Alex Drake relationship is that the opposites-attract dynamic is posited as much on class as on gender politics. Gene regards Alex as a 'posh bird' and there are numerous instances throughout *Ashes to Ashes* where his misogyny seems to arise from class antagonism as much as gender difference: his recurring nickname for her is 'Bollinger knickers' or 'Bolly knickers' and he variously refers to her as a 'posh mouthy tart' and a 'messed-up, clenched-arse, toffee-nosed bitch'. Gene's sexism arises not so much from a reluctance to accept women in senior positions (he expresses admiration for Prime Minister Margaret Thatcher on several occasions) as from a deep-rooted social conservatism about what he considers appropriate gender roles. His frequent references to Alex's dress – 'If that skirt was hitched any higher, I could see what you had for breakfast' and 'DI Bolly knickers, you appear to be drunk in charge of a handbag and dressed like a tart' – suggest that Gene has a fairly traditional view of feminine propriety. Alex, for her own part, is simultaneously repelled and attracted by Gene's hyper-masculine worldview. He is able to read this ('Now then, Bollinger knickers, you gonna kiss me or punch me?'), although he never takes it so far as to sleep with her (despite a drunken opportunity to do so approximately once per series). It might be argued that Gene's sexism is a form of old-fashioned chivalry: he accepts that Alex is a capable police officer but does not like her placing herself in danger.

There are two contexts to consider in analysing the gender politics of *Ashes to Ashes*: the context of real policing and television's representation of women police officers. These two contexts intersect in various ways in the series. *Ashes to Ashes* is set in the period following the Equal Pay Act (1970) and Sex Discrimination Act (1975) and the abolition of the Metropolitan Police's A4 (Women's Police) Division which had effectively segregated female officers into performing specific roles. Nevertheless, there is ample evidence that sexism persisted in the police force, and early episodes of *Ashes to Ashes* make reference to this. For example, Gene tells Alex that he intends 'to stamp your bum' – a reference to the infamous initiation ritual whereby new women police officers would have their buttocks stamped with 'Property of the Metropolitan Police' (1.2). Shaz, like Annie in *Life on Mars*, seems willing to accept the sexist 'banter' of her male colleagues. At the same time *Ashes to Ashes* is set during the period (the early 1980s) that saw the first female-centred police series on British television in the form of ITV's *The Gentle Touch* and the BBC's *Juliet*

Bravo. *The Gentle Touch* makes a particularly apposite comparison to *Ashes to Ashes*: it starred Jill Gascoigne as London-based DI Maggie Forbes and the series had focused as much on her home life as her police work (she was a widow with a 'difficult' teenage son). *Juliet Bravo* – created by Ian Kennedy Martin, who also devised *The Sweeney* – was about a female inspector who becomes head of a rural police station in the North: Ray's incredulity in *Ashes to Ashes* ('The new DI's a *woman*!') recalls the response of male officers to Jean Darblay's (Stephanie Turner) arrival in the first episode of *Juliet Bravo*. However, Alex Drake is less able to exercise her agency than her female predecessors in the 1980s: she is cast in the role of sidekick to the 'Gene Genie' rather than playing the leading role. And the fact that she struggles to assert her agency in her own imaginary world – 'Will you just shut up and listen!? This is my bloody fantasy, and I will be listened to!' (1.2) – might be taken as an expression of the wider societal repression of professional women.

Ashes to Ashes occasionally addresses the more serious side of institutionalized sexism within the police force. A particularly acute example of this occurs early in the first series (1. 3) in an episode that examines the police's treatment of rape victims. Gene is dismissive of a middle-aged prostitute who makes an allegation of rape:

Gene: Raped? Who's she trying to kid?
Alex: They say it's difficult for rape victims to be believed. I wonder why?
Gene: She gets paid for having sex.
Alex: It's not about sex, is it? It's about control – and power – and revenge.
       (*She sees that Gene is about to question the woman*).
       An interview room? Where's the rape suite?
Gene: Rape suite? Is that with or without a minibar? (1.3)

Here the strategy of *Ashes to Ashes* is the same as in *Life on Mars*: in highlighting reactionary attitudes in the past it also demonstrates how police culture has changed since with a better understanding of the trauma of rape victims and the introduction of special interview facilities. In this context the historical period of *Ashes to Ashes* is significant: it is set in the same year as the production of the observational documentary series *Police*. This was produced by the BBC's regional documentary unit at Bristol and followed the work of E Division of the Thames Valley Police based in Reading: the Home Office had seen it as a public relations exercise following the race riots of 1981 but this backfired when one episode featured officers dismissing an allegation of rape made by a woman with a history of mental illness (one of the male officers describes it as 'the biggest bollocks I've ever heard') and pressuring her into withdrawing it. 'A Complaint of Rape' prompted a public outrage and has been credited with changing the way in which the police deal with rape victims.[13]

Yet in most other respects *Ashes to Ashes* sidesteps the question of sexism within the police force – and by implication within society at large. And for this the character of Alex Drake herself is largely responsible. On one level Alex demonstrates progressive credentials: she is introduced as a modern career woman juggling work and motherhood and she is shown to be no less capable than her male colleagues. But in her fantasy world she is willing to accept not only her subordinate position but also the sexism of her colleagues: she even allows Gene to stamp her bottom (though this is a *quid pro quo* to get him to accept her line of enquiry into a case). It is as if Alex abandons her feminism when she enters her fantasy world: freed from the constraints of motherhood (despite her repeated assertions of wanting to see her daughter) she embraces the lifestyle of a single woman with apparent glee. She becomes sexually promiscuous – in one episode she allows herself to be seduced by 'some Thatcherite wanker' (1.3) – and is often drunk. And she dresses in a highly sexualized way: tight leather trousers or jeans in preference to the sober trouser suit of her contemporary self. Of course, this behaviour might be claimed as pro-feminist in the sense that Alex is asserting her own freedom: the counter-argument is that her behaviour merely serves to reinforce sexual and gender stereotypes. A series in which a major character can express her femininity only by dressing 'like a tart' – *Ashes to Ashes* takes an almost perverse delight in finding situations where Alex is undercover as a bunny girl or an escort – would hardly seem to be a site of progressive gender politics. In the event the excesses of Alex's behaviour – and the sexualized nature of her outfits – were toned down after the first series of *Ashes to Ashes*: this might have been in response to viewers who felt (rather like Gene) that she was too 'tarty'.

Ashes to Ashes therefore represents a problematic text for feminist scholars because it does not conform to the expected narrative of the female-centred police drama which should be to challenge the institutionalized sexism of the workplace and to provide characterizations of strong women who are able to assert themselves in a man's world. The paradigmatic texts in this narrative are *Cagney & Lacey* (for America) and *Prime Suspect* (for Britain). Lynda La Plante's *Prime Suspect* was produced intermittently between 1991 and 2006: the character of DCI Jane Tennison (Helen Mirren) became a means of exploring wider social discourses around feminism, sexism and the challenges faced by women police officers. It also became a yardstick against which to judge other female-centred police dramas (which are often found wanting). There is a sense in which the 'problem' with *Ashes to Ashes* is that it was not *Prime Suspect*. A number of explanatory frameworks have been put forward for this. On a broad level it has been suggested that police dramas since *Prime Suspect* have moved from a feminist to a post-feminist discourse: that the urgency of gender equality as a political issue has been acknowledged and that dramas have since returned to a more personalized and (in conventional terms) feminized arena. Charlotte Brunsdon, for example, whose previous work on *Prime Suspect* was instrumental in setting the terms of academic debate, has argued that early 2000s series such as *The Ghost Squad*, *Murder in Suburbia* and *Scott & Bailey* have introduced 'a postfeminist sensibility' into the genre insofar as their female protagonists are more concerned about their personal than their professional lives in marked contrast to the driven career woman Jane Tennison.[14] Hannah Hamad, one of the few feminist scholars to write specifically about *Ashes to Ashes*, offers a nuanced reading of the series in which she argues that 'the resident postfeminist discourse of early *Ashes* shifted over time, and that these changes manifested with the advent of recessionary culture.[15] She suggests that the first series of *Ashes to Ashes* is more critical of the sexist and patriarchal culture of the police but that later episodes become more accepting of Gene's 'recidivist masculinity', which she attributes to the financial crisis of 2008 reaffirming the traditionally male characteristics of strength and leadership at a time of economic uncertainty. As Alex tells Gene in the last episode: 'You're the most difficult, stubborn, obnoxious, misogynistic and reckless human being I've ever met. And yet, somehow, you make us all feel safe.'

However, the issue of gender did not feature as prominently as one might expect in the critical reception of *Ashes to Ashes* which focused more on whether it was better or worse than *Life on Mars*. The jury was out. On the one hand, there were those who thought it a worthy sequel. John Preston (*Sunday Telegraph*) felt that it 'came served with enormous energy and inventiveness on screen' and that it 'looks set to be as richly exuberant – and enjoyable – as the series that spawned it'.[16] Gerard O'Donovan (*Daily Telegraph*) felt that Gene Hunt's return 'virtually guaranteed the success of the much anticipated sequel *Ashes to Ashes*' and that the 1980s setting 'opened up a cornucopia of new possibilities for nostalgic irony'.[17] At the end of the first series O'Donovan averred that 'the series was always watchable, often intriguing and usually highly amusing. And the mad Eighties fashions and atmospheric soundtrack had a way of wafting us along every episode'.[18] For Robert Hanks (*The Independent*): 'At bottom, this is the mixture as before: a bit of pop culture, a bit of sci-fi, a bit of weirdness, and a lot of Philip Glenister hamming it up as old-style macho copper DCI Hunt. This time around, though, there's a bit more self-awareness.'[19] And Matthew D'Ancona (*The Spectator*) similarly felt that '[it] looks as if *Ashes to Ashes* will be more camp, more knowing and even more post-modern than its predecessor'.[20]

On the other hand, others felt that *Ashes to Ashes* was too derivative or that – in the popular parlance of television fan culture – it had 'jumped the shark'. Andrew Billen (*The Times*) found that 'much is second-hand' and complained that 'the action sequences are no longer taken seriously'.[21] Brian Viner (*The Independent*) felt that 'it never quite hit the same sublime notes as the original ... It was reasonable enough to give DCI Hunt and his unreconstructed coppers another planet to inhabit after *Life on Mars*, but the time-travel element has become an annoying distraction'.[22] Kathryn Flett (*The Observer*) asked: 'How post-modern are we these days? Watching *Ashes* I felt as though *Mars*'s tongue-in-cheek joie de vivre had been all but sacrificed.' She was particularly critical of Keeley Hawes, whom she felt 'has either been spectacularly miscast or woefully misdirected' and accused her of 'over-acting, with a performance pitched just short of hysteria ... [She] shrieked her way through the entire hour, to the point where I started wincing'.[23] Hawes's performance was a common complaint – especially for female critics. Hermione Eyre (*Independent on Sunday*), for example, found her 'grating – overwrought where John Simm was serene' and noted the 'lack of chemistry between Glenister and Hawes'.[24] Sam Woollaston (*The Guardian*) felt that *Ashes to Ashes* was 'actually pretty bad. Philip Glenister, who stole the show last time around as the thuggish Gene

Hunt, is still here. But his unreconstructed sidekicks are so over the top and the innuendo and groan-inducing jokes come so fast that the whole thing can't decide whether it's a police drama or a comedy parody of *The Professionals*'.[25] When the second series aired, Woollaston compared it unfavourably with Channel 4's *Red Riding* – a trilogy of television films about the Yorkshire police force during the 1970s and 1980s based on the books by David Peace – which 'as a picture of police corruption from around the same time, was everything that this isn't – proper, dark, scary, convincing. Next to *Red Riding*, *Ashes to Ashes* looks like *Grange Hill*'.[26]

Although Matthew Graham teased the press that there would be a third series called *The Laughing Gnome* set in the 1960s and featuring a young Gene Hunt this did not – perhaps fortunately – come to pass. However, there was an unusual coda to *Ashes to Ashes* which demonstrated the extent to which the series had become part of the wider cultural landscape in early-twenty-first-century Britain. The last series of *Ashes to Ashes* coincided with the general election campaign of 2010: the incumbent Labour government – in power since 1997 but with its opinion poll ratings declining following its handling of the financial crisis of 2008 and an unpopular Prime Minister in Gordon Brown – faced a challenge from a resurgent Conservative Party. During the election campaign, the Labour Party referenced *Ashes to Ashes* in a poster which took a publicity still of Gene Hunt sitting on the bonnet of his Audi Quattro, replacing him with Conservative leader David Cameron alongside the line: 'Don't let him take Britain back to the 1980s.'[27] The aim had been to raise the spectre of the social unrest and unemployment of the early Thatcher period. But the tactic backfired: the Conservative Party was happy to associate itself with Gene Hunt's robust approach to policing and Cameron was reported to have been 'flattered' by the comparison to the macho policeman.[28] The Conservatives reappropriated the image by issuing the same poster but now with the line: 'Fire up the Quattro, it's time for a change.' Hence, the character of Gene Hunt was claimed as both a reactionary throwback to the past and an impetus for change – an instance of how the political and cultural meanings attached to popular culture can be shaped by the ideological contexts in which they circulate as much as by the texts themselves.

Downton Abbey

Downton Abbey (2010–15) was by any measure one of the most successful costume dramas not just of the early twenty-first century but in the history of British television.[1] In Britain it regularly drew audiences over 11 million in its Sunday-evening primetime slot and won three National Television Awards – voted for by the public – while in the United States its success was nothing short of remarkable: it attracted record audiences for the non-commercial Public Broadcasting Service (PBS) and was nominated for over fifty Emmy Awards over its six seasons. Its roll-call of honours included the Primetime Emmy Award for Outstanding Miniseries, the Golden Globe for Best Miniseries, the Broadcasting Press Guild Award for Best Drama Series and the Producers' Guild of America's Award for Best Short Form Television Series. It was sold to over 100 countries and by 2012 was reckoned to be one of the most-watched television series in the world with an estimated global audience of 120 million.[2]

It will be clear that *Downton Abbey* represents more than just a successful television series – both critically and commercially – but that it was also a cultural phenomenon of the first order. Highclere Castle in Hampshire, which doubled for the fictional stately home of the title, saw a significant increase in visitors on the strength of its association with *Downton Abbey*, while the series is credited with fuelling a demand for English butlers in America and China.[3] Its creator Julian Fellowes claimed that 'we had no idea' why *Downton Abbey* was such a success: 'Exactly why the series has had such an impact, reached so many people around the world, all nationalities, all ages, all types, I cannot begin to explain.'[4] As with other popular dramas, however, the success of *Downton Abbey* was no accident but should be placed in its institutional and cultural contexts. On the one hand, *Downton Abbey* might be seen to exemplify the persistence of residual forms even in the age of the new

British Quality Television: the costume series after all has a long history and cultural pedigree. On the other hand, the social politics and stylistic practices of *Downton Abbey* demonstrate how a residual genre can be reinvented in line with the ideological and formal demands of television drama in the early 2000s. To this extent *Downton Abbey* can be understood – rather like the otherwise entirely dissimilar *Life on Mars* – as a transformative example of its genre.

The costume drama has enjoyed a distinguished presence in British television culture over many years. Its history – like that of the police series – can be mapped through different cycles since the 1950s. The early history of the costume drama was dominated by the BBC, which specialized in the production of classic serials – themselves an inheritance from radio – adapted from canonical texts of English literature: Austen, Dickens, Eliot, Thackeray et al.[5] The advent of commercial television in the 1950s did not immediately challenge the BBC's monopoly in this field of cultural production as the ITV network initially preferred telefilm adventure series such as *The Adventures of Robin Hood* rather than the studio-based literary adaptations associated with the BBC. It was in the late 1960s that the costume drama really came into its own: the BBC spent £250,000 on a serialization of John Galsworthy's family chronicle *The Forsyte Saga* in 1967 (the last major serial to be shot in black and white), while its adaptation of William Thackeray's *Vanity Fair* the same year was the first in colour. The advent of colour broadcasting ushered in a golden age for the genre in the 1970s, including *The Six Wives of Henry VIII, Elizabeth R, Upstairs, Downstairs, The Pallisers, I, Claudius, Poldark* and *Edward and Mrs Simpson*. By now British-made costume serials were regularly being screened on American television via the PBS as part of its *Masterpiece Theatre* strand: to this extent serials such as *Upstairs, Downstairs* were direct predecessors of *Downton Abbey* which also came to the attention of American audiences in this way.[6] Granada Television's *Brideshead Revisited* and *The Jewel in the Crown* were the major landmarks of the genre in the 1980s: both were expensively produced and won great critical and popular acclaim. The 1990s saw a revival of the Sunday-evening classic serial with the BBC's *Middlemarch* and its much-loved *Pride and Prejudice*, a tradition that continued into the new millennium with *Cranford* and *Lark Rise to Candleford*.

The prevalence of the costume drama has placed the genre at the heart of critical discussions in British television studies. In particular, it has become the focus of debates over the nature of 'quality' television. On the one hand, the costume drama is seen as representing television's engagement with 'culture' (through its source material in canonical literary texts) and 'quality' (in terms of its high production values, literate scripting and casting recognized actors often with a pedigree in the theatre). In this sense the costume drama may be seen as a middle-brow alternative to supposedly more low-brow and culturally less respectable genres such as the soap opera. It also represents what might be termed the 'best of British' television in contrast to imported American fare such as the cop series or the glossy super-soaps of the 1980s such as *Dallas* and *Dynasty*. On the other hand, however, the costume drama is sometimes regarded by more progressive critics as a conservative genre in both its content and aesthetics. It is held that the costume drama distances itself from the social problems of the present through recourse to cultural nostalgia for the past. In particular, the lovingly recreated period *mise-en-scène* is seen as a safe alternative to the more agitational style of contemporary social realist plays and serials. John Caughie, for example, argues that costume drama 'has avoided its historical appointment with modernism, with naturalism or with critical realism'.[7] The critical discourses of television drama mirror a similar debate in film studies over what has come to be known as 'heritage film': indeed, the term 'heritage drama' is now often used in relation to both film and television.

Charlotte Brunsdon identifies four 'quality components' associated with the heritage drama on British television: a literary source which lends it cultural respectability; the best of British acting talent – performers who invest costume drama with a degree of 'class', usually imported from their background in legitimate theatre; money, which enables the budget to be put on the screen through high production values; and what she terms 'heritage export' – 'a certain image of England and Englishness…in which national identity is expressed through class and imperial identity'.[8] While many costume dramas do indeed conform to these four criteria – serials such as *The Forsyte Saga*, *Brideshead Revisited*, *The Jewel in the Crown* and *Pride and Prejudice* are all paradigmatic examples – there are some that problematize the scheme if it is applied too rigidly. *Upstairs, Downstairs*, for example, was an example of a costume drama not based on a literary source text but written specifically for television – as indeed was *Downton Abbey* – while *Lark Rise to Candleford* quickly exhausted its original source material in the semi-autobiographical novels of Flora Thompson and invented new stories based around the same characters. And the literary sources of many costume dramas also problematize the question of television authorship: the BBC's *Pride and Prejudice*, for instance, was as much Andrew Davies's *Pride and Prejudice* as Jane Austen's.[9]

Downton Abbey was a co-production between Carnival Films and WGBH-TV Boston. Carnival Films was a well-established independent producer which, like its newer competitor Kudos, had supplied programme content for the major British broadcasters for several decades: its best-known drama productions included *Agatha Christie's Poirot*, *Jeeves and Wooster*, *Bugs*, *Hotel Babylon* and *Whitechapel*. In 2008 Carnival Films was bought by the US media conglomerate NBS Universal as 'part of a strategy by the US network and Hollywood studio bosses to move into production outside America'.[10] WGBH-TV Boston is a non-commercial US broadcaster that provides approximately two-thirds of drama content for PBS and coordinates *Masterpiece Theatre* (now known simply as *Masterpiece*). Gareth Neame, the co-executive producer of *Downton Abbey*, explained the production ecologies involved:

> The model is that shows such as *Downton* are overwhelmingly conceived and realised in the UK, with the UK broadcaster paying the lion's share of the budget and the producer supplying any deficit finance required (in other words, any gap between the total budget and the license fee paid by the broadcaster). As a non-profit organisation, Masterpiece and PBS's pockets are not deep and they generally have contributed relatively small percentages of the budgets ... They offer relatively small amounts of money for the rights to broadcast these shows, frankly because (traditionally) almost no-one else wanted them.[11]

When it began in 2010, the reported cost of *Downton Abbey* was £1 million per episode: this put it squarely in the top-budget bracket of British drama, although it was still cheaper than the costs of US network drama which could be up to £3 million per hour and for prestige HBO series such as *Boardwalk Empire* and *Game of Thrones* might be significantly more.[12] ITV's response to complaints from some viewers that the first (ninety-minute) episode of *Downton Abbey* was interrupted by too many commercial breaks was that it was 'only by doing this that they can afford to run high-quality drama like *Downton Abbey*.[13]

Downton Abbey certainly exemplifies the old industry adage of putting the budget on the screen: its expensive production values are evident in the sumptuous high-definition photography and the lush period décor. The series made extensive use of real locations: as well as Highclere Castle these included Waddesdon Manor in Buckinghamshire, Byfleet Manor in Surrey, Inveraray Castle in Argyll, Alnwick Castle in Northumbria, the heritage Bluebell Railway and the Historic Dockyard at Chatham. The casting of *Downton Abbey* also exemplified the 'best of British' acting talent that constitutes one of the characteristics of quality drama. As one American reviewer remarked: 'The diversity and excellence of *Downton*'s casting is what brings us back each week: Hugh Bonneville, Elizabeth McGovern, Maggie Smith, Michelle Dockery, Dan Stevens, Jim Carter, Phyllis Logan etc etc.'[14] While Maggie Smith, the *grande dame* of British stage and screen, was invariably singled out for her role as the outspoken Dowager Countess of Grantham, and won both a Golden Globe and an Emmy for Best Supporting Actress, *Downton Abbey* was essentially an ensemble drama: indeed, one of its many awards was for Outstanding Performance by an Ensemble in a Drama Series from the Screen Actors' Guild.

It is significant that most of the series' major awards were in the United States: in Britain its first series was nominated for Best Drama Series at the British Film and Television Academy Awards but lost to *Sherlock*. The success of *Downton Abbey* in the United States and other overseas markets also marks it out as what Brunsdon terms a 'heritage export'. It is important to recognize that the international television market is much more than just America. Indeed, Gareth Neame reacted against the idea that *Downton Abbey* was packaged to appeal specifically to American audiences: 'It always annoys me when people say "oh, this is done with one eye on the American market". There are more territories around the world that have little or no interest in the country house and the British class system – and those that do think they're too old-fashioned and full of ugly people.'[15] (The same point had been made in the 1960s by writer Dennis Spooner, who contributed to a range of ITC's action-adventure series including *Man in a Suitcase*, *The Champions*, *Department S* and *Randall and Hopkirk (Deceased)*, which were all sold internationally: 'During the Sixties I was bitterly attacked by somebody who said: "Look! There's Spooner sitting at

Elstree pandering to the Americans." I wrote him a letter saying: "You're quite wrong. I'm pandering to the Japanese and the Germans and everybody.'")[16]

Nevertheless, there has always been a sense that the American market represents a sort of Holy Grail for British film and television producers: and in this context the success of *Downton Abbey* was quite remarkable. Shown in the Sunday-evening *Masterpiece* strand on PBS, *Downton Abbey* drew some of the biggest audiences for a drama series in two decades. The first episode of the second series, for example, attracted 'a staggering audience of 6.3 million viewers' – twice the usual audience for its slot – and was 'the second-watched program at 9 p.m. on Super Bowl Sunday – a primetime coup for a period drama that airs on PBS, of all places'.[17] This was surpassed by the fourth-series première which was seen by 10.2 million viewers – more than competing dramas on the main networks and the highest audience for PBS since Ken Burns's acclaimed documentary series *Civil War* in 1990.[18] It was 'a godsend for public television in America, where it has delivered PBS's *Masterpiece* program its largest-ever viewership'.[19] There is no doubt that the arrival of *Downton Abbey* was timely for PBS, which had recently suffered cuts in its funding but now found itself 'at the center of a national cultural conversation' for the first time in many years.[20]

However, in one important respect *Downton Abbey* did not fit Brunsdon's schema of 'quality components': it was an original television drama rather than a literary adaptation. The series' credits declare that it is 'written and created by Julian Fellowes': to this extent it can be seen as an example of authored drama in much the same way as – to take a number of contrasting examples – Alan Bleasdale's *Boys from the Blackstuff*, Dennis Potter's *The Singing Detective*, Lynda La Plante's *Prime Suspect* or Anthony Horowitz's *Foyle's War*. Fellowes was a character actor known for playing upper-class 'snob' roles turned scriptwriter who had won an Academy Award for Best Original Screenplay for *Gosford Park* (2002), a country house film drama set in 1932. Fellowes, who hails from an upper-class background and who was ennobled in 2011 as Baron Fellowes of West Stafford, said – actually in relation to his novel *Snobs* though the point would apply equally well to both *Gosford Park* and *Downton Abbey* – that 'I decided to write about what I knew ... to write about my own past and the world I'd grown up in'.[21] There are a number of parallels between *Gosford Park* and *Downton Abbey*: both feature an ensemble cast, Maggie

Smith is common to both, and both focus equally on life 'above' and 'below' stairs in the institution of the English country house. If *Gosford Park* is more cynical, even brutal, in its representation of the social values and hypocrisy of the English aristocracy – in contrast, *Downton Abbey* affords a much more sympathetic portrait – this may probably be attributed to the agency of its American director, Robert Altman, rather than Fellowes. What Fellowes did bring to both *Gosford Park* and *Downton Abbey*, however, was a particular interest in the minutiae of social observation: 'I think I have a very detailed sense of observation ... I am interested in the details of people's lives and what information these details give us.'[22]

Some British reviewers compared *Downton Abbey* to *Upstairs, Downstairs* (1971–75), which, although set in a London town house rather than a country estate, similarly chronicled the lives of an aristocratic family and their servants against a background of real historical events either side of the First World War. Indeed, some of the characters of *Downton Abbey* are almost precise duplicates of those in *Upstairs Downstairs*: the authoritarian butler (Hudson/Carson), the pretty young maid (Sarah/Anna), the eager-to-please valet (Edward/Mosley), the avuncular head of the household (Lord Richard Bellamy/Robert, Earl of Grantham), his wife (Lady Marjorie/Lady Cora) and their daughter with a colourful love life (Lady Georgina/Lady Mary). Like *Downton Abbey*, *Upstairs, Downstairs* was written by actors: Eileen Atkins and Jean Marsh. However, the production discourse of *Downton Abbey* sought to position it more in relation to contemporary rather than period dramas. Gareth Neame suggested that a more appropriate comparison was to the American political drama *The West Wing*: '*The West Wing* is about a city state, the White House building, what goes on inside, the lives and relationships of the people who staff it ... [*Downton Abbey*] is in the same family as a hospital show or one set in a police station, with hierarchies, rivalries and politics.'[23]

While *Downton Abbey* certainly belongs in the lineage of heritage drama exemplified by series such as *Upstairs, Downstairs* and *Brideshead Revisited*, however, it also represents a shift in the genre away from some of the traditional heritage characteristics and towards embracing certain aspects of contemporary drama. This is most apparent in terms of its form and narration. Most costume dramas adhere to a highly pictorialist visual style in which the material trappings of the past – imposing stately homes, elegant costumes,

vintage motor cars and all other manner of lovingly recreated period detail –
are displayed as a form of spectacle through a combination of slow pacing
and languorous camerawork which allows the spectator to wallow in the
sumptuous *mise-en-scène*. Paul Kerr argues that 'in classic serials props are
employed specifically as signifiers of the past and its faithful reconstruction.
Such ambitions of authenticity serve to factify [*sic*] the fiction, literally to
prop it up, performing a positivist role as the tangible trace of a lost era'.[24]
Downton Abbey certainly includes its fair share of pictorialism – there is
no shortage of beautifully composed long shots of Highclere Castle, which
features throughout the series as a signifier of place and the persistence of
tradition – but otherwise the series largely eschews the slow pace of many
heritage dramas for a more fluid style of narration. Like *Gosford Park*, *Downton
Abbey* is far from static in its camera set-ups: the direction makes extensive
use of Steadicam to keep close to the actors, following the movements and
overhearing their conversations. The visual spectacle and period splendour
of the heritage drama are therefore combined with a sense of closeness and
intimacy that in its way owes as much to the tradition of studio drama.

The 'intimacy' of *Downton Abbey* also exemplifies another way in which it
represents a point of change for the costume drama on television. As it is not
a literary adaptation, *Downton Abbey* is free from the tyranny of fidelity to the
text that inevitably dominates the critical discourses around the classic serial.
Instead, it draws upon the conventions of other genres, particularly the soap
opera. It would perhaps not be too much of an exaggeration to suggest that
Downton Abbey is to all intents and purposes a period equivalent of the famous
American super-soap *Dallas*: the Granthams are the Ewings (just with different
accents) and Downton Abbey is Southfork ranch. The main narrative of the
first series of *Downton Abbey*, for example, is the acceptance and assimilation
of an outsider, Matthew Crawley, a distant third cousin who becomes the heir
presumptive to the Grantham title and estate following the loss of the previous
heir on the *Titanic*. The arrival of an outsider into a tightly knit and initially
unwelcoming family or other social community is a typical motif of the soap
opera: early episodes of *Dallas* had also focused on the gradual acceptance
of the initially unwelcome newcomer (Pamela Barnes Ewing) into the family.
The rivalry between the three Grantham sisters – Lady Mary, Lady Edith and
Lady Sybil – mirrors that between the Ewing brothers, while a recurring theme

of *Downton Abbey* is the threat to the estate itself from fluctuating economic fortunes just as the ownership of Southfork was sometimes at stake in *Dallas*.

Downton Abbey has recourse to the melodramatic conventions of soap opera perhaps to a greater degree than any previous costume drama. Soap opera is characterized by its 'overdramatic excess': it is driven by tabloid-style sensationalism and feeds on animosities, feuds and scandals.[25] *Downton Abbey* may lack the histrionics of *Dallas* and *Dynasty* but it employs similar plot devices. Among the soap-opera plots that feature in the series are the shaming of Lady Mary when she is seduced by a visiting Turkish diplomat who then dies in her bed ('I'll be ruined, mama – ruined and notorious – a laughing stock, a social pariah ... Is that what you want for the family?') and the subsequent threat of blackmail by her suitor Sir Richard Carlisle who comes into possession of an incriminating letter written by Lady Edith; the miscarriage of Lady Cora when she slips on a bar of soap deliberately left under her bath by the scheming maid O'Brien who wrongly believed she was about to be dismissed from service; the pregnancy out of wedlock of the flighty housemaid Ethel; Matthew Crawley's somewhat improbable recovery from a supposedly crippling injury during the Great War just in time to prevent Lady Mary from being obliged to marry Carlisle; the imprisonment of Lord Granthan's valet John Bates for the murder of his estranged wife; the cross-class romance between Lady Sybil and the family's Irish chauffeur Tom Branson; Lady Sybil's death in childbirth; and Matthew Crawley dying in a car accident immediately after the birth of his son and heir. The most notorious and sensational of the many soap-opera moments in *Downton Abbey* was the rape of the maid Anna by a visiting guest's valet in series four: this prompted over 400 complaints to the network and to broadcasting regulator Ofcom 'from people who did not think the storyline was necessarily an appropriate theme to be exploring in a Sunday-night period drama'.[26]

While some critics may (indeed did) deride the 'soap-opera' elements of *Downton Abbey*, it might be argued that this strategy actually allows a more progressive representation of social politics than classic serials such as *Brideshead Revisited* or *Pride and Prejudice* which are bound by their status as adaptations to reproduce something of the social values of the original (notwithstanding the fact that literary critics have identified elements of social criticism in both Waugh and Austen). *Downton Abbey* is not unique as a costume drama that affords equal narrative space to both the upper and the lower classes but it is a relatively rare example. It is surely significant that other costume dramas which do this in television and film, including *Upstairs, Downstairs* and *Gosford Park*, are also original dramas rather than adaptations. As Julianne Pidduck has observed: 'An "upstairs/downstairs" architecture for the house of fiction invites an interrogation of class difference.'[27] *Gosford Park* in particular is notable for its aspects of social critique: the aristocracy is characterized as snobbish, elitist, exclusive and utterly indifferent to the feelings of their servants. *Downton Abbey* is much more sympathetic to the aristocracy than *Gosford Park*: the Earl of Grantham (Hugh Bonneville) is characterized as a benevolent paternalist who shows a genuine concern in the welfare of his tenants and servants. Nevertheless, the series is concerned with the nature of the class system: like many dramas with an institutional setting the house and its inhabitants can be read as a set of archetypal characters who represent different social values.

Downton Abbey configures social relationships in two broad ways. The first strategy is to focus on the relationships within the house itself. A particular characteristic of *Downton Abbey* – which, as it is shared with *Gosford Park*, may reasonably be attributed to Fellowes – is that the social structure below stairs mirrors that above stairs in its hierarchies and groups. There is a clear pecking order of both male servants (butler, valet, footman) and female servants (housekeeper, lady's maid, housemaid). The middle-aged butler Carson and housekeeper Mrs Hughes act *in loco parentis* to the servants under their charge. Again consistent with *Gosford Park* is the idea that servants in the English country house are often just as socially conservative as their employers. Carson, for example, is a butler of the old school, unwilling to let maids serve at dinner even when faced with a shortage of footmen during the Great War. He identifies so closely with his employer that when the future of Downton Abbey is in jeopardy he even refers to 'our family threatened with the loss of all they hold dear ... They're the only family I've got'. And Lady Cora's maid O'Brien is as shocked as the Dowager Countess at the idea that the new heir to the earldom – which is bestowed exclusively through the male line – is 'a doctor's son from Manchester. Gentlemen don't work – not real gentlemen'. It is significant that the more sympathetic characters below stairs, such as Anna, tend to be those who accept their place in the social order, while the less sympathetic characters, such as scheming footman Thomas Barrow, are ambitious for social improvement.

This might seem to point towards a social structure that is rigid and fixed. However, *Downton Abbey* does offer the possibility of social mobility: this is exemplified above stairs by Matthew's acceptance both as heir apparent and as a legitimate suitor for Lady Mary, and below stairs by Anna's promotion from housemaid to lady's maid. The Earl of Grantham is initially horrified when his youngest daughter Lady Sybil begins an affair with Irish chauffer Tom Branson: he disowns her, then accepts her back into the family with her husband, who by the end of the series has been accepted as a member of the family. *Downton Abbey* is also notable for a relatively liberal attitude – certainly more so than the social values of the time – towards those on the margins or periphery of society. It is sympathetic to the plight of homosexuals – Barrow, for example, becomes a much more likeable character in series three as he comes to terms with his homosexuality – and to those who are trapped by legal and social situations, such as John Bates, whose duplicitous wife refuses him a divorce so he can marry Anna, and Lady Edith's suitor Charles Edwards, whose wife has been consigned to an asylum on account of her dementia. In common with heritage films such as *Howards End* (1992) and *The Remains of the Day* (1993), *Downton Abbey* represents characters who are trapped by social conventions. Even the Earl of Grantham himself occasionally expresses a sense of frustration with the weight of social responsibility: 'I've given my life to Downton. I was born here and I expect to die here. I claim no career beyond the nurturing of this house and its estates. It is my third parent and my fourth child.'

The second narrative strategy of *Downton Abbey* is to present the house and its people in the context of the wider social and political landscape of the time. In this regard it does bear a particularly close comparison with *Upstairs, Downstairs*, which similarly chronicled the fortunes of an aristocratic family and their servants against the background of national events. The first series of *Downton Abbey* begins with the news of the sinking of the *Titanic* (April 1912) and ends with the outbreak of the First World War (August 1914). Other events referred to in the series include the Marconi scandal of 1913, the Easter Rising of 1916, the Russian Revolution, the Spanish Influenza pandemic of 1919, the formation of the Irish Free State and the Beer Hall *putsch* of 1924. However, unlike, say, *Days of Hope* (1975), the BBC's acclaimed drama about the history of the Labour movement, *Downton Abbey* is not really concerned with the events themselves except insofar as they help to structure the narrative's time frame. This point was well made by American reviewer Ben W. Heineman Jr: 'The ideas of the time – class distinction, the horror of war, Irish nationalism, the equal rights of women – are just simplified and stylized bits of kaleidoscopic narrative, used more to move the story along than to explain their complexities and nuances.'[28]

Nevertheless, the strategy of locating fictional characters against a background of real historical events serves a specific ideological function in *Downton Abbey*. The underlying narrative that emerges across its six series is the effect of historical processes of change on the institution of the English country house. The Edwardian era is generally seen as the twilight of the great country houses, whose very social and economic fabric would be rendered asunder by the social changes of the First World War. *Downton Abbey*, strictly speaking, is post-Edwardian as the narrative begins in 1912, although the term 'Edwardian' is often applied imprecisely in reference to the pre-war decade described by George Dangerfield in his book *The Strange Death of Liberal England* (1936). The series is replete with references to social and historical change: perhaps the most sustained narrative is the rise of first-wave feminism as Lady Edith joins the Suffragist movement during the war and later challenges gender conventions by taking up journalism. On occasion the politics of *Downton Abbey* seem to have been as much influenced by present-day concerns: in series five, for example, the Earl of Grantham arranges for a separate plaque to honour Mrs Patmore's nephew who had been unjustly executed for cowardice during the war and whose name had been left off the village war memorial. This reflects the changing culture of remembrance in the twenty-first century and the campaign to rehabilitate those who were 'shot at dawn' now that the nature of 'shell shock' was better understood. The politics of *Downton Abbey* are perhaps best described as Liberal Tory: the series suggests a residual sympathy for the aristocracy and its traditions while accepting that change is not only inevitable but ultimately is for the better. Again it was an American reviewer, Jerry Bower, who perhaps summed this up best: 'The world has to change; he [the Earl of Grantham] knows it, but he wants the world to change more slowly than it wants itself to change.'[29]

The reception discourses of *Downton Abbey* serve to illustrate the wider critical and cultural debates over heritage drama. While most reviews in the press, especially for the first series in 2010, were generally favourable, they nevertheless highlighted contrasting attitudes towards the costume drama. On the one hand, there were those critics, such as Sam Wollaston (*The Guardian*), who welcomed it as a classy, quality drama series: 'It's beautifully made – handsome, artfully crafted and acted … This is going to be a treat if you like lavish period drama of a Sunday evening.'[30] (Many of the British reviews made some reference to the idea of Sunday-evening drama: this has traditionally been a slot for costume dramas – including *Pride and Prejudice*, *Cranford* and *Lark Rise to Candleford* – though for some unfathomable reason the BBC put its last series of *Spooks* on Sundays against the second series of *Downton Abbey*.) Similar views were echoed by Ceri Radford in the *Daily Telegraph* ('another Sunday evening national fixation, and a significant source of cheer as the nights start drawing in') and by Jan Moir in the *Daily Mail* ('most delicious Sunday evening entertainment … the most popular costume drama of recent times').[31] These responses suggest that it was the 'quality' aspects of *Downton Abbey* that reviewers enjoyed. On the other hand, there were other critics who disliked the series for much the same reasons. Rachel Cooke (*The New Statesman*), for example, complained after the first episode that 'virtually every costume-drama cliché one can think of has been concentrated into a little over an hour's worth of television.'[32] And A.A. Gill (*Sunday Times*), in a characteristically waspish review, declared that it exemplified 'everything I despise and despair of on British television: National Trust sentimentality, costumed comfort drama that flogs an embarrassing, demeaning and bogus vision of the place I live in.'[33]

Like all costume dramas, *Downton Abbey* raised the question of whose past is being represented. In 2012 – a year when events such as the Diamond Jubilee of Queen Elizabeth II and the Olympic Games in London focused attention on British history and cultural identity – *Downton Abbey* became the focus of a minor controversy over its representation (or rather its non-representation) of ethnic minority groups. Lara Pawson (*The Guardian*) suggested that its image of a Britain 'homogenous and hermetically sealed' from immigration compared unfavourably with the work of black British artists such as John Akomfrah and Kimathi Dankor whose work explored the multicultural legacy of Britain's past:

In a year in which Danny Boyle was congratulated for using Windrush arrivals in his Olympic opening ceremony, watching *Peripeteia* [a video film by John Akomfrah] reminded me how shortsighted a representation that was. Black people have been in Britain for hundreds of years, possibly thousands, and it is a sad indictment of us all that the work of artists such as Akomfrah and Dankor still seems so radical, so new and so political – while *Downton*'s aristocratic agitprop goes largely unnoticed.[34]

It was really a criticism of mainstream historical fictions in general, but *Downton Abbey* was seized upon as the example as it represented the most successful example of that genre at the time. Fellowes responded by introducing a sympathetic black character in series four in the form of jazz musician Jack Ross (Gary Carr) in order to 'open up the show's ethnicity'.[35] However, it is difficult to avoid the impression that this was a form of tokenism. The wider question of whether a costume drama like *Downton Abbey* was the right sort of vehicle to address multiculturalism went unanswered. A comment attributed to the Australian comedian Barry Humphries that *Downton Abbey* was popular in America 'because there are no black people in it' should perhaps not be taken too literally.[36]

The American critical reception was revealing in different respects. Most American critics highlighted the British parentage of *Downton Abbey* and saw it as a worthy heir to previous *Masterpiece* presentations such as *Upstairs, Downstairs* and *Brideshead Revisited*. Otherwise, the reviews tended to focus on what its popularity in the United States said about the cultural tastes of American audiences. James Parker (*The Atlantic*), for example, concluded that '*Downton Abbey* is a harmless, anachronistic masque of manners, in which the players keep obedient to their roles and thereby gratify the innate conservatism of the audience'.[37] Jerry Bower (*Forbes*) felt that its success demonstrated that 'there is no inherent need for good TV to be left of center. Stories sympathetic to virtue, preservation of property and admiration of nobility and of wealth can be told beautifully and to wide audiences.'[38] James Fenton (*New York Review of Books*) found it 'welcome counter-programming to the slow-burning despair and moral ambiguity of most quality drama on television right now'.[39] And Maureen Ryan (*The Huffington Post*) suggested that it was 'one of television's most constructed confections' but also offered an assessment of how it worked as drama:

Julian Fellowes is not all that interested in human nature as such and has an upper-class Englishman's horror of [*withering Dowager Countess voice*] 'psychology'. Fellowes is interested in people in so far as he can put them in situations that force them to react in certain ways: provoking the depths and complexities of those reactions just isn't his thing.[40]

There are interesting differences, therefore, in the British and American reception discourses of *Downton Abbey*. In Britain the series was seen very much as mainstream Sunday-evening drama and was understood (even by those who disliked it as old-fashioned and clichéd) squarely in the tradition of quality costume drama. In America, while it was also understood as quality drama, it was seen as representing a different type of quality: its British heritage and social conservatism marked it out as qualitatively different from American drama series. Or to put it another way: *Downton Abbey* was admired in Britain because it was like *Upstairs, Downstairs* or *Brideshead Revisited*, whereas in America it was admired because it was not like *Breaking Bad* or *House of Cards*.

In March 2015 the network and producer announced that the sixth series of *Downton Abbey* would be the last. According to Neame: 'Inevitably there comes a time when all shows should end and *Downton* is no exception. We wanted to close the doors of Downton Abbey when it felt right and natural for the story lines to come to an end and while the show was still being enjoyed so much by its fans.'[41] The final episode was the Christmas special of 2015: this was generally regarded as a fan-pleasing resolution to the family saga as it allowed a happy ending for the unlucky-in-love Lady Edith and rounded off most of the continuing subplots.[42] Fellowes went on to write the four-part mini-series *Titanic* (2012) and to adapt *Half a Sixpence* and *The Wind in the Willows* for the stage. Following *Downton Abbey* it was announced that he would write *The Gilded Age* – described as an 'American *Downton Abbey*' – for NBC.[43] At the time of writing a film of *Downton Abbey* is in pre-production: it seems a safe prediction – especially given the success of other recent British heritage films such as *The King's Speech* (2011) – that it will be popular on both sides of the Atlantic.

The success of *Downton Abbey* prompted a revival of the historical television drama. In particular, there was a vogue for what might be called heritage soap operas for Sunday evenings. ITV followed *Downton Abbey* with *Mr Selfridge* (2013–16), Andrew Davies's adaptation of Lindy Woodhead's biography of the founder of the London department store, which spanned much the same historical period as *Downton Abbey* and similarly set its semi-fictional drama against a landscape of real events. The BBC's popular *Call the Midwife* (2012–), created and written by Heidi Thomas and loosely based on the memoirs of Sister Jenny Worth, an Anglican midwife who worked in the Poplar district of London's East End, has regularly drawn audiences of over 10 million. *Call the Midwife* combines its period nostalgia – the series is set during the 1950s and 1960s – with social commentary as it explores issues such as working-class poverty, disease, epidemics, abortion, prostitution, racism, lesbianism and homosexuality. However, the most ambitious post-*Downton* historical drama was the Anglo-American series *The Crown* (2016–), commissioned by Netflix, the subscription-based online streaming service which since 2012 had ventured successfully into original film and television drama. *The Crown*, a royal biopic chronicling the reign of Queen Elizabeth II, was devised and written principally by Peter Morgan, writer of the feature film *The Queen* (2006) and the play *The Audience*. It reportedly cost £100 million and has been planned as a six-series arc.[44] Daniel J. Fienberg (*The Hollywood Reporter*) suggested that *The Crown* 'marks Netflix's strongest push to date into real of prestige drama' and that it represented 'costume drama at its most lush and addictive'.[45] Angela Lugo (*UWIRE*) felt that it 'exudes grace and refined taste'.[46] It remains to be seen whether the subscription model will take off in Britain in the way that it has in the United States. But it seems reasonable to say that Netflix might never have ventured into British costume drama on such an ambitious scale had it not been for the prior success of *Downton Abbey*.

Sherlock

Sherlock (2010–17), a modern reinterpretation of Sir Arthur Conan Doyle's famous Baker Street detective, represents perhaps the zenith of the new British Quality Television.[1] While its first series in the summer of 2010 drew respectable if unspectacular audiences (an average of 7.3 million across three ninety-minute episodes), its second series in January 2012 averaged 10.2 million and its third in January 2014 averaged 11.8 million. The third-season première 'The Empty Hearse' broadcast on 1 January 2014 recorded the highest audience for any BBC drama since the method of calculating ratings changed in 2001.[2] *Sherlock* also won critical plaudits and, following a raft of nominations in 2011 and 2012, won Emmy Awards in 2014 for Outstanding Writing for a Miniseries or Movie (Steven Moffat), Outstanding Lead Actor (Benedict Cumberbatch as Sherlock) and Outstanding Supporting Actor (Martin Freeman as John Watson). With its fast-paced storytelling, glossy visual style and irreverent approach to adaptation, *Sherlock* builds upon the innovations of series such as *Spooks* and *Hustle* and takes them even further: to date there has probably not been another British television drama that employs such a dazzling array of narrational tricks and elliptical devices. That it has done this without losing sight of the traditional virtues of clever writing and strong dramatic performances is one reason why *Sherlock* has been so enormously successful.

The character of Sherlock Holmes has a long history of adaptation into other media. The famous American stage actor William Gillette performed his play *Sherlock Holmes* from 1899 and appeared in a film version in 1916, while in Britain Eille Norwood starred in a series of three-reelers and two feature films for the Stoll Film Company in the early 1920s. In the talkie period there were acclaimed portrayals of the Great Detective by Arthur Wontner in five films in Britain in the 1930s and by Basil Rathbone in fourteen films – two for Twentieth Century Fox and twelve for Universal Pictures – between 1939 and 1946.[3] Among the many other actors to have donned the Great Detective's trademark deerstalker hat over the years are Peter Cushing (*The Hound of the Baserkvilles*), Christopher Lee (*Sherlock Holmes and the Deadly Necklace*), John Neville (*A Study in Terror*), Robert Stephens (*The Private Life of Sherlock Holmes*), George C. Scott (*They Might Be Giants*), Alan Arkin (*The Seven Per Cent Solution*), Roger Moore (*Sherlock Holmes in New York*), Christopher Plummer (*Murder by Decree*), Robert Downey Jr (*Sherlock Holmes* and *Sherlock Holmes: Game of Shadows*) and Ian McKellen (*Mr Holmes*). Indeed, it is reckoned that Sherlock Holmes is the most adapted fictional character in the history of cinema: he is one of those archetypes – alongside Tarzan, Dracula and Robin Hood – who are particularly amenable to critical reinterpretation and cultural reinvention at different times and in different contexts.[4]

Sherlock Holmes has also been adapted frequently for television. Ronald Howard starred in an American-financed telefilm series shot in France in 1954 and broadcast on the NBC network in the United States in 1954–55, while Douglas Wilmer and Peter Cushing both starred as Holmes for the BBC in the 1960s. Granada's *The Adventures of Sherlock Holmes* (1984–94) starring Jeremy Brett is widely regarded as the definitive television adaptation: a handsomely mounted heritage costume drama notable (for the most part) for its fidelity to the source texts. In the early 2000s there had already been two British television films written by Alan Cubitt starring Richard Roxburgh (*The Hound of the Baskervilles*) and Rupert Everett (*Sherlock Holmes and the Case of the Silk Stocking*) and four Canadian television films with Matt Frewer (*The Hound of the Baskervilles, The Sign of Four, The Royal Scandal, Sherlock Holmes and the Case of the Whitechapel Vampire*), while following the BBC's success with *Sherlock* the CBS network produced its own modernized version, *Elementary* (2012–19), set in New York and starring British actor Jonny Lee Miller as Holmes and Chinese-American Lucy Liu as a female Watson. There is some suggestion that CBS had originally wanted to remake *Sherlock* for American consumption – as per the American remake of *Life on Mars* – although in the event it opted for 'a contemporary take on Sherlock Holmes that will be based on Holmes and other characters in the public domain'.[5]

Sherlock was a product of the same stable as the BBC's successful revival of *Doctor Who*. Steven Moffat, the co-creator of *Sherlock* with Mark Gatiss, had succeeded Russell T. Davies as the 'showrunner' of *Doctor Who* in 2009, while Gatiss himself had written several episodes and had appeared in the series as an actor. It was during their many train journeys between London and the *Doctor Who* production base in Cardiff that Moffat and Gatiss hit upon the idea of *Sherlock*.[6] Both writers were drawn to Victorian Gothic fiction: Moffat had written *Jekyll* (2007), a modernized version of Robert Louis Stevenson's *The Strange Case of Dr Jekyll and Mr Hyde*, while Gatiss wrote the Victorian-themed *Doctor Who* episode 'The Unquiet Dead' as well as penning a pastiche novel, *The Vesuvius Club*, and adapting H.G. Wells's *The First Men in the Moon* for BBC4 in 2010. The BBC commissioned a one-hour pilot episode in 2008 at a reported cost of £800,000 with a view to producing a series of six one-hour episodes if the pilot was successful.[7] After seeing the pilot, however, Jay Hunt, the Controller of BBC1, and Ben Stephenson, the head of Drama Commissioning, 'decided to develop it into a bigger series ... It is understood they wanted to change the tone of the original production, make it more complex and introduce additional characters'.[8] *Sherlock* was commissioned as a series of three feature-length episodes rather than one-hour episodes. The original pilot 'A Study in Pink' was expanded and entirely reshot to the extent that it was 'completely reimagined in look, pace and sound'.[9] There are several possible reasons for this decision. One is that the feature-length format was consistent with other successful detective series at the time, including *Foyle's War*, *Lewis* (ITV's follow-up to *Inspector Morse* which proved nearly as popular as the original) and *Wallander* (the BBC's adaptations of Henning Mankell's Swedish detective starring Kenneth Branagh). Another factor was undoubtedly economic: *Sherlock* was commissioned at a time when the BBC was facing considerable external pressure to institute economies – the licence fee would be frozen by the Conservative-Liberal Democrat coalition government that came into office in 2010 – and one of the consequences of this was retrenchment in the commissioning of new drama. The cost of one ninety-minute episode would be rather less than two one-hour episodes. Ben Stephenson sought to present this as a strategy of product differentiation: 'In the US, the assumption is you have to make 12 or 24 episodes. *Sherlock* has made nine episodes over the course of three years, yet it's been such a big hit. Ultimately, it comes down to creativity – whatever its shape or size, creativity does drive commerciality.'[10]

Sherlock would be a co-production between the BBC, BBC America and WGBH-TV Boston. It was produced by Hartswood Films, an independent production company whose directors were Beryl Vertue and her daughter Sue Vertue (Steven Moffat's wife) and which specialized in situation comedy – including *Men Behaving Badly* and Moffat's own *Coupling* – as well as dramas including *Jekyll*, *The Guilty* and *Lady Chatterley's Lover*. Like *Downton Abbey*, there is no official confirmation of the amount of the budget that was provided by the American co-production partner, but according to a well-sourced article on the entertainment industry website *Den of Geek* 'there is a difference between a show like *Sherlock*, which was conceptualized as mostly a British production with some international funding (from America's PBS *Masterpiece* arm) that doesn't translate to much transnational creative control vs. a production like *The Night Manager* [2016], which was conceptualized as a collaborative co-production with funding, scripting, and casting decisions made with a global – at least British/American – context in mind'. The same article suggests that 'the typical model for *Masterpiece* co-production through WGBH involves putting up 10 per cent of the budget. This grants *Masterpiece*/WGBH the right to be consulted on casting and other creative decisions, but the final word ultimately lies with the major UK producer'.[11] There are also no official sources to confirm the budget of *Sherlock*, although the figure of $8 million (around £5.4 million) per series or $2.67 million (around £1.8 million) per episode quoted on one American website seems a reasonable estimate in comparison to other dramas at the time: this would place *Sherlock* at the high end of British drama production if not quite as expensive as HBO-produced dramas such as *Mad Men* ($2.3 million per one-hour episode) or *Game of Thrones* (which reportedly cost $8 million per episode).[12]

Like *Downton Abbey* – and like the tradition of British-made action-adventure series extending back to the early years of ITV such as *The Adventures of Robin Hood* in the 1950s and *Danger Man*, *The Saint* and *The Avengers* in the 1960s – *Sherlock* can be understood as a vehicle for both the economic and the cultural export of Britishness. While the BBC does not release sales figures for individual series, it has declared that the profits of its overseas sales arm BBC Worldwide since 2010 have been driven largely by four programmes – *Sherlock*, *Doctor Who*, *Top Gear* and *Strictly Come Dancing* (licensed for the United States as *Dancing with the Stars*) – and that for BBC Drama '*Sherlock* is our best selling programme' and had made a 'huge amount of money'.[13] It came at a time when British television was enjoying a higher profile in the US market due to the expansion of online streaming and 'on demand' television services such as Netflix and Amazon Prime which signalled a shift in viewing habits and enabled audiences to experience a wider range of British series than just those bought by the networks. In 2012 American broadcasters and other platforms spent a reported £475 million on British drama: *Downton Abbey* remained by some distance the most popular with audiences over 10 million on PBS, but *Sherlock* (4.2 million for the second series on PBS), the fantasy adventure *Merlin* (5.3 million on the NBC network) and *Doctor Who* (5 million via BBC America) were all successful in appealing to a viewership that may have been small by the standards of the networks but represented what might be considered a more educated and culturally discerning niche market. The appeal of *Sherlock* in America was attributed to it being a 'quintessentially British detective show'. According to Richard de Croce of BBC America: 'For decades, British TV was just about quality costume drama and funny accents for Americans. Now it is really becoming part of their popular culture.'[14]

At the same time – again like *Downton Abbey* – *Sherlock* was sold to broadcasters around the world: up to 224 countries according to the series' own publicity. (This is quite an achievement given that the United Nations officially recognizes only 195 countries.) It seems to have done particularly well in East Asia: the standalone episode 'The Abominable Bride' (2016) was released as a feature film in South Korea and China – a strategy also used by the BBC for the fiftieth-anniversary *Doctor Who* special 'The Day of the Doctor' in 2013 – and was reported to have grossed £21 million from cinema exhibition.[15] The international success of *Sherlock* is testament to two things: a general interest in British culture – *Sherlock* might not have coincided with the branding of 'Cool Britannia' in the 1990s but it represents much the same sort of phenomenon – and the enduring popularity of the character of Sherlock Holmes. Holmes is indisputably one of the most famous characters in fiction, and Sir Arthur Conan Doyle's stories have remained continuously in print since their original publication. It has been suggested that the Holmes stories represented the origin of modern fandom: publication of the *Strand Magazine* stories was eagerly awaited, and when Doyle notoriously killed off Holmes in 'The Final Problem' in 1893 men in London reportedly wore black armbands. The BBC's view of the success of *Sherlock* was that it 'has stoked the most passionate strand of Holmes fandom for a time'.[16] Retailers reported a spike in sales of the Belstaff woollen coat worn by Benedict Cumberbatch, while Speedy's sandwich shop on Gower Street (doubling for Baker Street) has become a mecca for fans of the series.[17]

Yet again it is tempting to ascribe the success of *Sherlock* to some form of television alchemy. The casting of Cumberbatch and Freeman was certainly adroit: the former was cast on the strength of his performance in the film *Atonement* (2007), while the latter, best known for his role as the nice-but-dim Tim in the sitcom *The Office*, made a perfect foil as a Watson who is more of an 'everyman' character than the loveable buffoon incarnated by Nigel Bruce. A particular feature of the Cumberbatch–Freeman partnership is that they restore the relative youth of Holmes and Watson following the middle-aged characters in some other versions. Cumberbatch plays Sherlock as a 'high-functioning sociopath': he is more socially awkward than the more clubbable characterizations by other actors such as Basil Rathbone and Peter Cushing. (Douglas Wilmer, who had played an excellent Holmes for the BBC in the 1960s, had a cameo as an elderly member of the Diogenese Club in 'The Reichenbach Fall'.) Like other successful dramas, however, the success of *Sherlock* was no accident but can be seen as the outcome of a considered and well-executed project to produce a high-end 'event' drama. The short series of three episodes meant that it did not suffer from the mid-season viewer fatigue that affected longer-running series including even *Doctor Who*. The increasingly long gaps between series – due partly to Moffat's concurrent commitment to producing *Doctor Who* and the availability of the two lead actors who were both much in demand – meant that audiences remained hungry for new episodes, while the scheduling shift after the first series meant that *Sherlock* became a much-anticipated highlight of the New Year drama schedules. Rather like *Doctor Who*, the launch of the series was supported by a range of spin-offs including new editions of the Conan Doyle stories with introductions by the series' writers. And the BBC launched two websites – *The Personal Blog of Dr John H. Watson* and *The Science of Deduction* – which helped to build up a para-text around the series.[18]

Sherlock also differed from all previous television adaptations of the Holmes stories – including the BBC's *Sherlock Holmes* of the 1960s, Granada's

The Adventures of Sherlock Holmes and the BBC's most recent ventures into Holmesiana by Alan Cubitt – insofar as it was a contemporary version rather than being set in the late Victorian period. Indeed, the series' production discourse was at pains to distance itself from what its creators evidently regarded as the too-faithful style of those period adaptations. Gatiss suggested that Holmes films and television series had 'become so much about the trappings – the hansom cabs, the fog, somewhere Jack the Ripper will creep in' [*sic*] – Holmes did indeed investigate the Ripper murders in the films *A Study in Terror* and *Murder by Decree* – while Moffat felt that modernizing Holmes allowed viewers 'to see the original stories the way the original reader would have read them – as exciting, cutting edge, contemporary stories, as opposed to these relics they've become'.[19] In fact, the idea of modernizing Holmes was not new. Most of the Holmes films of the 1920s and 1930s had been set in the present: it was not until Twentieth Century-Fox's *The Hound of the Baskervilles* and *The Adventures of Sherlock Holmes* that cinema placed Holmes in the late Victorian era of the original stories.[20] The Universal series starring Basil Rathbone and Nigel Bruce was set during and immediately after the Second World War: the first three films – *Sherlock Holmes and the Voice of Terror*, *Sherlock Holmes and the Secret Weapon*, *Sherlock Holmes in Washington* – see Holmes co-opted into the war effort to battle Nazi spies and saboteurs. An opening caption in these films avers that 'Sherlock Holmes … is ageless, invincible and unchanging. In solving significant problems of the present day he remains – as ever – the supreme master of deductive reasoning.' *Sherlock* bears a similar relationship to the source texts as the Universal series insofar as the films were all really original screenplays but employed some characters, plot devices and dialogue from the originals: some of the films even claimed to be based on specific stories – *Sherlock Holmes and the Voice of Terror* on 'His Last Bow', *Sherlock Holmes and the Secret Weapon* on 'The Dancing Men', *Sherlock Holmes Faces Death* on 'The Musgrave Ritual', *The Pearl of Death* on 'The Six Napoleons' and *The House of Fear* on 'The Five Orange Pips' – although this was largely to satisfy the studio's contractual obligations to the Doyle estate as the films' relationship to their notional source texts was distant to say the least.[21]

The modernization strategy of *Sherlock* is employed imaginatively. Moffat and Gatiss – along with third writer Stephen Thompson – decided that some aspects of Holmes's world were too iconic to leave out: hence, they retained the anachronistic 221B Baker Street address and Benedict Cumberbatch's Sherlock dons the famous deerstalker cap in 'A Scandal in Belgravia' in order to hide his face from the photographers and television crews drawn to Baker Street by his new-found celebrity. (The moment where John persuades Sherlock to wear the deerstalker might be understood as one of the series' many direct or indirect references to the Universal films: in *Sherlock Holmes and the Voice of Terror* Holmes is about to put on the deerstalker when Watson reminds him that 'You promised!' and he adopts a modern hat and coat instead.) The producers found a direct parallel between the Holmes canon and the present day insofar as the first novella *A Study in Scarlet* begins with Dr John Watson newly invalided out of the British army having been wounded during the Second Afghan War: the Watson of *Sherlock* is similarly an army medic who has been wounded in Afghanistan. (Doyle – who could be a notoriously sloppy writer – later forgot the nature of Watson's injury: in *A Study in Scarlet* he has been 'struck on the shoulder by a Jezail bullet', but in *The Sign of Four* he 'sat nursing my wounded leg. I had had a Jezail bullet through it some time before ... '[22] Moffat's script for 'A Study in Pink' acknowledges this continuity error – and in the process wins over Holmes aficionados – when Sherlock deduces that John's injury is partly psychosomatic.) Otherwise, the modernization strategy of *Sherlock* is manifest on several levels. It includes finding modern equivalents for aspects of the original stories – Sherlock's 'homeless network', for example, is the series' counterpart of the 'Baker Street Irregulars' – and substituting modern technology for the trappings of the Victorian period: John writes a blog rather than keeping a journal, Sherlock communicates by text message rather than telegram, and he deduces John's family history by examining his mobile phone rather than his pocket watch. The prominence of technology in *Sherlock* also allows the series to make use of innovative narrational techniques such as the on-screen 'flash' messages that represent text messages. As the series' production discourse was again keen to assert, however, this was consistent with the original stories in which Holmes is a modern character who embraces the latest investigative techniques.

Granada's *The Adventures of Sherlock Holmes* had exemplified what might be termed 'heritage Holmes': the series was characterized by its period authenticity, languorous camera style, pictorialist *mise-en-scène* and above all by its fidelity to the source texts. *Sherlock* on the other hand represents 'postmodern Holmes': it is notable for its less-than entirely faithful rendering of the source texts and for its employment of pastiche. This is a style that emerged into the mainstream of popular television in the 1990s with the success of the telefantasy series *Buffy the Vampire Slayer* – though it has been argued (including by myself) that similar characteristics can be found in later episodes of *The Avengers* in the 1960s.[23] Postmodern television drama is characterized by its awareness of its own status as drama: it reminds us constantly of its own status as a fictional text by making direct and conscious allusions to other cultural texts. In *Sherlock* this takes the form of an extreme use of pastiche: episodes are replete with references to the original stories, to other Sherlock Holmes adaptations and to other popular culture texts including film, television and music.

Moffat and Gatiss wisely determined that the first series of *Sherlock* should include familiar elements of the Holmes mythology, including his first meeting with Dr Watson ('A Study in Pink') and the introduction of his arch enemy 'Jim' Moriarty ('The Great Game'). 'A Study in Pink' – loosely based on the first Holmes novella *A Study in Scarlet* – concerns the investigation of a series of apparently unconnected suicides: the broadcast version introduces the character of Sherlock's brother Mycroft (played by Gatiss) who holds 'a minor position in the British government' – Mycroft had not featured in the original pilot episode – and hints at the shadowy figure of a master criminal known as Moriarty. 'The Blind Beggar' is less tied to a specific story – though the plot device of Sherlock decrypting a secret code represented as spray-paint graffiti has echoes of both 'The Dancing Men' and *The Valley of Fear* – but invokes the memory of the Universal series, particularly *The Spider Woman*. And 'The Great Game' – the title has been understood as a reference to the work of Holmesian scholars who research their subject as if he had been a real person – includes aspects of several Doyle stories, including 'The Five Orange Pips' (a countdown of pips from Greenwich heralds each new challenge for Sherlock), 'The Bruce Partington Plans' (a missile defence system rather than a submarine) and 'The Final Problem' (the much-anticipated confrontation between Sherlock and Moriarty), as well as a monstrous assassin known as the Golem who is nothing if not an homage to the Creeper in the film *The Pearl of Death*.

For the second series the production team again played safe by choosing three of the best-known Holmes stories. 'A Scandal in Belgravia' was based on 'A Scandal in Bohemia' – the first of the short stories published in the *Strand Magazine* – and as per the original has Sherlock tasked to retrieve some compromising photographs from *femme fatale* Irene Adler (Lara Pulver) – here cast in the role of a high-society dominatrix – on behalf of an unnamed member of the British royal family. 'The Hounds of Baskerville' adapts the most famous of Doyle's stories: here the legend of the giant spectral hound is related to hallucinations arising from experiments in psychological warfare and the Gothic house of the original becomes a secret military base on Dartmoor. This episode can be seen in a lineage of British television narratives about the existence of a secret state with sinister facilities hidden away in the countryside: other examples include *Quatermass II* and *Edge of Darkness*. And 'The Reichenbach Fall' – which sees the return of Moriarty who breaks into the Tower of London in order to convince the authorities he has developed a computer code that can penetrate the most secure security systems and which ends with a discredited Sherlock apparently falling to his death from the roof of St Bart's Hospital – is loosely based on 'The Final Problem' in which Doyle resolved to kill off Holmes by consigning him to a watery grave at the Reichenbach Falls, but also includes aspects of Fox's *The Adventures of Sherlock Holmes* (Moriarty plots to steal the Crown Jewels) and Universal's *The Woman in Green* (Moriarty attempts to discredit Holmes and have him commit suicide by jumping to his death).

The critical response to the first two series of *Sherlock* was overwhelmingly positive: the performances of the two leads were much admired and critics seem to have regarded the modernization strategy as a success. Sarah Crompton (*Daily Telegraph*) felt that it was 'the perfect depiction of Holmes for our times'.[24] For Thomas Sutcliffe (*The Independent*): '*Sherlock* is a triumph, witty and knowing, without ever undercutting the flair and dazzle of the original ... Flagrantly unfaithful to the original in some respects, *Sherlock* is wonderfully loyal to it in every way that matters'.[25] Dan Martin (*The Guardian*) found the first episode 'brilliantly promising. It has the finesse of *Spooks*, but is indisputably Sherlock Holmes ... *Sherlock* has done something quite remarkable: it's taken television's Sunday night and made it sexy'.[26] Terry Ramsey (*Daily Telegraph*) felt that 'the script is sharp and witty and the updating is clever, while remaining true to the original. A modern classic'.[27]

Chris Tilly (on entertainment media website *IGN*) described 'The Great Game' as 'spellbinding' and 'gripping... true drama the like of which British TV rarely produces'.[28] Tilly also rhapsodized over 'The Reichenbach Fall', which he thought provided 'a grandstanding conclusion to the brilliant BBC series, packed to the rafters with smart dialogue, audacious plotting, stylish direction and some truly wonderful performances'.[29] The revelation at the end of 'The Reichenbach Fall' that Sherlock is alive (he is seen briefly at the edge of the graveyard while John stands by his grave) prompted much speculation as to how Moffat and Gatiss would write their way out of the corner they had boxed themselves into.

For the third and fourth series there is evidence that the production team was starting to look further than the Holmes stories and adaptations for their points of reference. There is also a marked shift away from stories focusing on deduction and problem-solving to place the relationship between Sherlock and John (and to a lesser extent Sherlock and Mycroft) at the heart of the drama. This coincided with Moffat and Gatiss sidelining Stephen Thompson (who is credited only as co-writer of 'The Sign of Three') and writing more of the scripts themselves. 'The Empty Hearse' – based on Doyle's resurrection story 'The Empty House' – is notable for its refusal to provide a definitive explanation as to how Sherlock survived his fall from the roof at the end of series two: Sherlock's own oblique explanation ('You know my methods... I am well known to be indestructible') is a reference to the 1965 film *A Study in Terror* in which Holmes offers the same account for his escape from a burning warehouse. 'The Sign of Three' is less an adaptation of *The Sign of Four* than a murder mystery variant of wedding comedies such as *Four Weddings and a Funeral* and *My Best Friend's Wedding* in which the highlight is Sherlock's embarrassing best-man's speech at John's wedding to Mary Morstan (played by Martin Freeman's then wife Amanda Abbington). 'His Last Vow' is a reworking of Doyle's 'Charles Augustus Milverton' – with Danish actor Lars Mikkelsen as the master blackmailer Magnussen – rather than 'His Last Bow', although it does include a brief reference to the 'east wind' speech. The revelation that John's wife Mary is a highly trained ninja assassin owes rather more to *Nikita* and *Alias* than Conan Doyle.

The response to the third series was still generally positive, although some reviewers felt that 'The Empty Hearse' cheated on the explanation of how Sherlock survived at the end of 'The Reichenbach Fall'. At the end of the series, Neela Debnath (*The Independent*) was concerned that it had 'pushed the realm of believability a little too far … It felt implausible and too much of a coincidence without being clever'. In particular she felt that the bizarre crimes and ingenious solutions that had characterized the first two series were now becoming secondary to the focus on the relationships between the lead characters. 'If *Sherlock* wants to return to its once dizzying heights of brilliance,' she concluded, 'it needs to stick to the mystery and the intrigue. It is a compelling formula, and one not be messed around with.'[30] Myles McNult (for the American website *AV/TV*) detected 'some stylistic fatigue' and saw evidence of a change of emphasis that was not wholly satisfying: 'A conflict of style and substance has always been at the heart of PBS' *Sherlock … Sherlock*'s third season never quite reconciles its traditional stylistic excess and its storytelling goals, but it embraces that tension as it shifts towards a more character-centric storytelling model.'[31]

Following 'The Abominable Bride' – in which the period setting is actually Sherlock entering his 'mind palace' to investigate an unsolved Victorian mystery – series four further developed the personal narrative at the expense of deductive reasoning and (it has to be said) storytelling logic. 'The Six Thatchers' has only a tangential link to 'The Six Napoleons' – here it is a memory stick rather than a priceless pearl hidden in the plaster busts – though the main reference point seems to have been John O'Hara's novel *Appointment in Samarra*. The primary concern of 'The Lying Detective' is the reconciliation between Sherlock and John following Mary's death in the previous episode, although it does feature villain Culverton Smith (Toby Jones) from 'The Dying Detective' who is here recast as a psychopathic serial killer. And 'The Final Problem' was partly based on 'The Musgrave Ritual', although there are also aspects of 'The Three Garridebs', 'The Dancing Men' and 'The Disappearance of Lady Frances Carfax'. The episode draws together a number of narrative threads – including the distinctly non-canonical revelation that Sherlock has a hitherto unknown sister called Eurus (Greek for 'east wind') who murdered his childhood best friend and who is incarcerated in a high-security prison where she has nevertheless managed to 'turn' the governor and guards – into a heady potpourri of *The Silence of the Lambs*, *Carrie* and *Sophie's Choice*. *Sherlock* had never made a virtue of narrative plausibility but there was a feeling that it had now finally 'jumped the shark'. A review for the entertainment website *Vox* summed up the consensus on the last episode:

'The Final Problem'... collapses into a muddled mess of melodrama and confusion... There's ultimately not a lot of substance behind all of the *sturm und drang* that has led to this final episode, and there's even less logic. There is, however, a lot of high drama and plot shenanigans, and much of it is confusing. Full of frenzied plot twists, 'The Final Problem' closed out the season and maybe the series with an episode that – if it really is the last – feels like a huge anticlimax that substitutes implausible drama and showiness for meaningful character development and kind of narrative payoff.[32]

Another issue might have been a perennial problem for all Holmes adaptations: that the original canon is of variable quality and all the best stories had been used. It is not presently clear whether 'The Final Problem' will indeed be the last of *Sherlock*: it does not feature the usual cliffhanger that had marked the end of all the previous series. Instead, the last image – Sherlock and John running towards the camera in slow motion in the manner of Batman and Robin with a myth-making voice-over monologue from the deceased Mary ('It's all about the legend – the stories – the adventures') – hints strongly at closure.

Notwithstanding the more equivocal response to the fourth series, *Sherlock* represents a triumph of high-concept drama and imaginative adaptation. The strategy of modernizing the material works on several levels. *Sherlock* reconfigures the social politics of the original stories in several ways. Most obviously, the formality of the Holmes–Watson relationship in Doyle's stories is transformed into a 'buddy' narrative of the sort familiar from American cop series such as *Starsky and Hutch* and *Miami Vice* and represented in films such as the *Lethal Weapon* series and the two Sherlock Holmes films directed by Guy Ritchie starring Robert Downey Jr as Holmes and Jude Law as Watson. Perhaps the nearest equivalent of this relationship on British television was the early 1970s action-adventure series *The Persuaders!* which had starred Tony Curtis and Roger Moore as a pair of playboy crime-fighters. The 'buddy' narrative is usually understood as one that focuses on 'a closely bonded platonic relationship between two men who share professional and domestic intimacy, who form two halves of one powerhouse whole, but whose frequent looks and physical proximity must constantly struggle against their own romantic implications'.[33] The simplest aspect of the modernization is that

'Holmes' and 'Watson' become 'Sherlock' and 'John': the use of first names
might have offended some purists but is entirely consistent with the period
in which *Sherlock* is set. Like other buddy narratives the main threat to the
male pairing comes not from villains but from the intrusion of women into the
comfortable male world. It is significant in this regard that Sherlock's return
from the dead in 'The Empty Hearse' has him disrupting a romantic dinner
where John is about to propose to his fiancée Mary Morstan. In this reading
it is Sherlock's fear of losing his best friend that accounts for his ambivalent
attitude towards Mary. Some critics disliked the killing-off of Mary in 'The Six
Thatchers' and the ease with which John begins a new relationship (albeit it
turns out in retrospect with a disguised Eurus): however, this was consistent
with the original stories in which Mary was written out after *The Sign of Four*.
At the heart of *Sherlock* is the story of a friendship between two men: 'my Baker
Street boys' as Mary refers to them (courtesy of a pre-recorded posthumous
message) in 'The Final Problem'.

An aspect of *Sherlock* that has attracted much academic commentary – and no
little degree of controversy – is its suggestion of a 'bromance' between Sherlock
and John. The relationship between Holmes and Watson in the original stories
should correctly be described as homosocial: it is a relationship between two
men who respect each other and are friends. (That there is a degree of affection
between Holmes and Watson is not in doubt, especially in the later stories:
'It was worth a wound – it was worth many wounds – to know the depth of
loyalty and love which lay behind that cold mask,' Watson reflects in 'The Three
Garridebs' in response to Holmes's 'You're not hurt, Watson? For God's sake,
say that you are not hurt?'[34] It is abundantly clear from the context that 'love'
is not being used in a romantic sense.) It has become a frequent – if somewhat
tiresome – practice of a certain kind of criticism to insist on interpreting male
friendships in popular culture as narratives of disguised homosexual desire – a
practice that is sometimes described as 'queering the canon'. Once this type of
reading was a stick with which to beat popular culture: the US psychiatrist Dr
Fredric Wertham described the *Batman* comic books as a 'wish dream of two
homosexuals living together' in support of his argument that comics were a
pernicious influence on juveniles.[35] More recently, it has become an ideological
and interpretational strategy of 'queer theory' to insist that gay subtexts are
present in many popular narratives where they represent the wider societal

repression of homosexuality. Sherlock Holmes and Dr Watson have not been free from such ideological appropriation.[36]

Sherlock addresses the issue of 'queerness' in contradictory ways. On the one hand, there are frequent references to the idea of Sherlock and John as a gay couple. Every episode of the first two series seems to contain some such reference: from their landlady Mrs Hudson's suggestion that they will not want the second bedroom ('A Study in Pink') to the scene in 'The Reichenbach Fall' where they are handcuffed together and have to hold hands to run ('Now people will definitely talk,' John observes). On the other hand, *Sherlock* also repeatedly distances itself from a gay reading: in particular, John – the more 'ordinary' of the two characters – asserts his heterosexuality in no uncertain terms: 'Who the hell knows about Sherlock Holmes, but, for the record, if anyone out there still cares, I'm not actually gay' ('A Scandal in Belgravia'). *Sherlock* has been seen as an example of the phenomenon known as 'queer baiting': to introduce the possibility of a gay relationship into a popular fictional text in order to attract gay viewers but without the intention of ever depicting such a relationship. Moreover, the stridency with which *Sherlock* denies the possibility of a gay relationship has even raised the spectre of homophobia around the series – though this is difficult to reconcile with the fact that one of its producers and writers (Gatiss) is an openly gay man. Nevertheless, the characterization of Moriarty – played by gay actor Andrew Scott – as 'queer' is more than a little problematic: Moriarty is openly flirtatious in his exchanges with Sherlock ('Is that a British Army Browning L9A1 in your pocket, or are you just pleased to see me?') and both his vocal delivery and mannerisms are knowingly camp. But in the twenty-first century this sort of association between homosexuality and criminality seems a retrograde step: it is as if Moriarty's deviant behaviour is being equated with 'deviant' sexuality.

Sherlock also attracted some controversy on account of its gender politics. 'A Scandal in Belgravia' prompted a number of complaints about the appearance of a naked Lara Pulver as Irene Adler – albeit that her nudity is artfully concealed by camera angles and body posture – though for *Guardian* blogger Jane Clare Jones the real problem went deeper. Jones felt that the characterization of Adler – whom Holmes in the original stories always referred to as '*the* woman' – was a 'regressive step' insofar as her power over men was sexual rather than intellectual. She felt this 'regressive' characterization was a symptom of an underlying sexism in the writing of the series which she laid squarely at Steven Moffat's door:

> In many ways the Holmes stories are a perfect fit for Moffat's skill-set. The puzzle-box plotting, the 24/7 bromance, the fetishisation of 'masculine' reason over pesky 'feminine' emotion, all suit him right down to the ground... More troubling still, Moffat's Adler blatantly fails to outwit Holmes. Despite identifying as a lesbian, her scheme is ultimately undone by her great big girly crush on Sherlock, an irresistible brain-rot that lead her to trash the security she has fought for from the start of the show with about as sophisticated – or purposeful – as scrawling love hearts on an exercise book. As a result, Moffat sends Adler out into the world without the information she has always relied on for protection, having made herself entirely vulnerable for the love of a man.[37]

Similar criticisms have been made of Moffat's *Doctor Who* and so this is not an isolated point: nevertheless, it does seem to me that Irene Adler has more narrative agency in the one episode in which she appears than she does in the original source text. And for all that she does not outwit Sherlock, as she does in Doyle's story, she does nevertheless get the better of every other man. Jones is also mistaken in describing her as a lesbian who succumbs to a 'big girly crush': she is characterized as bisexual rather than as lesbian.

A possibly more productive way of reading *Sherlock* is not through its sexual or gender politics – in neither can it be said to be particularly progressive but at the same time nor is it quite so regressive as some critics suggest – but rather in terms of class. Doyle's Holmes was to some extent a classless hero in an era very aware of class: his social origins are indeterminate, while his profession as a 'consulting detective' brings him into contact with all social classes from European royalty and the English aristocracy to the poorest members of society and the criminal underclass. Holmes is comfortable in all social contexts, while his mastery of disguise allows him to move up and down the social spectrum. *Sherlock* arguably takes this even further by presenting its titular protagonist as being outside the traditional class system: while his supercilious brother Mycroft is closely identified with the establishment ('He *is* the British government,' Sherlock tells John – a line taken directly from the source texts), Sherlock himself is very much a social outsider. He is regarded as a 'freak' and a 'psycho' by the police (terms used by the antagonistic Detective Sergeant Sally Donovan who appears in the first two series). At the same time he demonstrates his liberal credentials in associating with the homeless community ('The Great Game'). The fact that Cumberbatch's Holmes is less inclined to adopt disguise – the one exception is the comedy French waiter he impersonates in 'The Empty Hearse' – might be taken as an indication that there is less need for him to navigate the class system than his Victorian predecessor.

Another way of reading *Sherlock* is as a commentary on the culture of celebrity. The early twenty-first century saw a transformation in the nature of celebrity culture arising from the popularity of 'reality' shows such as *Big Brother* and the emergence of Internet-based social media: Andy Warhol's famous dictum that everyone will be famous for fifteen minutes has never seemed more true than in the age of Twitter and Instagram. *Sherlock* takes a theme hinted at in the original stories – the idea that Holmes becomes a public figure due to Watson publishing accounts of his cases – and places it at the centre of the narrative. On one level this idea is treated for comedic effect: a montage of cases that Sherlock solves without even leaving Baker Street in 'The Empty Hearse' demonstrates the trivial subject matter that some clients bring to him. But on another level *Sherlock* is concerned with the distinction between the public and the private. At times Sherlock is uncomfortable with the public persona that has been created for him: in 'The Great Game' he cautions John against hero-worship ('Don't make people into heroes, John. Heroes don't exist – and if they did, I wouldn't be one of them'). But on other occasions he plays up to his public image: in 'The Hounds of Baskerville' John even admonishes him for this ('Can we not do this this time? ... You being all mysterious with your cheekbones and turning your coat collar up so you look cool.') The conspiracy plot of 'The Reichenbach Fall' revolves around Moriarty's desire to combat Sherlock not by killing him but by destroying his reputation, while the opening scenes of 'The Empty Hearse' concern the rehabilitation of his reputation.

Finally – at least for its place in the emergence of British Quality Television (there are many other aspects of the series that deserve commentary: this chapter has only scratched the surface) – *Sherlock* can be read as a vehicle for the cultural export of Britishness. It is highly significant in this regard that the two most successful British television exports of the 2010s, *Sherlock* and *Downton Abbey*, both represent different versions of an imaginary Britain: the modern, classless Britain of *Sherlock* and the traditional, aristocratic Britain of *Downton Abbey*. These images both respond to the carefully packaged image of Britain as a dynamic combination of modernity and heritage promoted by organizations such as Visit Britain.[38] In particular, *Sherlock* functions as a showcase for Britain's capital. Gatiss said that the series aims 'to fetishize modern London in the way that the period versions fetishize Victorian London'.[39] *Sherlock* represents Britain's capital within the visual discourses of tourism: the opening titles feature iconic London landmarks – the London Eye, River Thames and Big Ben – while time-lapse effects simulate the effect of speeding through the city's traffic. The London of *Sherlock* is a city constantly on the move: a recurring motif of the earlier episodes is the conversations between Sherlock and John while travelling by taxi. It is also an emphatically modern metropolis: in place of gaslight and fog we have the shiny tower blocks of Canary Wharf with their clean reflective surfaces ('The Blind Banker') and the open spaces of the South Bank ('The Great Game'). Like his Victorian predecessor, the modern Sherlock is very much at home in this environment: in 'A Study in Pink', for example, he can visualize a map of the backstreets of Soho to head off a taxi carrying a murder suspect (who in the event turns out to be an innocent American tourist: 'Welcome to London' says Sherlock – pretending to be a policeman). The representation of London in *Sherlock* bears some comparison with the James Bond film *Skyfall* (2012), which features (unusually for the Bond movies) extensive sequences in the capital: the shot of Daniel Craig's Bond on a rooftop looking over the London skyline towards St Paul's Cathedral near the end of *Skyfall* – shot from the roof of the Department for Energy and Climate Change in Whitehall Place – is mirrored precisely at the end of 'The Empty Hearse'.

At the time of writing the possibility of further episodes of *Sherlock* seems a distant prospect: there has been persistent speculation about a fifth series in the media but no official confirmation. It might be that Moffat and Gatiss have gone as far with reinventing *Sherlock* as they can: its thirteen feature-length episodes over seven years include just about the full range of story templates and plot devices within the genre. Benedict Cumberbatch and Martin Freeman have made only one film fewer than Basil Rathbone and Nigel Bruce did over a similar period. And 'The Final Problem' does seem to suggest a degree of, well, finality to the story of 'a junkie who solves crimes to get high and the doctor who never came home from the war'. But in any event *Sherlock* is surely destined to be regarded as one of the highpoints of contemporary British television and as the series that perhaps to a greater extent than any other marked the height of the modern 'high-concept' drama.

Broadchurch

Broadchurch was one of the television 'events' of 2013 in the United Kingdom: the eight-part weekly serial drew an average audience of 9.3 million – its final episode was watched by 10.4 million (representing a 34 per cent audience share) – attracted wide critical acclaim and won a host of awards including Best Drama Series from BAFTA, Best Drama at the National Television Awards, Best New Drama at the TV Choice Awards, Best Drama Serial from the Royal Television Society and Best Drama Series from the Broadcasting Press Guild.[1] In its way *Broadchurch* was as much of a critical and popular success as either *Sherlock* or *Downton Abbey*, although it was very different from both. It was neither a glossy, fast-paced high-concept drama nor a 'safe' heritage drama. With its serial format, slow-paced narration and its privileging of character development and psychological realism, *Broadchurch* instead represented something of a throwback to the style of thriller serials such as *Tinker, Tailor, Soldier, Spy* and *Edge of Darkness*, while its 'difficult' content, concerning the investigation of a child murder and its effects on the community, placed it in a lineage of psychologically oriented crime dramas including *Prime Suspect* and *Cracker*.

The production of *Broadchurch* demonstrates different institutional and cultural contexts from some other series included in this book. *Broadchurch* was produced by Kudos for ITV1. It was funded mostly by ITV but with some investment from BBC America and the German broadcaster ZDF (Zweites Deutsches Fernsehen).[2] Notwithstanding ITV's success with *Downton Abbey*, the commercial network lagged behind its public sector competitor in terms of both its share of the viewing audience and the cultural standing of its programme content. According to statistics compiled by the independent Broadcasters' Audience Research Board (BARB), in 2012 the BBC had a 33.6

per cent share of the total audience compared to ITV's 22.3 per cent.³ ITV was particularly associated with low-brow but popular light entertainment formats – these included 'talent' shows, notably *The X Factor* and *Britain's Got Talent*, and 'reality' shows such as *I'm a Celebrity, Get Me Out of Here!* – but had less of a reputation for quality drama. *Downton Abbey* and *Mr Selfridge* were the main exceptions in a drama output that tended towards generic fare, especially police series, whether those conceived in a 'heritage' style, such as *Midsomer Murders, Foyle's War* and *Lewis*, or the more 'gritty' mode of *The Vice, Rebus* and *Wire in the Blood*. To this extent the commissioning of *Broadchurch* was something of a departure for the network. Its producer and writer Chris Chibnall averred that ITV 'never saw it as a ratings winner. They didn't want it to be that, they wanted it to be just really classy, was what they said'.⁴

Ross P. Garner has argued that *Broadchurch* should be understood within the context of a corporate rebranding initiative by ITV during 2012–13 which saw the network attempt to position itself as the place 'Where Drama Lives'.⁵ *Broadchurch* was promoted as a flagship 'new' drama for the network that was both similar to yet different from other returning crime dramas such as *DCI Banks, Vera, Scott & Bailey* and *Endeavour*. This strategy was adopted from American networks where the crime drama was often seen as a means of appealing to a mainstream audience while also reaching out to specific or niche audience groups. ITV's own market research had established that its audience was skewed towards women in their mid-thirties and older: hence, its promotional strategy for *Broadchurch* sought to position it simultaneously as a melodrama with particular appeal for women (hence, the television trailer afforded prominence to the characters played by Olivia Colman and Jodie Whittaker and highlighted especially emotional scenes) and as something that would also appeal to younger male and female viewers (through the casting of David Tennant, star of the BBC's popular telefantasy series *Doctor Who*). Garner suggests that '*Broadchurch* represented a "new" series for ITV in early 2013, and its marketing and promotion deserve to be read in light of such rebranding discourses because of how it combines crime drama iconography with appeals to audience groups that ITV has previously overlooked, like cult TV fans'.⁶

The commissioning of *Broadchurch* can therefore be understood as an investment in 'quality' by ITV but a different kind of quality than *Downton*

Abbey. Its scheduling on Monday evenings suggested that it was not expected to be a major ratings success: this has not traditionally been a major drama slot (unlike Sunday and Wednesday evenings) but it did sometimes tend to be reserved for 'darker' or more troubling dramas. Another relevant factor in the positioning of *Broadchurch* was the adoption of the fixed-length serial format: this can be seen as a means of differentiating it from both open-ended serials with no narrative start or end point (such as soap operas) and episodic series featuring recurring characters. John Caughie suggests that the serial drama displaced the standalone single play when the latter became too expensive to produce in sufficient quantity to fill weekly anthology series such as *Armchair Theatre, The Wednesday Play* and *Play for Today.* He compares it to the literary novel in the sense that serial drama allows the narrative to develop over a longer running time than the single play and is structured into chapters or episodes that allow audiences to experience it in convenient segments. He elaborates:

> Whatever generic form it takes, the extension in time of an interrupted dramatic narrative seems to me to be one of television's specific contributions to the long history of the novelistic. Bakhtin's biographical narrative in which characters are taken on a spiritual or intellectual journey through time and space – whether it be through the historical environment of *Our Friends in the North* or the paranoid environment of *Edge of Darkness* – reaches a particularly developed form in the television dramatic serial.[7]

The crime or detective drama is particularly amenable to the serial form: the setting up of the social place and key characters, the discovery of the crime, the process of investigation and interviews with witnesses and suspects, and the final dramatic *denouement* are played out at a more natural pace than a standalone episode of fifty or ninety minutes. The idea of *Broadchurch* being the televisual equivalent of a long-form novel is further reinforced by Chibnall's own account of the writing process: 'It was like the material was speaking to me and telling me what it should be. It felt so inevitable then, and so right, and everything I wanted to talk about within the piece was served by that idea as well.'[8]

For Chibnall – whose previous television work had included episodes of *Torchwood, Doctor Who* and *Law & Order: UK* – *Broadchurch* represented the opportunity to write a crime drama that was more than just another 'whodunnit'. His aim was to explore the effects of a murder on the wider community and the psychological consequences for those most closely connected to it. In an interview for the *Radio Times* he elaborated:

> I knew the start would be a body being found. How did this affect this person, and that person? In that first episode are the ripples, that's how you meet everybody, how they hear, how they are affected. I don't let anyone off. At every point of plotting I'd ask myself, 'What would the characters do?' It was never 'Here's a big plot twist'. I wasn't looking at it structurally. Everything in this came from character.[9]

This emphasis on psychologically realistic characterization can be understood as a means of differentiating *Broadchurch* from more generic detective dramas, while the police procedural framework also distanced it from the high murder-count of series such as *Midsomer Murders* which were determinedly non-realist in their content. Insofar as it would afford as much narrative space to the supporting characters as well as to the process of the investigation, *Broadchurch* also adopted certain elements of the British soap opera: the tightly knit community, the narrative focus on the domestic space and the diverse range of characters whose lives are interconnected and most of whom have something to hide.

   Broadchurch has a number of possible antecedents and influences. On one level it suggests a comparison with Troy Kennedy Martin's *Edge of Darkness* (1985) as an authored serial drama that uses the conventions of a familiar genre (political thriller/police procedural) to explore wider social and psychological issues. *Edge of Darkness* concerned a policeman, Craven (Bob Peck), whose investigation of the murder of his daughter uncovers a high-level conspiracy involving the British government and an American nuclear power company which has covered up the illegal manufacture of plutonium. It was initially broadcast on BBC2, suggesting that the corporation regarded it, rather like ITV did with *Broadchurch*, as a niche rather than a mainstream drama, but it drew larger than expected audiences for the second channel which secured a quick repeat on BBC1 and doubled the audience to 8 million.[10] Like *Broadchurch*, *Edge of Darkness* was critically acclaimed and won Best Drama Series from BAFTA and the Broadcasting Press Guild. There are also some quite specific parallels between *Broadchurch* and *Edge of Darkness* including the murder that sets the narrative in motion, the psychologically damaged detective and the slow pacing. *Edge of Darkness* was more directly political than *Broadchurch* – it caught a mid-1980s *Zeitgeist* of growing social and political discontent with the Conservative government of Margaret Thatcher – but the two serials nevertheless share common ground in terms of form and style. Lez Cooke could be talking about *Broadchurch* when he writes: 'The epic scale of *Edge of Darkness* ... three times longer than the average feature film, enabled not only a greater complexity than is often achieved in a feature film but also the playing out of some scenes at greater length than one might normally expect.'[11]

Another, more recent cultural reference point for *Broadchurch* was the emergence in the international television market of Scandinavian crime drama – a genre sometimes called 'Nordic *noir*'. Since around 2008 imported television dramas such as *Wallander* (Sweden), *Forbrydelsen/The Killing* (Denmark) and *Broen/The Bridge* (Denmark) had acquired something of a cult following in Britain where they were picked up by digital channels such as BBC4 and attracted more viewers than might have been expected for subtitled television series. Nordic *noir* – which also draws upon the literary fiction of crime writers such as Peter Høeg, Henning Mankell and Stieg Larrson – is characterized by its existential content, slow narration and pictorialist *mise-en-scène* which places a particular emphasis on bleak natural landscapes. It employs landscape as a metaphor for expressing the psychological state of its protagonists: the physical environment reflects the moral bleakness of a world that explores the dark underside of the Scandinavian Social Democratic ideal. Glen Creeber sees Nordic *noir* as a form of product differentiation insofar as it 'stands out from the television "flow" by appearing so different from other programmes'. 'In particular,' Creeber suggests, 'it is the opposite of what John Caldwell refers to as "televisuality", a contemporary aesthetic style typified by a faster narrative pace and a tendency towards visual and aural hyperactivity.' [12]

Broadchurch can be seen as a British cousin of Nordic *noir* in its content and style: its slow pacing, its morose detective protagonist and its pervading atmosphere of gloomy melancholy all serve to locate it alongside (if not actually within) this tradition. 'Like Nordic *noir*,' Creeber attests, '*Broadchurch* employs its complex narrative structure to reveal the hidden connections that are at play in society, but hints that those connections may sometimes work on a level beyond all human rationality.'[13] *Broadchurch* also evokes the *mise-en-scène* of Scandinavian crime dramas, especially *Wallender*, in its atmospheric use of location: the geologically distinct Jurassic Coast of south west Dorset. The association with Nordic *noir* is further heightened by the choice of Icelandic composer Ólafur Arnalds to write the music. Arnalds wanted to avoid the too lush sound of a full orchestra and instead wrote the score for a string quartet and a piano: a reviewer in the *New York Times* described the result as 'a tasty icing of gloom and foreboding'.[14]

For his part, however, Chibnall downplayed the Scandinavian connection and instead suggested that *Broadchurch* was particularly influenced by two American television series of the 1990s: *Twin Peaks* and *Murder One*.[15] *Twin Peaks* (1990–91) had been created by avant-garde filmmaker David Lynch: it used the detective-mystery formula – following the investigation of a murder in the Pacific Northwest – as a means of exposing the dark underside of small-town America that Lynch had previously explored in his film *Blue Velvet* (1986). *Broadchurch* would echo *Twin Peaks* in its location (a picturesque small community) and in the motif of the outside investigator (FBI Agent Dale Cooper/DI Alec Hardy) whose arrival puts the local police force out of joint. There are other echoes of *Twin Peaks* in the series' advertising ('Broadchurch – a town wrapped in secrets') and in the structuring of the narrative. In both *Twin Peaks* and *Broadchurch* what apparently starts out as a conventional murder mystery narrative – 'Who killed Laura Palmer?' (*Twin Peaks*) and 'Who killed Danny Latimer?' (*Broadchurch*) – transforms into something else in which uncovering the identity of the killer does not provide the sense of narrative resolution and closure expected of the classical detective story. In its second series *Twin Peaks* veered into the realm of surreal fantasy as it transpired that the killer (the victim's father) was possessed by an evil spirit known as 'Demon Bob': ratings declined and the series was cancelled without ever reaching a resolution. (A much-belated third series of *Twin Peaks* did follow in 2017: its broadcast in the United Kingdom followed the third series of *Broadchurch*.)

Murder One (1995–7) was a legal drama created by Steven Bochco – also responsible for *Hill Street Blues* and *NYPD Blue* – for the ABC network. It differed from other legal dramas, such as Bochco's own *LA Law*, in that it followed one case (the trial of a Hollywood actor for the rape and murder of a fifteen-year-old girl) through the whole season. *Murder One* succeeded initially because the single-case serial narrative was an innovation and through the charismatic lead performance of Daniel Benzali as lawyer Ted Hoffman:

ratings slipped during the second season which did not feature Benzali and which had a series of separate cases spread over several episodes (one was a loosely disguised version of the O. J. Simpson murder trial) and the series was cancelled. *Broadchurch* was also a serial narrative: its first series followed the investigation of the murder of eleven-year-old Danny Latimer, while its second series followed the subsequent trial and the third series featured a different crime that reunites the two lead detectives for a final time. A particular link between *Murder: One* and *Broadchurch* is their focus on the relationship between law and the media: they both document (in fictional form) the respective legal and judicial processes while at the same time reflecting upon how serious crime is understood and interpreted by the media. Jason Bainbridge has suggested that *Murder: One* and *Broadchurch* (and another US procedural drama, the long-running *CSI: Crime Scene Investigation*) 'operate as part of this "public archive" of popular visual media representations of law that self-reflexively depict the saturation of law by the media'.[16]

Broadchurch was shot on location in and around the towns of Clevedon in Somerset and West Bay in Dorset. Chibnall described the series as 'a love letter to the Jurassic coast': key scenes were set on the beach and cliff tops.[17] Unusually for filmed television drama it was shot in narrative sequence: this was in order to allow the actors to develop their performances and to react plausibly and persuasively to unfolding events. In fact, Chibnall had completed only the first few episodes before shooting began: he waited until casting was complete and he had seen the actors performing their roles before completing the script. The identity of the killer was withheld from most of the cast and crew: *Broadchurch* was shot under conditions of great secrecy and for once the 'secret' was not leaked prior to broadcast of the last episode. The shooting period ran from September to November 2012 and the time frame of the serial covers a similar period of fifty-six days from the night of the murder to the solving of the case: the sequential shooting meant that the serial's photography reflects the seasonal transition in the changing light and weather conditions of autumn.

Broadchurch is a highly visual serial: not in the flashy sense of *Sherlock* or *Hustle* but in terms of its pictorialist photography and carefully arranged *mise-en-scène*. The direction makes extensive use of slow motion, slow dissolves, non-match cuts and oblique angles. The visual style and framing of shots suggest a relationship between characters and the natural landscape: isolated figures placed on the beach or the cliff-top are repeated motifs throughout the serial. According to co-director James Strong:

> When Chris and I first walked the Jurassic cliffs at West Bay, the incredible Dorset landscape was immediately embedded into the visual identity of *Broadchurch*. These are characters connected to the natural landscape (the cliffs, the sea, the field), so we chose locations that showed the world 'outside' and allowed us to embrace the changing seasons as the story progresses ... TV crime drama can tend towards the grim (urban and gritty) or a sanitised 'chocolate box' view. We wanted the duality of real life, which is somewhere in between: beautiful waves shot through a piece of barbed wire, litter on a beach. The British seaside seems riddled with these contradictions.[18]

Strong therefore positions *Broadchurch* within a discourse of space and place – a discourse that currently holds a great degree of intellectual currency in television studies. Historically television drama has been characterized by a studio-bound aesthetic: production modes and technologies privileged interiors and intimate spaces. The transition from live drama to film allowed more possibilities for shooting on location – often in a 'heritage' style exemplified by costume dramas such as *Brideshead Revisited* and *Pride and Prejudice* – though even so many filmed series and serials still often gravitated to the studio. *Broadchurch* exemplifies a trend towards predominantly location shooting (a few interiors were still shot in television studios in Bristol and London) that was an outcome of various technological, economic and aesthetic determinants: other examples – all occupying similar generic terrain within the detective/police procedural framework – include BBC Wales' *Y Gwyll/Hinterland*, Channel 4's *Southcliffe* and the BBC's *Shetland*. All these dramas were broadcast for the first time in 2013: *Broadchurch* should therefore be seen as part of a cycle of location-based procedural dramas on British television rather than as a unique or standalone example.

Les Roberts argues that the police procedural genre 'provides a rationale for thinking critically about landscape' in television drama.[19] Some genres lend themselves more readily to an expressive use of location, while others (such as the soap opera) do not. In this regard it is significant that the police procedural drama on British television has shifted from the urban settings of *Prime Suspect* and *Cracker* in the 1990s to a preference for communities on the geographical and cultural peripheries of the United Kingdom: West Dorset (*Broadchurch*), Ceredigon (*Hinterland*), the Thames Estuary marshes (*Southcliffe*) and the Shetland Islands. Landscape functions in several ways in these dramas: as a distinctive and regionally specific iconography that differentiates them from other genres, especially the urban crime drama; as a means of emphasizing the social and geographical remoteness of these communities; as a visual expression of the psychological state of their protagonists; and as a form of televisual tourism which represents non-metropolitan areas through the lens of a 'tourist gaze'. It is a feature of these series that they use location as more than just picturesque scenery but as an extension of the drama: landscape becomes an existential space as well as a physical space. In *Broadchurch* this is expressed through the beach at the foot of the cliff where Danny Latimer's body is found: the two detectives – DI Alec Hardy (David Tennant) and DS Ellie Miller (Olivia Colman) – return repeatedly to this space for 'meaningful' conversations.

Broadchurch challenges – indeed it can be argued that it subverts – the paradigm of the detective/procedural drama. It does this in several ways. For one thing it focuses as much on the effects of the murder on the victim's family and on the wider community as it does on the actual investigative process. Consequently, *Broadchurch* represents a move away from the semi-documentary mode of most procedurals – exemplified on British television historically by *Fabian of the Yard* and *Dixon of Dock Green* and also including modern examples of the form such as *Taggart*, *Prime Suspect*, *Cracker* and *Law & Order: UK* – to what might be described as a more melodramatic mode. This can also be conceptualized as a shift from the public to the private. For Chibnall this was evidently an entirely conscious process:

> I kept thinking that there was something we'd never seen in British crime drama – the impact on the family. But also, as I started thinking about it, how much it was in the news, victims' rights, things like Sarah's Law, Megan's Law. So it felt right to do a drama that moved us in this direction.[20]

It is rare in crime drama to consider the emotional effects of murder on the victim's family and friends. As Celia Wren remarked in her review for *Commonweal*: 'The show does stray from classic whodunit territory in focusing frequently on the grief of Danny's mother, Beth (Jodie Whittaker):

in one heart-wrenching scene, we see her trying to distract herself by grocery shopping, only to find her eyes straying to Danny's favourite cereal. In another, we see her jogging desperately along the beach, as if trying to outrun her agony.'[21]

The focus on the wider community in *Broadchurch* differentiates it from other crime series and orients it towards the conventions of the soap opera. A feature of the soap opera – especially the British soap opera as exemplified by *Coronation Street* and *EastEnders* but also by regional daytime soaps such as the long-running Welsh language serial *Pobol y Cwm* – is its focus on community: even the BBC's much-derided Spanish adventure *Eldorado* in the early 1990s fit this paradigm. Like the soap opera, *Broadchurch* creates a community where everyone knows each other and where their lives all intersect. This idea is established formally in a sequence near the beginning of the first episode where director James Strong employs a continuous mobile Steadicam shot – recalling whether intentionally or not the celebrated opening shots of Orson Welles's *Touch of Evil* (1958) and Robert Altman's *The Player* (1992) – which follows Mark Latimer as he walks along the high street: along the way he meets and interacts briefly with most of the characters who will play important roles in the drama. The first people Mark encounters are Ellie and Joe Miller with their son Tom: these are followed (in sequence) by the reclusive Susan Wright, the Reverend Paul Coates, journalist Olly Stephens who works for local paper the *Broadchurch Echo* and the newspaper's editor Maggie Radcliffe, local hotelier Becca Fisher and, lastly, Mark's work partner Nigel Carter, with whom he shares a plumbing business. Roberts argues that the opening scene 'can be regarded as paradigmatic of the drama as a whole'. 'Taken as a microcosm,' he explains, 'this spatial vignette depicts a landscape reduced to the functional mechanics of setting: space serves as a container or backdrop within or against which social action can be rehearsed and transacted.'[22]

Like the soap opera, *Broadchurch* revolves around a tension between the public and the private: the public interest (the murder investigation) mandates intrusion into individuals' privacy. As Hardy tells the first press conference at the end of episode one: 'Danny's life touched many people – we'll be looking at all those connections.' Broadchurch (the place) is a community where everyone has something to hide: these secrets are exposed during the course of the investigation. For example, suspicion initially falls upon Danny's father

Mark: he has lied about his whereabouts on the night of the murder. It emerges that he has been having an affair with Becca Fisher and was with her at the time of the murder. The local newsagent Jack Marshall becomes a suspect when the press reveals he was once imprisoned for a sexual offence: Jack is hounded by the townspeople and is driven to commit suicide. Reverend Coates is a recovering alcoholic who also cannot account for his whereabouts on the night of the murder. Susan Wright has concealed evidence from the crime scene in order to protect her estranged son Nigel whom she thinks may have killed Danny: Nigel's father was a paedophile who had abused their daughter and Susan thinks this may be hereditary. Many characters conceal knowledge in order to protect others: even Ellie's son Tom deletes text messages and smashes his laptop to conceal emails.

The narrative around the media in *Broadchurch* needs to be understood in relation to this public/private dichotomy. *Broadchurch* continually reflects on the role of the media – including press, television and social media – in reporting crime and in mediating public knowledge. This is apparent from the first episode when the identity of the dead boy is leaked on Twitter and when Danny's sister Chloe has set up a Google alert for 'Broadchurch and death'. It would be fair to say that the representatives of the media are for the most part not represented in a particularly favourable light: Olly Stephens attempts to exploit his family connection (he is Ellie Miller's nephew) to gain information about the investigation and national journalist Karen White seems more focused on pursuing a vendetta against DI Hardy over his alleged mishandling of a previous murder case than in genuinely helping the family. The case throws Broadchurch into the spotlight of the national media in a wholly unwanted way ('Now we're a murder town!' declares a pub bore) and there is an undercurrent of public resentment that the slow investigation is affecting the tourism on which the town's seasonal economy largely depends. The investigation begins with Hardy appealing for privacy for the family ('We ask the media to respect the family's privacy at this time') and concludes with a similar plea to leave the community alone to come to terms with the trauma ('I would respectfully ask that the town is now left alone to come to terms with what took place here ... Now is the time for Broadchurch to be left, to grieve and heal away from the spotlight'): the irony that these appeals are made via televised press conferences is not lost on viewers.

On one level the prominence accorded to the role of the media in *Broadchurch* might be seen as accurately representing the contemporary media environment: we have become used to public appeals for information from the police in high-profile investigations and to the use of crime reconstruction and CCTV in television programmes such as the BBC's long-running *Crimewatch UK* (1984–2017). But it seems to me that something more is going on in *Broadchurch*. Some reviewers suggested that *Broadchurch* had echoes of real cases, notably the murder of teenager Milly Dowler and the Soham child murders, which had received wide coverage on television (including being featured cases on *Crimewatch*) and in the press.[23] *Broadchurch* was written at a time when there was growing scrutiny of the media, especially in wake of the *News of the World* phone-hacking scandal which came to a head in 2011. In *Broadchurch* the press is presented as carrying out a parallel investigation to the police but without appropriate restraint or consideration of their actions – the very essence of the fourth estate manifesting 'power without responsibility'. Hence, it is the press that uncovers Jack Marshall's past which the under-resourced police investigation had not picked up: but their action in 'outing' him as a paedophile (Jack had been imprisoned for a sexual relationship with a fifteen-year-old girl whom he subsequently married after his release) prompts a witch hunt against him and is indirectly responsible for his death.

At the heart of *Broadchurch* is the 'odd couple' pairing of DI Alec Hardy and DS Ellie Miller. In contrast to the 'buddy' narratives of so many detective dramas, however, the relationship between Hardy and Miller is riddled with tension. Miller resents Hardy because he has been preferred over her for the senior detective's position ('You got my job', she states bluntly when they meet for the first time at the murder scene) and because she feels that an out-of-town detective will not be able to penetrate the secrets of a tightly knit, insular community. Hardy is marked as an outsider on account of his Scottishness (David Tennant's natural accent) and his social awkwardness. From the moment of his arrival it is apparent that there is a cloud hanging over him: he had been the senior investigating officer on another murder case that collapsed when it came to trial (the reason is initially unspecified: later it transpires that Hardy's ex-wife lost a key piece of evidence and he took the blame to cover for her). Hardy also represents a fragile masculinity that is uncommon in the police/detective drama: his authority has been compromised and his health is threatened by a heart condition which nearly incapacitates him during the course of the investigation. Accordingly, questions are constantly being asked whether he is a suitable person to lead a complex murder case. Miller is also compromised in the course of the investigation, although in a different way than Hardy. She is so embedded in the community that she cannot detach herself. When Hardy tells her that she has to look at her friends as potential suspects, Ellie is unable to do so:

> *Hardy:* You have to learn not to trust … You have to learn to look at your community from the outside now.
>
> *Miller:* I can't be outside of it and I don't want to be.

Like the opening of episode one, this scene becomes more significant in hindsight: it turns out that Miller is indeed too close to the community to have been able to see the truth.

The revelation of the identity of Danny's killer in the last episode of *Broadchurch* is surely one of the defining moments of contemporary television drama. It is neither a cleverly disguised formal storytelling trick (as in Agatha Christie's *The Murder of Roger Ackroyd*) nor a ratings-driven 'shock' moment (such as killing off a favourite character in soap opera) but rather the inevitable conclusion of a psychologically complex narrative. The discovery of Danny's missing mobile phone confirms Hardy's suspicion that it was Ellie's husband Joe who killed him: Joe confesses to developing an unusually close relationship with Danny and killing him in a violent rage. Chibnall said: 'I didn't want it to feel we've been shielding [Joe Miller] all along. I think there's enough clues in there that you can pick it up and work it out. I never wanted it to be cheat. I wanted it to feel like you could piece this together and you could have your suspicions and they could be proved correct.'[24] There are several visual and narrative 'clues' in previous episodes. In the episode one tracking shot, for example, Joe has his arm around his son Tom's neck as if he were 'strangling' him (the actors had been told to improvise some father-and-son horseplay: it is possible that the 'clue' was not intentional as actor Matthew Gravelle who plays Joe had not yet been told that his character was the killer). Perhaps the biggest clue is in episode seven where Miller is questioning Susan Wright, who reveals that her ex-husband abused their own daughter. Miller is incredulous that Susan could not have known what was happening: 'Like you didn't see what your husband was up to? ... Back then, in your own home, how could you not know?' Beth Latimer repeats the same question when she confronts Ellie after the revelation: 'How could you not know?'

Some sense of the dramatic and emotional impact of the last episode can be gleaned from reviews at the time. For *Guardian* blogger Tim Dowling:

> The eight-week roller coaster ride ended in mid-air. Instead of a car chase, a manhunt or a clock running down, we were left to watch the tragedy that began with Danny's murder finally rip what was left of Broadchurch to shreds. Like the first episode, this was not so much a police procedural as a despairing exploration of grief, its scabbed-over wounds torn open by the revelation that Joe Miller had been patiently, assiduously grooming Danny Latimer, that the murder was done in a blind rage born of guilt and panic. There was no satisfaction, no sense of justice served, to be derived from the outcome. Joe Miller's guilt simply added to the tally of victims, most notably his wife. As the betrayed and bewildered Ellie, Olivia Colman went over the top in style. It was, in the end, horribly believable.[25]

A similar point was made by Serena Davies, the television editor of the *Daily Telegraph*:

> *Broadchurch* has gradually laid hold of the nation's imagination, and by the start of the final instalment it held it in a sure, vice-like grip. Seven episodes earlier, a small Dorset town had been shaken by the murder of an 11-year-old boy, Danny Latimer. In the last episode, the murderer, in a scene of a bone-crunching tension that fully justified its slo-mo presentation, was unveiled as Joe Miller, a suppressed paedophile and husband to one of the detectives on the case, Ellie Miller (Colman).
>
> Did it matter that Joe was the suspect that many already had in their sights, after a couple of pointers in episode seven? I don't think so. It made the viewer feel clever, for once, rather than their being thrown an explanation they couldn't have possibly thought of, involving glass eyes or magic bullets, as is usually the case in whodunits. Also, it set the stage for a scene of great power.[26]

The critical response was therefore couched in terms of psychological realism rather than the pleasures of the 'whodunnit': there is little or no intellectual satisfaction to be gained from having guessed the identity of the murderer correctly as there is in the classic detective story. Instead, the response seems to have been that the resolution was psychologically realistic insofar as it explains the 'who' and the 'how' but not really the 'why': Joe is a broken man at the end of the episode – literally so when Ellie kicks him onto the floor – who is unable to articulate the nature of his 'love' for Danny or to express his shame and grief.

Broadchurch had drawn a bigger audience than ITV had expected. More to the point the viewing figures indicated that audiences had stayed with the serial throughout: the lowest consolidated audience of 8.8 million (including both the 'overnight' viewers and those who watched it either through recording it or via catch-up services) was only half a million less than the average across the eight episodes. There is both statistical and anecdotal evidence to suggest that *Broadchurch* may have contributed to a change in viewing habits. Over recent years the trend had been towards a steady decline in overnight audiences and a concomitant increase in the percentage of viewers time-shifting: this was largely a consequence of the advent of a new generation of television sets with in-built personal video recording (PVR) facilities. While news and sport were usually watched 'live', drama was the type of television most amenable to time-shift viewing. In 2013 BARB reported that over 20 per cent of drama was watched later (usually within twenty-eight days) and that time-shifting was more common in younger and more affluent households.[27] In this regard there is an instructive comparison between *Broadchurch* and another popular British drama: *Doctor Who*. For the eight episodes of *Doctor Who* broadcast in the spring and early summer of 2013, the overnight audience accounted for 73 per cent of the consolidated audience on average: the number of time-shift viewers was therefore slightly above average for drama, which probably reflects the nature of the audience for a family-oriented Saturday-evening telefantasy series. In contrast, the overnight audience accounted for around 86 per cent of the total for *Broadchurch*: the overnight audience also increased from 84 per cent for the first episode to 89 per cent for the last episode indicating that more viewers were watching it 'live' as the series drew towards its conclusion. This trend is also supported by anecdotal evidence. As Caroline Crampton (*The New Statesman*) observed: 'Unlike the way I react to almost all of the other programmes I keep up with, I wanted to watch *Broadchurch* live ... DVD box sets and on-demand services are brilliant, but *Broadchurch* showed me that they are also often lonely.'[28] And Nick Curtis (*Evening Standard*) similarly averred that 'the concept of must-see TV was so stirringly reaffirmed, not by some import or an obscure satellite channel championed by the chatterati but by a mass audience ITV Monday night drama'.[29]

ITV had not necessarily expected *Broadchurch* to be such a success: its critical and popular acclaim meant that Chibnall was able to continue what he later claimed he had seen all along as a three-serial story arc through to the end. There were some reservations about this decision: some critics felt that the first series was such an exemplary standalone event that it would be unwise to attempt to repeat or continue it. Indeed, one reviewer had even declared that '*Broadchurch* – perhaps wisely – has been created as a one-off series, which won't return for a sequel'.[30] However, it was announced at the end of the concluding episode of series one that '*Broadchurch* will return'. Chibnall decided not to write another murder-investigation story: *Broadchurch* was not *Midsomer Murders* and it would have stretched credulity to have another murder in the same community. He told the press: 'It's going to be a different type of story and hopefully it will be just as compelling and bold ... It will take us a little while, but hopefully it will be secrets and lies up to [the quality of] the first run'.[31] The second *Broadchurch* followed two years later and was both a sequel and a prequel to the first. It interweaves two separate stories – the trial of Joe Miller, who, to wide disbelief, pleads not guilty to Danny's murder – and Hardy's continuing but unofficial investigation of the Sandbrook case. Most of the cast of the first series returned: they were complemented by Charlotte Rampling as retired Queen's Counsel Jocelyn Knight and Eve Myles (*Torchwood*) as Claire Ripley, the key prosecution witness in the Sandbrook case who has gone into hiding following the acquittal of her ex-husband Lee Ashworth (James McAvoy).

The institutional and cultural contexts of the second *Broadchurch* were different from the first series: *Broadchurch* was now a 'brand' that carried certain associations for critics and audiences.[32] The promotional discourse of series two ('Same town – new secrets') set out to position it as the same yet different: a familiar setting but more revelations. The trial of Joe Miller results in his acquittal: the jury returns a not guilty verdict when weaknesses in the prosecution's case – including the revelation that he was beaten up while in custody by his own wife and the fact that Ellie paid her sister to make a witness statement – are exposed. The trial verdict undermines the end of series one: the closure offered by Joe's arrest turns out to have been illusory and the Latimer family and the wider community find themselves having to relive the trauma of Danny's murder. As the narrative progresses new secrets come to light: Mark Latimer has developed a close bond with Ellie's son Tom, the Reverend Coates has been providing spiritual guidance for Joe and it is revealed that Ellie's sister Lucy has a gambling addiction. This is paralleled with the reopening of the Sandbrook case which had tarnished Hardy's reputation and had also collapsed due to tainted evidence. It emerges that the original suspect in the Sandbrook case was guilty after all but was aided and abetted by his wife Claire who provided false testimony at his trial. In this sense the second series of *Broadchurch* is a narrative of rehabilitation and redemption: Hardy is able to resume his career in the police, Ellie comes to terms with the fact that her husband killed Danny, and Beth and Mark Latimer are reconciled when she gives birth to a baby girl.

The second series of *Broadchurch* had a more equivocal reception than the first. The national television critics were split more or less down the middle. Some, such as Mark Lawson (*The Guardian*), thought it 'an ingeniously seamless reboot' and praised Chibnall for writing a continuation story that explored other aspects of criminal justice: most murder suspects do indeed plead not guilty which forces the victim's family to relive the events.[33] But James Delingpole (*The Spectator*) thought the second series was 'a bit of a dud'.[34] And Rachel Cooke (*The New Statesman*) felt that '*Broadchurch* has gone completely loopy'.[35] Vicky Frost (*The Guardian*) summed up the last episode as 'a packed finale that showcased the strengths and the weaknesses of *Broadchurch* ... Parts were breathtaking, but at other times this was as uneven as the rest of the second season, the cast acting out of their skins, but the script and plotting not always helping them out'.[36] The consolidated audience for the first episode was 11.3 million – nearly a million more than for the last episode of the first series – but this had dropped to 9.2 million by the third episode, prompting the press to talk about a haemorrhaging of viewers.[37] Nevertheless, the average audience of 9.7 million was consistent with (in fact slightly higher than) the first series.

A third and final series of *Broadchurch* followed in 2017. This marked a return to the procedural narrative of the first serial as Hardy and Miller are reunited to investigate a new case: the rape of Trish Winterman (Julie Hesmondhalgh) during a weekend house party. The other new cast members included Charlie

Higson as the victim's ex-husband, Georgina Campbell as the abrasive DC Katie Hartford who clashes with Hardy and Miller, and Lenny Henry as her father Ed Burnett. Given the sensitivity of the subject matter, and perhaps mindful of the criticisms levelled against the inaccuracies in the representation of courtroom processes in the second series, Chibnall went to great lengths to ensure that the storyline was treated authentically and without sensationalism: to this end he sought advice from rape counselling services while writing the scripts. In particular, *Broadchurch* set out to challenge some dominant rape myths: that women are 'asking for it' and that all rape victims are necessarily attractive young women.[38] The victim in *Broadchurch* is middle-aged and dowdy: Ellie becomes the voice who reminds us that 'rape is not about sex, it's about power and violence'. There is a considered attempt to represent the treatment of the victim by the police in a sympathetic and sensitive manner: to this extent *Broadchurch* series three marks a shift back towards the more familiar semi-documentary mode of the police procedural. This perception informed the reception discourse of series three. Sally Newell (*The Independent*) called it a 'meticulous police procedural ... It was unflinching and forced us to confront any prejudices about who might be the victim of a sexual assault'.[39]

The third series of *Broadchurch* was the most successful of the trilogy: it drew an average audience of 10.7 million with a high of 11.6 million for the last episode. The critical consensus was that it marked a return to form and a fitting high point on which to conclude. 'After a disappointing second series,' wrote Michael Hogan (*The Telegraph*), 'this third chapter of Chibnall's trilogy represented a return to the fine form of the debut run. Another slow-burning manhunt with multiple suspects, it gripped the nation and built to a compelling climax'.[40] Again there is evidence that a large majority of viewers preferred to watch it 'live' rather than recording it or watching on demand. As Mark Lawson (*The Guardian*) observed:

> There will be delight among traditional broadcasters that – despite the increasing success of self-scheduling seasons on Netflix and Amazon Prime – the last series of *Broadchurch* and the latest series of *Line of Duty* have confirmed the enduring power of weekly serials that millions (up to 10 for *Broadchurch* and 7 for *Line of Duty*) watch at the same time every week, after seven days of wild anticipation and speculation. *Broadchurch* may be dead, but it has helped old-fashioned TV to live longer.[41]

Again this suggests a sense that *Broadchurch* was a form of 'event' television: ITV's press release for the last episode spoke about a 'nation tuning in'.[42] The 36 per cent audience share was significantly higher than ITV1's average (15.6 per cent in 2017) and was the second highest for any drama episode (including soaps) for the year (it was beaten by 'The Six Thatchers' – the New Year's Day episode of *Sherlock* – by around 100,000 viewers).[43]

The success of *Broadchurch* demonstrated, perhaps against the received wisdom, that there was still a place for the slow-paced, intense psychological drama in the era of the high-concept television series. But it also did more: it signalled the return of the fixed-length serial to British television. The six- or eight-part drama serial had been in decline in the decade or so before *Broadchurch*: Paul Abbott's six-part *State of Play* (2003) was perhaps the last to catch the public imagination in the way that *Edge of Darkness* or *Pride and Prejudice* had. There was a sense in which drama commissioners had become wary of too-long serials: even popular procedural dramas such as *Silent Witness* and *Waking the Dead* would usually be broadcast in two-part stories over successive evenings to guard against losing viewers to rival channels in what John Ellis has characterized as television's 'age of plenty'.[44] However, *Broadchurch* demonstrated that in the right circumstances a slow-burning drama could still build audiences over a period of eight weeks. And this has been reflected in the re-emergence of the serial form in the years since *Broadchurch*. It is no coincidence that there has been a particular vogue for psychological crime dramas and police procedurals. BBC2's five-part *The Fall* (2013) had been commissioned before *Broadchurch* aired, but the 'Broadchurch effect' might be seen as a factor in the commissioning of BBC2's five-part *Line of Duty* (2014) and BBC1's eight-part *The Missing* (2014) and six-part *The Night Manager* (2016) – the latter an adaptation of John le Carré's novel that can be placed in a tradition extending back to the celebrated adaptations of *Tinker, Tailor, Soldier, Spy* and *Smiley's People*. *The Fall* and *Line of Duty* were recommissioned: the latter has so far run to six series and increased its audience from 4 million to 9.5 million when it moved to BBC1 in 2017. The most successful drama serial of recent times, surpassing even *Broadchurch*, has been BBC1's six-part *Bodyguard* (2018), a political thriller in the mould of *State of Play*, created and written by Jed Mercury, which drew audiences of over 10 million. Its final episode, seen by an overnight audience of 10.4 million, rising to 14.3 million via catch-up after seven days and 17.1 million after twenty-eight days, was the biggest audience for any drama since the turn of the millennium, surpassing the previous records set by *Doctor Who* and *Sherlock*. As television historian John Cook observed: '*Bodyguard* proves that broadcasting, rather than catch-ups and box set binges, has a future… It shows that we still want to have a shared national experience. When it's done this well with drama, it can work really powerfully.'[45]

The idea of television drama as a national experience had once informed the response to *The Wednesday Play* and *Play for Today*. The form and style of contemporary drama have changed out of all recognition since the heyday of the single play, but the success of series such as *Downton Abbey*, *Sherlock* and *Broadchurch*, which all drew audience shares over 30 per cent at a time when viewers have more choice of channels than at any time before, demonstrates that television drama still holds a powerful grip on the public imagination. The institutional contexts and critical discourses of contemporary British television drama are very different from those of the 'golden age' half a century ago. But golden ages are usually only apparent in hindsight, and it would not surprise me if future television historians come to regard the early twenty-first century as at the least a silver age of British drama.

Notes

Introduction

1 'Julie Gardner and Claire Parker: In Conversation', in *Life on Mars: From Manchester to New York*, eds Stephen Lacey and Ruth McElroy (Cardiff: University of Wales Press, 2012), 181.

2 There is an extensive critical literature on American Quality Television: for a good introduction, see Janet McCabe and Kim Akass, eds, *Quality TV: Contemporary American Television and Beyond* (London: I.B. Tauris, 2005). For a wide-ranging discussion of the discursive terms of debate (including British as well as American television), see Christine Geraghty, 'Aesthetics and Quality in Popular Television Drama', *International Journal of Cultural Studies*, 6: 1 (2003), 25–45.

3 John Caughie, *Television Drama: Realism, Modernism, and British Culture* (Oxford: Oxford University Press, 2000), 13.

4 *The Observer*, 7 November 2010: www.theguardian/com/tv-and-radio/2010/nov/07/jimmy-mcgovern-tv-drama-irony (accessed March 2017).

5 The authors of these studies are Stephen Lacey (Tony Garnett), Dave Rolinson (Alan Clarke), John Tulloch (Trevor Griffiths), Kara McKechnie (Alan Bennett), Lez Cooke (Troy Kennedy Martin), Julia Hallam (Lynda La Plante), Sue Vice (Jack Rosenthal) and Steve Blandford (Jimmy McGovern). The series also includes studies of genre writer Terry Nation (by Jonathan Bignell and Andrew O'Day) and the master of adaptation Andrew Davies (by Sarah Cardwell). Full publication details can be found in the bibliography.

6 At the time of writing, Matt Hills's *Sherlock: Detecting Quality Television* is listed for publication by Bloomsbury, London, in 2020.

7 Mark Thompson, 'What's Wrong with Our TV', *The Guardian*, 24 August 2002, 18.

8 Andrew Billen, 'Why I Love American TV', *The Guardian*, 28 July 2002, 76.

9 Mark Duguid, 'TV Drama in the 2000s', *BFI Screenonline*: www.screenonline.org/uk/tv/id/1394013/index.html (accessed March 2017).

10 Robin Nelson, *State of Play: Contemporary 'High-End' TV Drama* (Manchester: Manchester University Press, 2007), 3.

11 The one major exception to this in recent times has been the new *Doctor Who*, which is produced 'in house' by BBC Wales.

12 *The Guardian*, 15 February 2010: www.theguardian.com/media/2010/feb/15/ stephen-garrett-kudos (accessed March 2017).

13 *The Guardian*, 28 August 2010: www.theguardian.com/media/2010/aug/28/paul-abbott-uk-tv-drama (accessed March 2017).

14 Lez Cooke, *British Television Drama: A History*, 2nd edn (London: British Film Institute/Palgrave Macmillan, 2015), 217.

15 *The Guardian*, 31 August 2014: www.theguardian.com/media/media-blog/2014/ aug/31/sherlock-downton-call-midwife-television-drama-america (accessed March 2017).

16 Since writing this, the last episode of BBC1's *Bodyguard* (23.09.2018) has overtaken the *Sherlock* episode 'The Empty Hearse' (01.01.2014) to become the most-watched television drama episode since 2002 with an overnight audience of 10.4 million rising to a consolidated total including time-shift and on-demand viewers of 17.1 million after 28 days.

17 Broadcasters' Audience Research Board, *The Viewing Report: Our Annual Exploration of the UK's Viewing Habits*, 27 April 2017: https://www.barb.co.uk/ download/?file=/wp-content/uploads/2017/04/Barb-Viewing-Report-2017.pdf (accessed February 2019).

Chapter 1

1 *Spooks*. Kudos Film and Television Productions for BBC1. *Created by:* David Wolstencraft and Howard Brenton. *Executive producers*: Stephen Garrett, Jane Featherstone. *Writers:* David Wolstencraft, Simon Mirren, Howard Brenton, Matthew Graham, Ben Richards, Rupert Walters, Raymond Khoury, David Farr, Zinnie Harris, Neil Cross, George Tiffin, Russell Lewis, Richard McBrien, Christian Spurrier, Sean Reilly, Dennis Kelly, James Dormer, Jonathan Bradley & Sam Vincent, Anthony Neilson, Sean Cook. *Directors:* Bharat Nalluri, Rob Bailey, Andy Wilson, Justin Chadwick, Ciaran Donnelly, Sam Miller, James Campbell, Cilla Ware, Bill Anderson, Alrick Riley, Antonia Bird, Jeremy Lovering, Omar Madden, Julian Simpson, Kenny Glenaan, Andy Haye, Julian Holmes, Charles Beeson, Brendan Mahon, Stefan Schwartz, Colm McCarthy, Peter Hoar, Edward Hall, Paul Whittington, Michael Caton-Jones, Paul Whittington. Series 1: 13 May–17 June 2002.

Series 2: 2 June–11 August 2003. Series 3: 11 October–13 December 2004.
Series 4: 12 September–10 November 2005. Series 5: 17 September–13
November 2006. Series 6: 16 October–18 December 2007. Series 7: 27
October–8 December 2008. Series 8: 4 November–23 December 2009.
Series 9: 20 September–8 November 2010. Series 10: 18 September–23
October 2011.

2   '*Spooks* to End This Autumn on BBC One', *BBC News*, 11 August 2011: http://.
    bbc.co.uk/news/entertainment-arts-14488634 (accessed May 2016).

3   'About Kudos', *Kudos Productions*: http://www.kudosproductions.co.uk/about
    (accessed December 2011).

4   *The Independent*, 13 February 2016: www.independent.co.uk/arts/entertainment/
    tv/features/a6872226.html (accessed May 2016).

5   David Buxton, *From 'The Avengers' to 'Miami Vice': Form and Ideology in
    Television Series* (Manchester: Manchester University Press, 1990), 77.

6   Sergio Angelini, 'Cold War Spies', *BFI Screenonline*: http://www.screenonline.org.
    uk/tv/id/1008415/index.html (accessed December 2011).

7   'Julie Gardner and Claire Parker in Conversation', in *Life on Mars: From
    Manchester to New York*, eds Stephen Lacey and Ruth McEloy (Cardiff: University
    of Wales Press, 2012), 181.

8   'The Terror Question', *Spooks* DVD Series 1 Disc 2 (BBC Worldwide/
    Entertainment One UK VFC45576).

9   *The Guardian*, 15 February 2010: www.theguardian.com/media/2016/feb/15/
    stephen-garrett-kudos (accessed May 2016).

10 Episodes of *Spooks* do not have individual titles but titles have been adopted in
    online episode guides. See *Spooks (A Titles & Air Dates Guide)*: http://epguides.
    com/Spooks/ (accessed December 2011).

11 *BBC Annual Report and Accounts 2008/9: The BBC Executives' Review and
    Assessment*: http://downloads.bbc.co.uk/annualreport/pdf/bbc_executive_08_09.
    pdf (accessed May 2016).

12 BBC Television Publicity release: '*Spooks*: MI5 not 9 to 5': www.bbc.co.uk/
    pressoffice/pressreleases/stories/2002/05_may/spooks-presspack.pdf (accessed
    May 2016). This document can also be found on the digitised microfiche for
    Spooks held by the BFI's Reuben Library.

13 Quoted in Christopher Andrew, *The Defence of the Realm: The Authorized History
    of MI5* (London: Allen Lane, 2009), 778.

14 David Shayler, 'Must Spy Harder', *The Guardian*, 15 May 2002, A4.

15 Michael Denning, *Cover Stories: Narrative and Ideology in the British Spy Thriller*
    (London: Routledge & Kegan Paul, 1987), 34.

16 BBC Television Publicity release: '*Spooks*: MI5 not 9 to 5'.

17 Ibid.

18 *The Guardian*, 12 August 2003, 22.

19 These five were the so-called 'Cambridge spy ring', recruited by the Soviet Union while at Cambridge University who all rose to senior positions in either the Foreign Office or the intelligence services MI5 and MI6.

20 *Time Out*, 16 May 2006: http.//www.timeout.com/london/books/features/339/David_Wolstencroft_on_London_spies.html (accessed May 2016).

21 However, see Peter Morey, 'Strangers and Stereotypes: The *Spooks* Controversy and the Framing of Muslims', *Journal of Postcolonial Writing*, 46: 5 (2010), 529–39.

22 *The Guardian*, 11 June 2003, 7.

23 *The Daily Telegraph*, 11 June 2003, 6.

24 *The Times*, 31 July 2003, 12.

25 *The Guardian*, 3 June 2002, 7.

26 Christian William Erickson, 'Thematics of Counterterrorism: Comparing *24* and *MI-5/Spooks*', *Critical Studies in Terrorism*, 1: 3 (2008), 344.

27 *The Guardian*, 15 October 2004: http://www.the guardian.com/media/2004/oct/15/Iraqdossier.bbc (accessed May 2016).

28 Ibid.

29 'Blair Defeated over Terror Laws', *BBC News*, 9 November 2005: news.bbc.co.uk/1/hi/uk_politics/4422086.stm (accessed May 2016).

30 *The Daily Telegraph*, 5 July 2008: http://www.telegraph.co.uk/news/uknews/2253398/Russian-spies-leaving-door-open-for-terrorists-in-Britain.html (accessed May 2016).

31 *The Guardian*, 14 May 2002, 22.

32 *The Independent*, 19 May 2002, 13.

33 *The Financial Times*, 15 August 2003, 13.

34 *The Guardian*, 7 June 2002, 52.

35 *The Times*, 5 August 2003, 27.

36 *The Daily Telegraph*, 11 June 2002, 22.

37 *The Guardian*, 4 December 2008, 32.

38 *Time Out*, 8 May 2002, 13.

39 *The Daily Telegraph*, 13 September 2005, 26.

40 *The Guardian: Media*, 2 December 2008, 5.

41 *The Daily Telegraph*, 23 October 2011, 24.

42 *The Sunday Telegraph*, 26 May 2002, 5.

43 *The Times*, 31 October 2005, 5.

44 Shayler, 'Must Spy Harder', A4.

45 *The Guardian*, 16 September 2011, 5.

46 *Daily Mail*, 8 December 2011, 7.

47 *The Guardian: Media*, 11 August 2011, 3.

48 Ibid.

49 The average audiences for *Spooks* by series were 7.5 million for series one (2002), 7.1 million for series two (2003), 5.8 million for series three (2004), 6.1 million for series four (2005), 6 million for series five (2006), 5.7 million for series six (2007), 5.4 million for series seven (2008), 5.1 million for series eight (2009), 6.3 million for series nine (2010) and 5.4 million for series ten (2011).

50 *Variety*, 8 May 2015: variety.com/2015/film/global/spooks-the-greater-good-review-kit-harington/201487729 (accessed May 2016).

Chapter 2

1 *Foyle's War*. Greenlit Productions for ITV1. *Created by:* Anthony Horowitz. *Executive producer:* Jill Green. *Producers:* Jill Green, Simon Passmore, Keith Thompson. *Writers:* Anthony Horowitz, Michael Russell, Rob Heyland, Michael Chappel, David Kane. *Directors:* Jeremy Silbertson, David Thacker, Giles Foster, Gavin Millar, Tristram Powell, Simon Langton, Stuart Orme, David Richards, Andy Hay. Series 1: 'The German Woman' (27.10.2002), 'The White Feather' (03.11.2002), 'A Lesson in Murder' (10.11. 2002), 'Eagle Day' (17.11.2002). Series 2: 'Fifty Ships' (16.11.2003), 'Among the Few' (23.11.2003), 'War Games' (30.11.2003), 'The Funk Hole' (07.12.2003). Series 3: 'The French Drop' (24.10.2004), 'Enemy Fire' (31.10.2004), 'They Fought in the Fields' (07.11.2004), 'A War of Nerves' (14.11.2004). Series 4 (Part 1): 'Invasion' (15.01.2006), 'Bad Blood' (22.01.2006). Series 4 (Part 2): 'Bleak Midwinter' (11.02.2007), 'Casualties of War' (15.04.2007). Series 5: 'Plan of Attack' (6.01.2008), 'Broken Souls' (13.04.2008), 'All Clear' (20.04.2008). Series 6: 'The Russian House' (11.04.2010), 'Killing Time' (18.04.2010), 'The Hide' (25.04.2010). Series 7: 'The Eternity Ring' (24.03.2013), 'The Cage' (31.08.2013), 'Sunflower' (7.04.2013). Series 8: 'High Castle' (4.01.2015), 'Trespass' (11.01.2015), 'Elise' (18.01.2015).

2 Since I first wrote about *Foyle's War*, other academic studies have confirmed that it is a site of significant cultural interest for television historians: see Siân Nicholas, 'History, Revisionism and Television Drama: *Foyle's War* and the

"Myth of 1940'", *Media History*, 13: 2–3 (2007), 203–19, and Stephen Lacey, 'The Blitz Detective: *Foyle's War*, History, Genre and Contemporary Politics', in *Contemporary British Television Crime Drama: Cops on the Box*, ed. Ruth McElroy (London: Routledge, 2016).

3   The critical literature on *Inspector Morse* includes Simon Barker, '"Period" Detective Drama and the Limits of Contemporary Nostalgia: *Inspector Morse* and the Strange Case of a Lost England', *Critical Survey*, 6: 2 (1994), 234–42; Helen Davis, '*Inspector Morse* and the Business of Crime', *Television and New Media*, 2: 2 (2001), 133–48; and Lucy Fife Donaldson, 'Series Spaces: Revisiting and Re-Evaluating *Inspector Morse*', *Journal of Popular Television*, 4: 1 (2016), 3–28.

4   *Broadcast*, 2 March 2001, 10.

5   *Broadcast*, 28 March 2003, 8.

6   British Film Institute Reuben Library digitized microfiche for *Foyle's War*: *Foyle's War* Press Pack (Greenlit/ITV, 2002), 20.

7   *Radio Times*, 21–27 January 2006, 10.

8   *The Daily Telegraph*, 26 October 2002, 26; *The Sunday Telegraph Review*, 3 November 2002, 6.

9   *Foyle's War* Press Pack Series 3 (Greenlit/ITV, 2004), 1.

10   *The Independent: Review*, 11 December 2003, 21.

11   This is the list of wartime crimes cited by Assistant Commissioner Summers (Edward Fox) in the first episode when Foyle requests a transfer as he believes 'I could be doing something a little more relevant for the war effort'.

12   *The Daily Telegraph*, 13 November 2002, 23.

13   *Foyle's War* Press Pack, 20.

14   Leslie Halliwell used the phrase 'friendly socialism' to describe Priestley's broadcasts in his introduction to a series of wartime films under the umbrella title *The British at War* on Channel 4 in 1984. Priestley's Dunkirk broadcast was actually on 5 June 1940. It sounds to my ear that the radio voice heard in the episode is not Priestley's but someone imitating him.

15   *The Independent: Review*, 18 November 2002, 21.

16   *The Sunday Telegraph: Review*, 3 November 2002, 6.

17   *The Times*, 25 October 2004, 23.

18   *The Times*, 16 November 2002, 25.

19   *The Age*, 28 November 2002, 14.

20   *The Daily Telegraph*, 28 November 2002, 14.

21   *Daily Mail*, 24 March 2003, 16.

22   *Daily Express*, 16 January 2006.

23   *Radio Times*, 17–23 January 2006, 13.

24 *The Independent*, 14 January 2006, 18.

25 *The Guardian*, 10 February 2009: www.theguardian.com/media/2008/apr/08/itv. television (accessed March 2017).

26 *Radio Times*, 11–18 April 2010, 33.

27 *The Guardian*, 14 April 2008: www.theguardian.com/media/2008/apr/14/ tvratings. television (accessed March 2017).

28 *The Daily Telegraph*, 18 January 2015: www.telegraph.co.uk/culture/tv-and-radio-review/11352906 (accessed March 2017).

29 *New York Times*, 13 September 2013: www.nytimes.com/2013/09/13/television-foyles-war-the-hero-switch-to-intelligence-wprk.html (accessed March 2017).

30 *Los Angeles Times*, 3 February 2015: http://www.latimes.com/entertainment/enveleope/emmys/la-en-st-case-for-foyles-war-20150528-story.html (accessed March 2017).

31 *Los Angeles Times*, 28 May 2015: http://www.latimes.com/entertainment/tv/la-st-foyles-war-20150203-column.html (accessed March 2017).

32 'Foyle's War: Series Creator Was Ready for UK Cancellation', *TV Series Finale*, 6 June 2016: www.tvseriesfinale.com/tv-show/foylers-war-series-creator-ready-uk-cancellation (accessed March 2017).

Chapter 3

1 *Hustle*. Kudos Film and Television Productions for BBC1. *Created by:* Tony Jordan. *Executive producers:* Karen Wilson, Howard Burch, Tony Jordan, Simon Crawford Collins. *Writers:* Tony Jordan, Matthew Graham, Ashley Pharoah, Howard Overman, Julie Rutherford, Steve Coombes, Danny Brown, David Cummings, Colin Blytheway, Nick Fisher, Fintan Ryan, Chris Hurford & Tom Butterworth, Chris Bucknall, Chris Lang, James Payne, Ryan Craig. *Directors:* Bharat Nalluri, Minkie Spiro, Robert Bailey, Otto Bathurst, Alrick Riley, John Strickland, Colm McCarthy, S. J. Clarkson, Lee MacIntosh, Stefan Schwartz, James Strong, Julian Simpson, Martin Hutchings, Iain MacDonald, Sarah O'Gorman, Luke Watson, John McKay, Roger Goldby, Colin Teague, Adrian Lester. Series 1: 24 February–30 March 2004. Series 2: 25 March–3 May 2005. Series 3: 10 March–14 April 2006. Series 4: 3 May–7 June 2007. Series 5: 8 January–12 February 2009. Series 6: 4 January–8 February 2010. Series 7: 7 January–18 February 2011. Series 8: 13 January–17 February 2012.

2 *The Observer*, 15 February 2004: www.theguardian.com/lifeandstyle/2004/feb/15/foodanddrink.television (accessed March 2017).

3 *The Times*, 21 February 2004, 29.

4 Ibid.

5 *The Guardian*, 25 October 2005: www.theguardian.com/media/2005/oct/25/ broadcast. bbc (accessed March 2017).

6 Umberto Eco, 'The Narrative Structure in Fleming', in *The Bond Affair*, eds Oreste Del Buono and Umberto Eco, trans. R. A. Downie (London: Macdonald, 1965), 58.

7 David Buxton, *From 'The Avengers' to 'Miami Vice': Form and Ideology in Television Series* (Manchester: Manchester University Press, 1990), 117.

8 'Adrian Lester', *DigitalSpy*, 20 September 2007: www.digitalspy.co.uk/movies/ a75810/adrian-lester.html (accessed March 2017).

9 Stephen Harper, '"When You Walk through These Doors, You Can Be Anything You Want": Authenticity, Fantasy and Neoliberal Ideology in *Hotel Babylon*', *Journal of British Cinema and Television*, 5: 1 (2008), 122.

10 *The Times: The Eye*, 21 February 2004, 28.

11 *The Daily Telegraph*, 25 February 2004, 28.

12 *The Guardian*, 16 February 2004, 16.

13 *The Daily Telegraph*, 30 March 2005, 25.

14 *The Independent*, 25 February 2004, 23.

15 *The Times: T2*, 25 February 2004, 22.

16 *The Times*, 4 May 2007, 23.

17 *The Independent: Review*, 30 March 2005, 21.

18 *The Daily Telegraph*, 15 January 2009, 20.

19 *Metro*, 4 May 2007, 39.

20 Stephen Bourne, *Black in the British Frame: Black People in British Film and Television 1896–1996* (London: Cassell, 1998), *passim*.

21 Rachel Carroll, 'Black Britain and the Classic Adaptation: Integrated Casting in Television Adaptations of *Oliver Twist* and *Little Dorrit*', *Adaptation*, 8: 1 (2015), 16–30.

22 *Black Film Maker*, 26: 27 (November/December 2004), 15.

Chapter 4

1 *Life on Mars*. 2006–7. Kudos Film and Television Productions for BBC Wales. *Executive producers:* Jane Featherstone, Julie Gardner, Matthew Graham. *Writers:* Matthew Graham, Ashley Pharoah, Tony Jordan, Chris Chibnall,

Julie Rutterford, Guy Jenkin, Mark Greig. *Directors:* Bharat Nalluri, John McKay, S. J. Clarkson, John Alexander, Richard Clark, Andrew Gunn. Series 1: 9 January–7 February 2006. Series 2: 13 February–10 April 2007.

2   Steve O'Brien, 'The nick of time', *SFX*, 139 (January 2006), 54.

3   'Julie Gardner and Claire Parker: In Conversation', in *Life on Mars: From Manchester to New York*, eds Stephen Lacey and Ruth McElroy (Cardiff: University of Wales Press, 2012), 172.

4   Ibid.

5   Quoted in Matt Hills, *Triumph of a Time Lord: Regenerating 'Doctor Who' in the Twenty-First Century* (London: I.B. Tauris, 2010), 48–9.

6   John Curzon, 'Sam Tyler and the "New North"', in *Life on Mars: From Manchester to New York*, ed. Stephen Lacey and Ruth McElroy, 69–77.

7   See, for example, 'Take a Look at the Lawman' (*Life on Mars* DVD Series 1 Disc 1, BBC Worldwide/Contender Home Entertainment VCF 89612) and 'The Return of *Life on Mars*' (*Life on Mars* DVD Series 2 Disc 1, BBC Worldwide/Contender Home Entertainment VFD 04238).

8   The website *Digital Spy* had a discussion forum entitled 'Hunt's Housewives' for female fans of the character (and actor Philip Glenister). The posts are archived at: https://forums.digitalspy.com/discussion/1112278/huntshousewives-roll-call (accessed June 2017).

9   Quoted in *Radio Times*, 13–20 January 2006, 9.

10   'Julie Gardner and Claire Parker: In Conversation', 170.

11   *I Love the 70s* was a 'nostalgia clip' show that featured various celebrities recalling their memories of growing up in the decade with particular reference to favourite television shows interspersed with archive excerpts: originally a cheap schedule-filler for BBC2 on Saturday nights in the summer of 2000 it proved so popular that it was quickly followed by *I Love the 1980s* and *I Love the 1990s*.

12   John Ellis, 'Watching Death at Work: An Analysis of *A Matter of Life and Death*', in *Powell, Pressburger and Others*, ed. Ian Christie (London: British Film Institute, 1978), 79–104.

13   Ibid., 101.

14   Ibid., 101–2.

15   *The Independent*, 10 January 2006, 44.

16   *The Times 2*, 11 April 2007, 23.

17   *The Times*, *Law* section, 17 January 2006, 5.

18   Clive Emsley, *The English Police: A Political and Social History*, 2nd edn (London: Routledge, 1996), 179.

19 See Christopher Booker, *The Seventies: Portrait of a Decade* (Harmondsworth: Allen Lane, 1980); Leon Hunt, *British Low Culture: From Safari Suits to Sexploitation* (London: Routledge, 1998); and Laurel Forster and Sue Harper, eds, *British Culture and Society in the 1970s: The Lost Decade* (Necastle-upon-Tyne: Cambridge Scholars, 2010).

20 John R. Cook and Mary Irwin, '"Moonage Daydreams": Nostalgia and Cultural Memory Contexts of *Life on Mars* and *Ashes to Ashes*', in *Life on Mars: From Manchester to New York*, eds Stephen Lacey and Ruth McElroy, 80.

21 Ruth McElroy, 'Consuming Retrosexualities: The Past Live on Screen, Online Now', in *Life on Mars: From Manchester to New York*, eds Stephen Lacey and Ruth McElroy, 119.

22 Bill Bryson, *Notes from a Small Island* (London: Black Swan, 1996), 23.

23 Bantam Press published two spin-off books from the series in 2007 *The Wit and Wisdom of Gene Hunt* 'by Ray Carling and Chris Skelton' and *The Handbook of Modern Policing (1973 Edition)* by 'DCI Gene Hunt'. The real author of both was Guy Adams.

24 *The Times*, 11 April 2007, 23.

25 *The Independent*, 13 April 2007, 22.

26 *Radio Times*, 7–13 January 2006, 70.

27 *Daily Star*, 9 January 2006, 22.

28 *The Guardian* G2, 10 January 2006, 32.

29 *The Sunday Telegraph* S7, 10 February 2006, 25.

30 *The Independent*, 10 January 2006, 44.

31 *Evening Standard*, 21 February 2006, 41.

32 For a discussion of the different formal and aesthetic styles of the British and American series of *Life on Mars*, see Elke Weissmann, *Transnational Television Drama: Special Relations and Mutual Influence between the UK and US* (Basingstoke: Palgrave Macmillan, 2012), 82–95.

Chapter 5

1 *Ashes to Ashes*. Kudos Film and Television Productions for BBC Wales. *Created by:* Ashley Pharoah and Matthew Graham. *Executive producers:* Jane Featherstone, Simon Crawford Collins, Matthew Graham, Piers Wenger. *Writers:* Matthew Graham, Ashley Pharoah, Julie Rutterford, Mark Greig, Mick Ford, Nicole Taylor, Jack Lothian, Tom Butterworth & Chris Hurforth,

James Payne. *Directors:* Jonny Campbell, Billie Eltringham, Catherine Morshead, Ben Bolt, Philip John, David Drury, Alrick Riley, Jamie Payne. Series 1: 7 February–27 March 2008. Series 2: 20 April–8 June 2009. Series 3: 2 April–21 May 2010.

2 Alex's monologue changes slightly in each series of *Ashes to Ashes*, reflecting the fact that the series moves into 1982 and 1983.

3 *Radio Times*, 2–8 February 2008, 16.

4 *Ashes to Ashes, BBC Press Office*, 28 January 2008: www.bbc.co.uk/pressoffice/ pressreleases/stories/2008/01_january/28/ashes.shtml (accessed April 2017).

5 *The Guardian: Media*, 7 January 2008, 2–3. See also the interview with Graham in 'Dust to Dust', *Ashes to Ashes: Series 3*, DVD Disc 4 (BBC Worldwide/Contender Home Entertainment VFD 43940).

6 Stephen Lacey and Ruth McElroy, 'Introduction', in *Life on Mars: From Manchester to New York*, eds Stephen Lacey and Ruth McElroy (Cardiff: University of Wales Press, 2012), 10–11.

7 Hannah Hamad, '"Don't Let Him Take Britain Back to the 1980s": *Ashes to Ashes* as Postfeminist Recession Television', *Continuum: Journal of Media and Cultural Studies*, 28: 2 (2014), 203.

8 Wheeler Winston Dixon, 'The Halfway House', in *Liberal Directions: Basil Dearden and Postwar British Film Culture*, eds Alan Burton, Tim O'Sullivan and Paul Wells (Trowbridge: Flicks Books, 1997), 111.

9 In fact, the new officer's arrival is not quite the last scene of *Ashes to Ashes*, as after the closing credits there is a short clip of Jack Warner's PC George Dixon signing off with his customary address to camera from an early episode of *Dixon of Dock Green*: 'So it was all sorted out in the end – and no bones broken, luckily … Now, I don't know about you, but I'm going to knock off.' The clip serves several purposes. It locates *Ashes to Ashes* (like *Life on Mars* had done) within the history of the British police series by invoking the memory of perhaps the most iconic 'copper' of all. It reminds us that what we have been watching is a fiction in which 'it was all sorted out in the end': this might refer to the idea that the last episode of *Ashes to Ashes* also resolves the loose ends of *Life on Mars*. But there is also another possible meaning. The character of PC Dixon had first appeared in the Ealing feature film *The Blue Lamp* (1950) – coincidentally also directed by Basil Dearden – when, like Gene, he had been shot and killed in the course of a robbery, only to be resurrected for the television series *Dixon of Dock Green*, which ran for twenty-one years from 1955 to 1976.

10 Caitlin Shaw, 'Remediating the Eighties: Nostalgia and Retro in British Screen Fiction from 2005 to 2011' (PhD thesis, De Montfort University, 2015), 73.

11 Clive Emsley, *The English Police: A Political and Social History*, 2nd edn (London: Routledge, 1996), 212.

12 *The Daily Telegraph*, 13 April 2007, 14.

13 Helen Piper, *The TV Detective: Voices of Dissent in Contemporary Television* (London: I.B. Tauris, 2015), 105.

14 Charlotte Brunsdon, 'Television Crime Series, Women Police and Fuddy-Duddy Feminism', *Feminist Media Studies*, 13: 4 (2013), 375–95.

15 Hamad, 'Don't Let Him Take Britain Back to the 1980s', 205.

16 *The Sunday Telegraph*, 10 February 2008, 29.

17 *The Daily Telegraph*, 8 February 2008, 36.

18 *The Daily Telegraph*, 28 March 2008, 34.

19 *The Independent: Extra*, 8 February 2008, 14.

20 *The Spectator*, 10 February 2008, 257.

21 *The Times 2*, 16 January 2008, 25.

22 *The Independent*, 21 April 2009, 19.

23 *The Observer*, 10 February 2008, 22.

24 *Independent on Sunday*, 10 February 2008, 58.

25 *The Guardian*, 8 February 2008, 27.

26 *The Guardian*, 28 April 2009, 41.

27 *The Guardian*, 2 April 2010: https://www.theguardian.com/politics/2010/apr/02/david-cameron-gene-hunt-labour-poster (accessed March 2017).

28 *The Independent*, 4 April 2010: https://www.independent.co.uk/news/uk/politics/labour-poster-turns-cameron-into-a-cult-hero-1935428.html (accessed March 2017).

Chapter 6

1 *Downton Abbey*. Carnival Films for ITV1. *Created and written by:* Julian Fellowes. *Executive producers:* Julian Fellowes, Gareth Neame, Rebecca Eaton. *Producers:* Liz Trubridge, Nigel Marchant. *Directors:* Brian Percival, Ben Bolt, Brian Kelly, Andy Goddard, James Strong, Ashley Pearce. Series 1: 26 September–7 November 2010. Series 2: 18 September–6 November 2011. Series 3: 16 September–4 November 2012. Series 4: 22 September–11 November 2013. Series 5: 21 September–9 November 2014. Series 5:

20 September–8 November 2015. There were also five Christmas Day 'specials' in successive years from 2011 to 2015.

2   *New York Times*, 3 January 2013: https://www.nytimes.com/2013/01/06/ arts/television/downton-abbey-reaches-around-the-world.html (accessed March 2017).

3   *Daily Mail*, 28 November 2012: http://www.dailymail.co.uk/news/article-2239672/Downton-Abbey-effect-Demand-British-butlers-DOUBLES-2-years-wealthiest-families.html (accessed March 2017).

4   'Carnival Films and ITV announce Season 6 to be the final *Downton Abbey*', *ITV Press Centre*, 26 March 2015: https://www.itv/com.presscentre/press-releases/carnival-films-and-itv-downton-abbey (accessed March 2017).

5   The critical literature on the British costume drama includes Robert Giddings and Keith Selby, *The Classic Serial on Television and Radio* (Basingstoke: Palgrave Macmillan, 2001); Sarah Cardwell, *Adaptation Revisited: Television and the Classic Novel* (Manchester: Manchester University Press, 2002); and James Leggott and Julie Anne Taddeo, eds, *Upstairs and Downstairs: British Costume Drama Television from 'The Forsyte Saga' to 'Downton Abbey'* (Lanham MA: Rowman and Littlefield, 2015).

6   Simone Knox, '*Masterpiece Theatre* and British Drama Imports on US television: Discourses of Tension', *Critical Studies in Television*, 7: 1 (2012), 29–48.

7   John Caughie, *Television Drama: Realism, Modernism, and British Culture* (Oxford: Oxford University Press, 2000), 216.

8   Charlotte Brunsdon, 'Problems with Quality', *Screen*, 31: 1 (1990), 86.

9   Sarah Cardwell, *Andrew Davies* (Manchester, 2005), 30–1, 119–20.

10 *The Guardian*, 20 August 2008: https://www.guardian.co.uk/media/2008/aug/20/ television.usa1 (accessed March 2017).

11 Email from Gareth Neame, 6 November 2013.

12 *Broadcast*, 27 August 2010, 23.

13 *MailOnline*, 29 September 2010: https://www.dailymail.co.uk/tvshowbiz/ articles-1315926 (accessed March 2017).

14 *The Atlantic*, 1 January 2013: https://www.theatlantic.com/entertainment/ magazine/2013/01/brideshead-regurgitated (accessed March 2017).

15 *Broadcast*, 27 August 2010, 23.

16 'Dennis Spooner' (interviewed by John Fleming), *StarBurst*, 4: 9 (1982), 47.

17 *Newsweek*, 14 February 2012: https://www.thedailybeast.com/articles/2012/02/14/ downton-abbey-and-how-pbs-got-cool (accessed March 2017).

18 '"Downton Abbey" Premiere Breaks Ratings Record', *CNN*, 7 January 2014: cnn. com/2014/01/06/showbiz/tv/downton-abbey-premiere-ratings-record (accessed March 2017).

19 *Vanity Fair*, December 2012: http://www.vanityfair.com/culture/1012/12/julian-fellowes-downton-abbey (accessed March 2017).

20 *Newsweek*, 14 February 2012.

21 *The Berkshire Eagle*, 20 February 2013: https://www.berkshireeagle.com/stories/julian-fellowes-abbey-owes-much-to-wharton,421116 (accessed March 2017).

22 *The New Statesman*, 14 October 2010: https://www.newstatesman.com/television/2010/10/downton-abbey-drama-lord (accessed March 2017).

23 *Broadcast*, 27 August 2010, 20.

24 Paul Kerr, 'Classic Serials: To Be continued', *Screen*, 23: 1 (1982), 13.

25 Anna McCarthy, 'Studying Soap Opera', in *The Television Genre Book*, ed. Glen Creeber (London: British Film Institute, 2001), 47.

26 *The Guardian*, 4 November 2013: https://www.theguardian.com/media/2013/nov/04/downton-abbey-rape-scene-will-not0face-investigation-despite-complaints (accessed March 2017).

27 Julianne Pidduck, *Contemporary Costume Film: Space, Place and the Past* (London: Routledge, 2004), 126.

28 *The Atlantic*, 1 February 2013: https://www.theatlantic.com/entertainment/magazine/2013/02/downton-is-entertainment-but-brideshead-was-art (accessed March 2017).

29 *Forbes*, 14 February 2013: https://www.forbes.com/sites/jerrybower/2013/02/14/down-on-downton-why-the-left-is-trashing-downton-abbey (accessed March 2017).

30 *The Guardian*, 27 September 2010: https://www.theguardian.co.uk/2010/sept/27/downton-abbey-and-all-new-celebrity-total-wipeout (accessed March 2017).

31 *The Daily Telegraph*, 30 July 2011: http://www.telegraph.co.uk/culture/tvandradio/8670941/Downton-Abbey-second-series-first-review.html (accessed March 2017).

32 *The New Statesman*, 14 October 2010: https://www.newstatesman.com/television/2010/10/downton-abbey-drama-lord.html (accessed March 2017).

33 *The Sunday Times*, 23 September 2012: https://www.thesundaytimes.co.uk/sto/culture/film_and_tv/article1129037.ece (accessed March 2017).

34 *The Guardian*, 4 November 2012: https://www.theguardian.com/commentisfree/2012/nov/04/downton-abbey-black-people.html (accessed March 2017).

35 *The Independent*, 26 February 2013: https://www.independent.co.uk/arts-entertainment/tv/news/downton-abbey-to-open-things-up-ethnically-with-introduction-of-first-black-character-8511265.html (accessed March 2017).

36 *The Independent*, 5 July 2018: https://www.independent.co.uk/arts-entertainment/tv/news/downton-abbey-popular-in-America-because-there-are-no-black-people-in-it-claims-Barry-Humphries-a679676.html (accessed March 2017).

37 *The Atlantic*, 1 January 2013.

38 *Forbes*, 14 February 2013.

39 *New York Review of Books*, 8 March 2012: https://www.nybooks.com/articles/2012/03/08/abbey-jumped-shark (accessed March 2017).

40 *The Huffington Post*, 1 February 2013, updated 4 March 2013: www.huffingtonpost.com/maureen-ryan/downton-abbey-season-3-review.html (accessed March 2017).

41 'Carnival Films and ITV announce Season 6 to be the final *Downton Abbey*.'

42 *The Guardian*, 25 December 2015: https://www.theguardian.com/tv-and-radio/2015/dec/25/downton-abbey-the-finale (accessed March 2017).

43 *The Hollywood Reporter*, 6 April 2015, 1.

44 *Variety*, 25 October 2016, 46.

45 *The Hollywood Reporter*, 11 November 2016, 96.

46 *UWIRE Text*, 19 November 2016, 1.

Chapter 7

1 *Sherlock*. Hartswood Productions for BBC1/WGBH TV Boston. *Created by:* Mark Gatiss and Steven Moffat. *Executive producers*: Mark Gatiss, Steven Moffat, Sue Vertue, Rebecca Eaton, Bethan Jones. *Writers:* Steven Moffat, Mark Gatiss, Stephen Thompson. *Directors:* Paul McGuigan, Euros Lyn, Toby Haynes, Jeremy Lovering, Colm McCarthy, Nick Hurran, Douglas Mackinnon, Benjamin Caron, Rachel Talalay. Series 1: 'A Study in Pink' (25.07.2010), 'The Blind Banker' (01.08.2010), 'The Great Game' (08.08.2010). Series 2: 'A Scandal in Belgravia' (01.01.2012), 'The Hounds of Baskerville' (08.01.2012), 'The Reichenbach Fall' (15.01.2012). Series 3: 'The Empty Hearse' (01.01.2014), 'The Sign of Three' (05.01.2014), 'His Last Vow' (12.01.2014). Special: 'The Abominable Bride' (01.01.2016). Series 4: 'The Six Thatchers' (01.01.2017), 'The Lying Detective' (08.01.2017), 'The Final Problem' (15.01.2017).

2   *Radio Times*, 22 January 2014: www.radiotimes.com/news/2014-01-22/sherlock-
    is-most-watched-BBC-drama-series-for-over-a-decade (accessed March 2017).

3   The Arthur Wontner films were *The Sleeping Cardinal* (1931), *The Missing
    Rembrandt* (1932), *The Sign of Four* (1932), *The Triumph of Sherlock Holmes*
    (1935) and *Silver Blaze* (1937). The Basil Rathbone series comprised two
    for Twentieth Century-Fox – *The Hound of the Baserkvilles* (1939) and *The
    Adventures of Sherlock Holmes* (1939) – and twelve for Universal Pictures:
    Sherlock Holmes and the Voice of Terror (1942), *Sherlock Holmes and the Secret
    Weapon* (1942), *Sherlock Holmes in Washington* (1943), *Sherlock Holmes Faces
    Death* (1943), *The Spider Woman* (1944), *The Scarlet Claw* (1944), *The Pearl of
    Death* (1944), *The House of Fear* (1945), *The Woman in Green* (1945), *Pursuit to
    Algiers* (1945), *Terror by Night* (1946) and *Dressed to Kill* (1946).

4   See David Stuart Davies, *Holmes of the Movies: The Screen Career of Sherlock
    Holmes* (London: New English Library, 1976); Alan Eyles, *Sherlock Holmes: A
    Centenary Celebration*; Alan Barnes, *Sherlock Holmes on Screen: The Complete
    Film and TV History* (London: John Murray, 2011); and Jeffrey Richards, *Cinema
    and Radio in Britain and America, 1920–60* (Manchester: Manchester University
    Press, 2010), 249–86.

5   *The Independent*, 15 February 2012: https://www.independent.co.uk/arts-
    entertainment/tv/6939158.html (accessed March 2017).

6   'Unlocking *Sherlock*', *Sherlock: Series 1* (BBC DVD VFD 46528).

7   *Broadcast*, 14 July 2009, 1.

8   *Broadcast*, 14 May 2010, 47.

9   *The Guardian*, 26 December 2010: https://www.theguardian.com/tv-and-
    radio/2010/sep/02/sherlock-mark-lawson (accessed March 2017). The original
    version of 'A Study in Pink' is included on the DVD of *Sherlock: Series 1* (BBC
    DVD VFD 46528).

10 *The Financial Times*, 26 August 2014: www.ft.com/content/3cc9afc4-2d0e-11e-
    911b-00144feabdc0 (accessed March 2017).

11 'Are International Co-Productions the Future of TV Drama?', *DenofGeek*,
    23 April 2016: www.denofgeek.com/us/tv/the-night-manager/253935 (accessed
    March 2017).

12 *Onstride Financial*, 31 March 2014: https://www.onstride.co.uk/blog/much-cost-
    produce-favorite-tv-show/ (accessed March 2017).

13 *The Financial Times*, 26 August 2014.

14 *The Guardian*, 19 July 2014: www.telegraph.co.uk/reviews/worldnews/
    northamerica/usa/10978139.html (accessed March 2017).

15 *The Guardian*, 14 January 2016: https://www.theguhttps://www.theguardian.com/ tv-and-radio/2016/jan/14/sherlock-abominable-bride-cinema-sales-worldwide (accessed March 2017).

16 'How Sherlock Holmes Changed the World', *BBC News*, 6 January 2016: www.bbc. co.uk/culture/story/20160106 (accessed March 2017).

17 *The Guardian: Weekend*, 4 September 2010, 49.

18 At the time of writing the websites are no longer active but their content is archived at: https://www.bbc.co.uk/programmes/profiles/5BnCVjDxp6fVMzLmn LLQxSQ/.

19 'Unlocking Sherlock', *Sherlock: Series 1* (BBC DVD VFD 46528).

20 The first Sherlock Holmes novel (*A Study in Scarlet*) was published in 1887 and the first short story ('A Scandal in Bohemia') in the *Strand Magazine* in 1891. Doyle continued writing new Holmes stories until 1927 but most were set in the 1880s or 1890s. 'His Last Bow' is set in 1914 on the eve of the First World War and features Holmes coming out of retirement to foil a German spy ring.

21 Amanda J. Field, *England's Secret Weapon: The Wartime Films of Sherlock Holmes* (Hendon: Middlesex University Press, 2009), 108.

22 Arthur Conan Doyle, *A Study in Scarlet* (Oxford: Oxford University Press, [1887], 1993), 5; Arthur Conan Doyle, *The Sign of the Four* (Oxford: Oxford University Press, [1889], 1993), 5.

23 James Chapman, '*The Avengers*: Television and Popular Culture during the "High Sixties"', in *Windows on the Sixties: Exploring Key Texts of Media and Culture*, eds Anthony Aldgate, James Chapman and Arthur Marwick (London: I.B. Tauris, 2000), 37–69.

24 *The Telegraph*, 1 January 2012: https://www.telegraph.co.uk/culture/tvandradio/ bbc/8987577/the-timeless-appeal-of-Sherlock-Holmess-sexy-logic.html (accessed March 2017).

25 *The Independent*, 25 July 2010: https://www.independent.co.uk/arts-entertainment/ tv/reviews/the-weekend-tv/4-2035302.html (accessed March 2017).

26 *The Guardian*, 23 July 2010: https://www.theguardian.com/tv-and-radioblog/2010/ jul/23/sherlock-steven-moffat-mark-gatiss (accessed March 2017).

27 *The Telegraph*, 6 January 2012: https://www.telegraph.co.uk/culture/tvandradio/ 8995909/sherlock-episode-two-BBc-One-preview.html (accessed March 2017).

28 *IGN*, 9 August 2010: https://uk-ign/com/articles/2010/08/09/sherlock-the-great-game-review (accessed March 2017).

29 *IGN*, 20 May 2012: https://uk-ign.com/article/2015/05/21/sherlock-the-reichenbach-fall-review (accessed March 2017).

30 *The Independent*, 12 January 2014: https://www.independent.co.uk/arts-entertainment/tv/review/sherlock-his-last-vow-a-disappointingly-desperate-finale-9052641.html (accessed March 2017).

31 *AV/TV Club*, 17 January 2014: https://tv.avclub.com/sherlock-turns-introspective-with-its-silly-sociopath-o-1798179209 (accessed March 2017).

32 *Vox*, 16 January 2017: www.vox.com/2017/1/16/14279588/sherlock-finale-final-problem-review (accessed March 2017).

33 Carlen Lavigne, 'The Noble Bachelor and the Crooked Man: Subtext and Sexuality in the BBC's *Sherlock*', in *Sherlock Holmes for the 21st Century: Essays on New Adaptations*, ed. Lynette Porter (Jefferson NC: McFarland, 2012), 17.

34 Arthur Conan Doyle, *The Case-Book of Sherlock Holmes* (Oxford: Oxford University Press, [1927] 1993), 132.

35 Fredric Wertham, *The Seduction of the Innocent: The Influence of the Comic Book on Today's Youth* (New York: Rinehart & Co., 1954), 190.

36 See Stephen Gunn, 'Queer (Mis)recognition in the BBC's *Sherlock*', *Adaptation*, 8: 1 (2013), 50–67; Judith Fathallah, 'Moriarty's Ghost: Or the Queer Disruption of the BBC's *Sherlock*', *Television and New Media*, 16: 5 (2015), 490–500; and Amandelin A. Valentine, 'Towards a Broader Recognition of the Queer in the BBC's *Sherlock*', *Transformative Works and Cultures*, 22 (2016): https://journal.transformativeworks.org/index.php/twc.

37 Jane Clare Jones, 'Is *Sherlock* sexist? Steven Moffat's wanton women', *The Guardian*, 3 January 2012: https://www.theguardian.com/commentisfree/2012/jan/03/sherlock-sexist-steven-moffat (accessed March 2017).

38 See *VisitBritain: The Official Tourism Website of Great Britain*: https://www.visitbritain.com/gb/en (accessed February 2019).

39 'Unlocking Sherlock'.

Chapter 8

1 *Broadchurch*. Kudos Film and Television Productions for ITV1. *Created and written by:* Chris Chibnall. *Executive producers:* Chris Chibnall, Jane Featherstone. *Directors:* James Strong, Euros Lyn (Series 1), Jessica Hobbs, Jonathan Teplitzky, Mike Barker (Series 2), Paul Andrew Williams, Daniel Nettheim, Lewis Arnold (Series 3). Series 1: 4 March–22 April 2013. Series 2: 5 January–22 February 2015. Series 3: 28 February–17 April 2017.

2 *Broadcast*, 1 March 2013, 23.

3 Broadcasters' Audience Research Board, 'Trends in television viewing: 2012', March 2013: http://www.barb.co.uk/download/?file/wp-content/uploads/2015/12/ Barb-Trends-in-Television-Viewing-2012 (accessed September 2017).

4 Quoted in Marianne Colbran, *Media Representations of Police and Crime: Shading the Police Television Drama* (Basingstoke: Palgrave Macmillan, 2014), 205.

5 Ross P. Garner, 'Crime Drama and Channel Branding: ITV and *Broadchurch*', in *Contemporary British Television Crime Drama: Cops on the Box*, ed. Ruth McElroy (London: Routledge, 2016), 139–53.

6 Ibid., 141–2.

7 John Caughie, *Television Drama: Realism, Modernism, and British Culture* (Oxford: Oxford University Press), 2000, 205–6.

8 *Entertainment Weekly*, 25 September 2013, 18.

9 *Radio Times*, 22–28 April 2013, 15.

10 Lez Cooke, *British Television Drama: A History*, 2nd edn (London: British Film Institute/ Palgrave Macmillan, 2015), 147.

11 Ibid., 144.

12 Glen Creeber, 'Killing Us Softly: Investigating the Aesthetics, Philosophy and Influence of Nordic *noir* Television', *Journal of Popular Television*, 3: 1 (2015), 25.

13 Ibid., 29.

14 *New York Times*, 6 August 2013: https://www.nytimes.com/2013/08/07arts/ television/broadchurch-a-dark-new-drama-arrives-on-bbc-america.html (accessed September 2017).

15 *Entertainment Weekly*, 25 September 2013, 18.

16 Jason Bainbridge, '"If It's Not Good TV, Believe Me, It's Not for a Jury": Representing the Media Saturation of Law', *Griffith Law Review*, 24: 3 (2015), 353.

17 'Broadchurch Postmortem', *Yahoo! News*, 13 July 2017: https://uk.news.yahoo. com/broadchurch-creator-chris-chibnall-seeing-hardy-new-light-030000456. html (accessed September 2017).

18 *Broadcast*, 1 March 2013, 22.

19 Les Roberts, 'Landscape in the Frame: Exploring the Hinterland of the British Procedural Drama', *New Review of Film and Television Studies*, 14: 3 (2016), 375.

20 Quoted in Colbran, *Media Representations of Police and Crime*, 205.

21 'Broken Compasses', *Commonweal*, 16 August 2013, 24.

22 Roberts, 'Landscape in the Frame', 376.

23 In 2002, two ten-year-old girls, Holly Wells and Jessica Chapman, were murdered in Soham, Cambridgeshire. School caretaker Ian Huntley, who spoke several

times to television reporters, was subsequently arrested and convicted of their murders. Milly Dowler, a thirteen-year-old schoolgirl, was murdered in Walton-on-Thames, Surrey, in 2002. In 2011 Levi Bellfield, already serving life sentences for two other murders in 2005, was convicted of her murder. At the same time it emerged that Milly's mobile phone had been hacked by a private investigator employed by tabloid newspaper the *News of the World* and that voicemail messages had been deleted (thereby interfering with evidence in a murder investigation).

24 'Broadchurch postmortem'.

25 *The Guardian*, 23 April 2013: http://www.theguardian.com/tv-and-radio/tvandradioblog/2013/apr/23/broadchurch-finale-work-out-killer (accessed September 2017).

26 *The Daily Telegraph*, 23 April 2013: https://www.telegraph.co.uk/culture/tv-and-radio/10011343/Broadchurch-final-episode-review.html (accessed September 2017).

27 Broadcasters' Audience Research Board, *The Viewing Report*, November 2013: https://www.barc.co.uk/content/downloads/2015/12/BarbViewingReport_Nov13.pdf (accessed September 2017).

28 *The New Statesman*, 26 April 2013, 13.

29 *Evening Standard*, 27 April 2013, 12.

30 *The Telegraph*, 23 April 2013: https://www.telegraph.co.uk/culture/tv-and-radio/10011343/Broadchurch-final-episode-review.html (accessed September 2017).

31 *Metro*, 23 April 2013: https://metro.co.uk/2013/04/23/broadchurch-finale-is-ratings-winner-5663122/ (accessed September 2017).

32 Paul Rix, 'The Interaction of Broadcasters, Critics and Audiences in Shaping the Cultural Meaning and Status of Television Programmes: The Public Discourse around the Second Series of *Broadchurch*', *Journal of Popular Television*, 5: 2 (2017), 225–43.

33 *The Guardian*, 6 January 2015: https://www.theguardian.com/tv-and-radio/tvandradioblog/2015/jan/06/broadchurch-2-i-could-have-done-with-more-spoilers (accessed September 2017).

34 *The Spectator*, 24 January 2015: https://www.spectator.co.uk/2015/01/broadchurch-review-unwatchable (accessed September 2017).

35 *The New Statesman*, 15 January 2015: https://www.newstatesman.com/culture/2015/01/onset-madness-broadchurch-has-gone-completely-loopy (accessed September 2017).

36   *The Guardian*, 23 February 2015: https://www.theguardian.com/tv-and-radio /2015/feb/23/broadchurch-recap-season-two-finale-episode-eight (accessed September 2017).

37   Rix, 'The Interaction of Broadcasters, Critics and Audiences', 236.

38   For a discussion of rape myths in British television drama (with particular reference to a storyline in *EastEnders*), see Rebecca Harrison's blog, 'The Blonde, White Woman and the Politics of Rape Survival in *EastEnders*; or, Why Skin, Hair and Colour Matter if You Want to Bust Rape Myths', 24 August 2016: www. writingonreels.uk/blog/archive/08-2016 (accessed September 2017).

39   *The Independent*, 28 February 2017: https://www.independent.co.uk/arts. entertainment/tv/broadchurch-series-3-episode-1-review-david-tennant-olivia -colman-a7601791.html (accessed September 2017).

40   *The Telegraph*, 18 April 2017: https://www.telegraph.co.uk/tv/0/broadchurch -series-3-finale-review (accessed September 2017).

41   *The Guardian*, 18 April 2017: https://www.guardian.com/tv-and-radio/2017/ apr/18/broadchurch-season-3-finale-bbc-legacy-mark-lawson (accessed September 2017).

42   '*Broadchurch* Finale: Nation Tunes in for Cliffhanger Ending', *ITV Report*, 17 April 2017: https://www.itv.com/news/meridian/2017-04-17/ broadchurch-finale-nation-tunes-in-for-cliffhanger-ending (accessed September 2017).

43   'Final *Broadchurch* Episodes Pull in Biggest ever Audience', *ITV Report*, 18 April 2017: https://www.itv.com/news/westcountry/2017-04-18/ final-broadchurch-episode-pulls-in-biggest-ever-audience/ (accessed September 2017).

44   John Ellis, *Seeing Things: Television in the Age of Uncertainty* (London: I.B. Tauris, 2000).

45   *The Sunday Post*, 23 October 2018: https://www.sundaypost.com/fp/final-episode -of-bodyguard-attracts-biggest-audience-for-uk-tv-drama-since-current-records- began (accessed February 2019).

Bibliography

References to primary sources, including newspaper articles, reviews, publicity materials and blogs, may be traced through the endnotes.

Andrew, Christopher, *The Defence of the Realm: The Authorized History of MI5*, London: Allen Lane, 2009.

Angelini, Sergio, 'Cold War Spies', *BFI Screenonline*: http://www.screenonline.org.uk/tv/id/1008415/index.html (accessed December 2011).

Bainbridge, Jason, '"If It's Not Good TV, Believe Me, It's Not for a Jury": Representing the Media Saturation of Law', *Griffith Law Review*, 24: 3 (2015), 351–78.

Barker, Simon, '"Period" Detective Drama and the Limits of Contemporary Nostalgia: *Inspector Morse* and the Strange Case of a Lost England', *Critical Survey*, 6: 2 (1994), 234–42.

Barnes, Alan, *Sherlock Holmes on Screen: The Complete Film and TV History*, London: Titan Books, 2011.

Bignell, Jonathan, and Andrew O'Day, *Terry Nation*, Manchester: Manchester University Press, 2004.

Bignell, Jonathan, and Stephen Lacey, eds, *Popular Television Drama: Critical Perspectives*, Manchester: Manchester University Press, 2005.

Blandford, Steve, *Jimmy McGovern*, Manchester: Manchester University Press, 2013.

Booker, Christopher, *The Seventies: Portrait of a Decade*, Harmondsworth: Penguin, 1980.

Bourne, Stephen, *Black in the British Frame: Black People in British Film and Television 1896–1996*, London: Cassell, 1998.

Brandt, George, ed., *British Television Drama in the 1980s*, Cambridge: Cambridge University Press, 1993.

Brunsdon, Charlotte, 'Problems with Quality', *Screen*, 31: 1 (1990), 67–90.

Brunsdon, Charlotte, 'Television Crime Series, Women Police and Fuddy-Duddy Feminism', *Feminist Media Studies*, 13: 4 (2013), 375–95.

Bryson, Bill, *Notes from a Small Island*, London: Black Swan, 1996.

Buxton, David, *From 'The Avengers' to 'Miami Vice': Form and Ideology in Television Series*, Manchester: Manchester University Press, 1990.

Cardwell, Sarah, *Adaptation Revisited: Television and the Classic Novel*, Manchester: Manchester University Press, 2002.

Cardwell, Sarah, *Andrew Davies*, Manchester: Manchester University Press, 2005.

Carroll, Rachel, 'Black Britain and the Classic Adaptation: Integrated Casting in Television Adaptations of *Oliver Twist* and *Little Dorrit*', *Adaptation*, 8: 1 (2015), 16–30.

Caughie, John, *Television Drama: Realism, Modernism, and British Culture*, Oxford: Oxford University Press, 2000.

Chapman, James, '*The Avengers*: Television and Popular Culture during the "High Sixties"', in *Windows on the Sixties: Exploring Key Texts of Media and Culture*, eds Anthony Aldgate, James Chapman and Arthur Marwick, London: I.B. Tauris, 2000, 37–69.

Clark, Jennifer, 'Postfeminist Masculinity and the Complex Politics of Time: Contemporary Quality Television Imagines a Pre-Feminist World', *New Review of Film and Television Studies*, 12: 4 (2014), 445–62.

Cobley, Paul, '"It's a Fine Line between Safety and Terror": Crime and Anxiety Re-Drawn in *Spooks*', *Film International*, 7: 2 (2009), 36–45.

Colbran, Marianne, *Media Representations of Police and Crime: Shading the Police Television Drama*, Basingstoke: Palgrave Macmillan, 2014.

Cooke, Lez, *Troy Kennedy Martin*, Manchester: Manchester University Press, 2007.

Cooke, Lez, *British Television Drama: A History*, 2nd edn, London: British Film Institute/Palgrave Macmillan, 2015.

Copelman, Dina M., 'Consuming *Downton Abbey*: The Commodification of Heritage and Nostalgia', *Journal of British Cinema and Television*, 16: 1 (2019), 61–77.

Corner, John, ed., *Popular Television in Britain: Studies in Cultural History*, London: British Film Institute, 1991.

Creeber, Glen, ed., *The Television Genre Book*, London: British Film Institute, 2001.

Creeber, Glen, 'Killing Us Softly: Investigating the Aesthetics, Philosophy and Influence of Nordic *noir* Television', *Journal of Popular Television*, 3: 1 (2015), 21–35.

Davies, David Stuart, *Holmes of the Movies: The Screen Career of Sherlock Holmes*, London: New English Library, 1976.

Denning, Michael, *Cover Stories: Narrative and Ideology in the British Spy Thriller*, London: Routledge & Kegan Paul, 1987.

Dixon, Wheeler Winston, 'The Halfway House', in *Liberal Directions: Basil Dearden and Postwar British Film Culture*, eds Alan Burton, Tim O'Sullivan and Paul Wells, Trowbridge: Flicks Books, 1997, 108–15.

Donaldson, Lucy Fife, 'Series Spaces: Revisiting and Re-Evaluating *Inspector Morse*', *Journal of Popular Television*, 4: 1 (2016), 3–28.

Downey, Christine, '*Life on Mars*, or How the Breaking of Genre Rules Revitalises the Crime Fiction Tradition', *Crimeculture*, 2007: http://www.crimeculture.com/Contents/Articles-Summer07/Life_on_Mars.html (accessed December 2011).

Doyle, Arthur Conan, *A Study in Scarlet*, 1887, Oxford: Oxford University Press, 1993.

Doyle, Arthur Conan, *The Sign of Four*, 1890, Oxford: Oxford University Press, 1993.

Doyle, Arthur Conan, *The Case-Book of Sherlock Holmes*, 1927, Oxford: Oxford University Press, 1993.

Duguid, Mark, 'TV Drama in the 2000s', *BFI Screenonline*: www.screenonline.org/uk/tv/id/1394013/index.html (accessed December 2011).

Eco, Umberto, 'The Narrative Structure in Fleming', in *The Bond Affair*, eds Oreste Del Buono and Umberto Eco, trans. R. A. Downie, London: Macdonald, 1965, 35–75.

Ellis, John, 'Watching Death at Work: An Analysis of *A Matter of Life and Death*', in *Powell, Pressburger and Others*, ed. Ian Christie, London: British Film Institute, 1978, 79–104.

Ellis, John, *Seeing Things: Television in the Age of Uncertainty*, London: I.B. Tauris, 2000.

Emsley, Clive, *The English Police: A Political and Social History*, 2nd edn, London: Routledge, 1996.

Erickson, Christian W., 'Thematics of Counterterrorism: Comparing *24* and *MI-5/Spooks*', *Critical Studies on Terrorism*, 1: 3 (2008), 343–58.

Eyles, Alan, *Sherlock Holmes: A Centenary Celebration*, London: John Murray, 1986.

Fathallah, Judith, 'Moriaty's Ghost: Or the Queer Disruption of the BBC's *Sherlock*', *Television and New Media*, 16: 5 (2015), 490–500.

Feuer, Jane, Paul Kerr and Tise Vahimagi, eds, *MTM 'Quality Television'*, London: British Film Institute, 1984.

Field, Amanda J., *England's Secret Weapon: The Wartime Films of Sherlock Holmes*, Hendon: Middlesex University Press, 2009.

Forster, Laurel, and Sue Harper, eds, *British Culture and Society in the 1970s: The Lost Decade*, Newcastle-upon-Tyne: Cambridge Scholars, 2010.

Garland, Jon, and Charlotte Bilby, '"What Next, Dwarves?": Images of Police Culture in *Life on Mars*', *Crime Media Culture*, 7: 2 (2011), 115–32.

Geraghty, Christine, 'Aesthetics and Quality in Popular Television Drama', *International Journal of Cultural Studies*, 6: 1 (2003), 25–45.

Geraghty, Christine, 'Discussing Quality: Critical Vocabulary and Popular Television', *E-Comps*, 6 (2008): http://dx.doi.org/10.30962/ec.v8i0.125 (accessed March 2019).

Giddings, Robert, and Keith Selby, *The Classic Serial on Television and Radio*, Basingstoke: Palgrave Macmillan, 2001.

Gunn, Stephen, 'Queer (Mis)recognition in the BBC's *Sherlock*', *Adaptation*, 8: 1 (2013), 50–67.

Hallam, Julia, *Lynda La Plante*, Manchester: Manchester University Press, 2005.

Hamad, Hannah, "'Don't Let Him Take Britain Back to the 1980s": *Ashes to Ashes* as Postfeminist Recession Television', *Continuum: Journal of Media and Cultural Studies*, 28: 2 (2014), 202–12.

Hammond, Michael, and Lucy Mazdon, eds, *The Contemporary Television Series*, Edinburgh: Edinburgh University Press, 2005.

Harper, Stephen, "'When You Walk through These Doors, You Can Be Anything You Want": Authenticity, Fantasy and Neoliberal Ideology in *Hotel Babylon*', *Journal of British Cinema and Television*, 5: 1 (2008), 113–31.

Hills, Matt, *Triumph of a Time Lord: Regenerating 'Doctor Who' in the Twenty-First Century*, London: I.B. Tauris, 2010.

Hills, Matt, '*Sherlock* "Content" Onscreen: Digital Holmes and the Fannish Imagination', *Journal of Popular Film and Television*, 45: 1 (2017), 68–78.

Hochscherf, Tobias, and Heidi Philipsen, eds, *Beyond the Bridge: Contemporary Danish Television Drama*, London: I.B. Tauris, 2017.

Kerr, Paul, 'Classic Serials: To Be Continued', *Screen*, 23: 1 (1982), 6–19.

Knox, Simone, '*Masterpiece Theatre* and British Drama Imports on US Television: Discourses of Tension', *Critical Studies in Television*, 7: 1 (2012), 29–48.

Lacey, Stephen, *Tony Garnett*, Manchester: Manchester University Press, 2007.

Lacey, Stephen, and Ruth McElroy, eds, *Life on Mars: From Manchester to New York*, Cardiff: University of Wales Press, 2012.

Leggott, James, and Julie Anne Taddeo, eds, *Upstairs and Downstairs: British Costume Drama Television from 'The Forsyte Saga' to 'Downton Abbey'*, Lanham, MA: Rowman and Littlefield, 2015.

Lewis, Jon E., and Penny Stempel, *The Ultimate TV Guide*, London: Orion Books, 2001.

McCabe, Janet, and Kim Akass, eds, *Quality TV: Contemporary American Television and Beyond*, London: I.B. Tauris, 2007.

McElroy, Ruth, ed., *Contemporary British Television Crime Drama: Cops on the Box*, London: Routledge, 2016.

Morey, Peter, 'Strangers and Stereotypes: The *Spooks* Controversy and the Framing of Muslims', *Journal of Postcolonial Writing*, 46: 5 (2010), 529–39.

Morley, David, 'Mediated Classification: Representations of Class and Culture in Contemporary British Television', *European Journal of Cultural Studies*, 12: 4 (2009), 487–508.

Nelson, Robin, *State of Play: Contemporary 'High-end' TV Drama*, Manchester: Manchester University Press, 2007.

Nelson, Robin, '*Life on Mars*', in *The Essential Cult TV Reader*, ed. David Lavery, Lexington: University Press of Kentucky, 2010, 142–9.

Nicholas, Siân, 'History, Revisionism and Television Drama: *Foyle's War* and the "Myth of 1940"', *Media History*, 13: 2–3 (2007), 203–19.

Oldham, Joseph, *Paranoid Visions: Spies, Conspiracies and the Secret State in British Television Drama*, Manchester: Manchester University Press, 2017.

Pidduck, Julianne, *Contemporary Costume Film: Space, Place and the Past*, London: British Film Institute, 2004.

Piper, Helen, *The TV Detective: Voices of Dissent in Contemporary Television*, London: I.B. Tauris, 2015.

Porter, Lynnette, ed., *Sherlock Holmes for the 21st Century: Essays in New Adaptations*, Jefferson, NC: McFarland, 2012.

Richards, Jeffrey, *Cinema and Radio in Britain and America, 1920–60*, Manchester: Manchester University Press, 2010.

Rives-East, Darcie, 'Watching the Detective: *Sherlock*, Surveillance, and British Fears Post-7/7', *Journal of Popular Culture*, 48: 1 (2015), 44–55.

Rix, Paul, 'The Interaction of Broadcasters, Critics and Audiences in Shaping the Cultural Meaning and Status of Television Programmes: The Public Discourse around the Second Series of *Broadchurch*', *Journal of Popular Television*, 5: 2 (2017), 225.

Roberts, Lee, 'Landscape in the Frame: Exploring the Hinterland of the British Procedural Drama', *New Review of Film and Television Studies*, 14: 3 (2016), 364–85.

Rolinson, Dave, *Alan Clarke*, Manchester: Manchester University Press, 2005.

Sangster, Jim, *Spooks Confidential: The Official Handbook*, London: Contender Books, 2003.

Shaw, Caitlin, 'Remediating the Eighties: Nostalgia and Retro in British Screen Fiction from 2005 to 2011', PhD thesis, De Montfort University, 2015.

Steine, Louisa Ellen, and Kristina Busse, eds, '*Sherlock*' *and Transmedia Fandom: Essays on the BBC Series*, Jefferson, NC: McFarland, 2012.

Sydney-Smith, Susan, *Beyond Dixon of Dock Green: Early British Police Series*, London: I.B. Tauris, 2002.

Thompson, Felix, '*Coast and Spooks*: On the Permeable National Boundaries of British television', *Continuum: Journal of Media and Cultural Studies*, 24: 3 (2010), 429–38.

Tincknell, Estella, '"A Sunken Dream": Music and the Gendering of Nostalgia in *Life on Mars*', in *Popular Music on British Television*, ed. Ian Inglis, London: Ashgate, 2010, 161–75.

Tulloch, John, *Trevor Griffiths*, Manchester: Manchester University Press, 2006.

Valentine, Amandelin A., 'Towards a Broader Recognition of the Queer in the BBC's *Sherlock*', *Transformative Works and Cultures*, 22 (2016): https://journal. transformativeworks.org/index.php/twc (accessed March 2017).

Vice, Sue, *Jack Rosenthal*, Manchester: Manchester University Press, 2009.

Weissmann, Elke, *Transnational Television Drama: Special Relations and Mutual Influence between the UK and US*, Basingstoke: Palgrave Macmillan, 2012.

Wertham, Fredric, *The Seduction of the Innocent: The Influence of the Comic Book on Today's Youth*, New York: Rinehart & Co., 1954.

Index

A-Team, The 53–4
A&E Network 51, 52
Abbington, Amanda 125
Abbott, Paul 6, 153
Adams, Kelly 54, 57–8
Addison, Paul 38
Adventures of Robin Hood, The 8, 100, 118
Adventures of Sherlock Holmes, The (film) 121, 124
Adventures of Sherlock Holmes, The (tv series) 45, 114, 121
Agutter, Jenny 14
Akomfrah, John 111–12
Altman, Robert 105, 144
Ambler, Eric 18
American Broadcasting Company (ABC) 53
AMC Network 9, 52
'American Quality Television' 1
Andrew, Christopher 17
Andrews, Dean 69, 83
Armchair Theatre 1, 137
Armitage, Richard 15
Arnalds, Olafur 140
Ashes to Ashes 1, 7, 8, 83–98
Atkins, Eileen 105
Austin Powers: International Man of Mystery 77
Avengers, The 2, 7, 12, 16, 59, 62, 92, 118, 123

Bailey, Rob 14
Bainbridge, Jason 141
Banks-Smith, Nancy 18
Basil Brush Show, The 76
Bennett, Alan 3
Benzali, Daniel 10
Bergerac 72
Between the Lines 72
Bill, The 34, 72, 73
Billen, Andrew 4, 73, 97

Blackpool 9
Blair, Tony 21, 23
Bleasedale, Alan 104
Blues and Twos 72
Boardwalk Empire 102
Bochco, Steven 140
Bodyguard, The 9, 153–4
Bolan, Marc 91
Bonneville, Hugh 103, 108
Bourne, Stephen 63
Bower, Jerry 110, 112
Bowie, David 66, 71, 87
Boyer, Charles 53
Brackley, Jonathan 29
Branagh, Kenneth 117
Brenton, Howard 14, 23
Brideshead Revisited 100, 101, 107, 112, 142
Bridge, The (Broen) 9, 81, 139
British Broadcasting Corporation (BBC) 22–4, 66, 80, 100, 118, 119, 135, 142
Broadcasters' Audience Research Board (BARB) 135–6, 149
Broadcasting Act (1990) 5, 11
Broadcasting Standards Commission 21
Broadchurch 1, 7, 8, 135–54
Brown, Gordon 21, 98
Bruce, Nigel 132
Brunsdon, Charlotte 96, 101–2, 104
Bryson, Bill 78–9
Buffy the Vampire Slayer 58, 123
Bugs 12
Burns, Ken 104
Bush, George W. 21
Buxton, David 12, 59–60

Cagney & Lacey 96
Calder, Angus 38
Call the Midwife 9, 45, 114
Callan 12
Camberwick Green 10, 76, 78

Cameron, David 98
Campbell, Georgina 152
Carnival Films 5, 60, 102
Carr, Gary 112
Casualty 6
C.A.T.S. Eyes 12
Caughie, John 2, 101, 137
Celtic Films 5
Chamberlain, Richard 58–9
Champions, The 12, 103
Chancellor, Anna 23
Channel 4, 12, 65–6, 142
Chariots of Fire 89
Chase, David 7
Chibnall, Chris 7, 137–8, 140, 141, 143,
    147, 150
City Central 67
Clarke, Alan 3
Clarke, Charles 25
Clemens, Brian 7
Collins, Andrew 76
Colman, Olivia 136, 143
Commander, The 72
Cook, John 77, 154
Cooke, Lez 6, 139
Cooke, Rachel 111, 151
Cooper, Glenda 92
Cops 72
Coronation Street 3, 77, 144
Cracker 72, 135, 142
Crampton, Caroline 149
Cranford 100
Crawford Collins, Simon 51
Creeber, Glen 139
Crime Traveller 34, 66, 87
Crimewatch UK 146
Crompton, Sarah 124
Crown, The 9, 114
CSI: Crime Scene Investigation 141
Cumberbatch, Benedict 115, 120, 132
Curtis, Nick 149–50
Curtis, Tony 127

D'Ancona, Matthew 97
Dallas 101, 106–7
Danger Man 12, 16, 59, 118
Dangerfield, George 110
Dankor, Kimathi 111
Dark Side of the Moon, The 81

Davies, Andrew 102, 113
Davies, Gavyn
Davies, Russell T. 7, 117
Davies, Serena 148
Day, Nick 17
Days of Hope 110
DC Banks 136
de Croce, Richard 119
Dearden, Basil 88
Debnath, Neela 128
Deighton, Len 18
Delingpole, James 151
Dempsey and Makepeace 72, 92, 127
Den of Geek 118
Department S 12, 103
Di Angelo, Matt 54
Dixon of Dock Green 72, 73, 143
Doctor Who 2, 3, 9, 52, 66, 87, 119, 130,
    137, 149
Dr Kildaire 59
Dodds, Megan 22
Dowler, Milly 146
Dowling, Tom 148
Downton Abbey 1, 2, 7, 45, 99–114, 119,
    135, 154
Doyle, Arthur Conan 115
Duguid, Mark 4
Dunn, Nell 2
Dyke, Greg 23
Dynasty 101

EastEnders 3, 51, 63, 144
Eco, Umberto 54–5
Edge of Darkness 13, 124, 135, 138–9, 153
Edge, Simon 44
Ehle, Jennifer 30
Eldorado 144
Elementary 116
Elliott, Nick 34
Endeavour 33, 136
Erickson, Christian 21–2
Eyre, Hermione 97

Fabian of the Yard 143
Fall, The 153
Faulkner, Lisa 21
Featherstone, Jane 28–9, 51, 53
Fellowes, Julian 7, 99, 104, 108, 113
Fennell, Albert 7

Fienberg, Daniel J. 114
Fincham, Peter 46
Firth, Peter 14, 30
Fleming, Ian 54
Flett, Kathryn 97
For Your Eyes Only 86
Forsyte Saga, The 100, 101
Foyle's War 1, 6, 8, 33–49, 117, 136
Freeman, Martin 115, 120, 132
Frost, Vicky 151

Game of Thrones 30, 102, 118
Game, Set and Match 13
Gardner, Julie 1, 4, 13, 66, 67–8
Garner, Ross P. 136
Garnett, Tony 3
Garrett, Stephen 5–6, 12
Gascoigne, Jill 94
Gatiss, Mark 112, 129, 132
Gentle Touch, The 72, 93–4
Get Carter 77
Get Smart 12
Gideon's Way 72
Gill, A.A. 111
Glenister, Philip 67, 83
Glenister, Robert 54
Gosford Park 104–5, 108–9
Graham, Alison 80
Graham, Matthew 7, 51, 65, 67, 83, 84, 98
Gravelle, Matthew 147
Graves, Peter 54
Green for Danger 39
Green, Jill 34, 37
Greene, Graham 18, 29
Greenlit Productions 5, 34
Griffiths, Trevor 3
Grifters, The 53
Guinness, Alec 15

Haddington, Ellie 41
Hale, Mike 48
Halfway House, The 88–9
Hamad, Hannah 85, 96
Hanks, Robert 97
Happy Valley 9
Harington, Kit 30
Harper, Stephen 60
Hartswood Films 5, 118
Hawes, Keeley 14, 83, 97

Head, Anthony 19
Heartbeat 72
Henry, Lenny 152
Hesmondhalgh, Julie 151
Higson, Charlie 152
Hills, Matt 3
Hinterland (Y Gwyll) 142
Hogan, Michael 152
Hoggart, Paul 44
Holby City 63
Holward, Leigh 27
Hornblower 52
Horowitz, Anthony 7, 34–5, 40, 45, 47,
    104
Hotel Babylon 9, 60
Hound of the Baskervilles, The 121
Hour, The 9
Howards End 109
Howell, Anthony 36
Humphries, Barry 112
Hunt, Jay 117
Hustle 1, 6, 7, 51–66
Hussein, Saddam 23
Hutton Report 23

I Love the 1970s 68
Incorporated Television Production
    Company 8
Independent Television (ITV) 33, 46, 100,
    102–3, 135–7
Inspector Morse 33–4, 45, 49, 72, 117
Irwin, Mary 77

Jacks and Knaves 72
Jaffrey, Raza 16
Jewel in the Crown, The 100, 101
Joel, Billy 90
Jones, Gemma 14
Jones, Jan Clare 129–30
Jones, Toby 126
Jordan, Tony 51, 52, 65
Joseph, Joe 62
Juliet Bravo 72, 93–4

Kamabawiwoole, Israel 72
Kelly, David 23–4
Kennedy Martin, Ian 94
Kennedy Martin, Troy 3, 138
Kerr, Paul 106

Killing, The (Forbrydelsen) 139
King's Speech, The 113
Kitchen, Michael 35
Knock, The 72
Kudos Film and Television Productions
    5–6, 11–12, 51, 135

La Plante, Lynda 3, 96, 104
Lacey, Stephen 84
Lancaster, Marshall 69, 83
Lark Rise to Candleford 9, 100, 102
Latif, Shazad 16
Laurie, Hugh 14
Law & Order: UK 137
Lawson, Mark 26–7, 151, 152
le Carré, John 15, 18, 28, 48
Left Bank Productions 5
Lester, Adrian 54, 60, 63–4
Lewis 33, 117, 136
Lewis-Smith, Victor 81
Life on Mars 1, 3, 6, 8, 45, 65–82, 83–6, 89,
    100, 118
Line of Duty 153
Litvinenko, Alexander 25
Liverpool One 72
Lombard, Montserrat 84
Love Thy Neighbour 78–9
Lovejoy 57
Lugo, Angela 114
Luther 9
Lynch, David 140

McAvoy, James 150
McBain, Kenny 34
McDiarmid, Ian 26
McElroy, Ruth 78, 84
McGovern, Jimmy 2, 3
McInnerny, Tim 14, 30
McNally, Kevin 21
McNamara, Mary 48
McNult, Myles 126
Macfadyen, Matthew 14, 15
Mad Men 118
Man from U.N.C.L.E., The 12, 51, 59
Man in a Suitcase 12, 103
Mark, Robert 76
Marsh, Jean 105
Martin, Dan 124
Masterpiece (Theatre) 100, 102, 112, 118

Matter of Life and Death, A 69–71
Mays, Daniel 88
Meades, Jonathan 44
Mercer, David 1
Mercurio, Jed 153
Merlin 119
Miami Vice 127
Midsomer Murders 33, 34, 136, 138, 150
Mikkelsen, Lars 125
Minghella, Anthony 33
Minogue, Kylie 58
Mirren, Helen 96
Missing, The 153
Mission: Impossible 12, 53–4
Mr Palfrey of Westminster 12
Mr Selfridge 113–14, 136
Mitchell, Julian 33
Moffat, Steven 7, 115, 116–18, 122, 130
Moir, Jan 111
Moonlighting 57, 92
Moore, Roger 127
Morgan, Frank 71
Morgan, Peter 114
Murder One 140–1
Murray, Jaime 54
Murray, John C. 45
Myles, Eve 150
Myles, Sophia 15

Nalluri, Bharat 14, 30, 51, 77
NBS Universal 102
Neame, Gareth 16–17, 105, 102, 103, 113
Nelson, Robin 4–5
Netflix 114
New Adventures of Robin Hood, The 58
New Avengers, The 12
New Tricks 72
Newell, Sally 152
News of the World 146
Night Manager, The 118, 153
Niven, David 53, 69
No Hiding Place 72
Norris, Hermione 15

O'Donovan, Gerard 44, 62, 97
O'Hara, John 126
Ocean's Eleven 53, 54
Okonedo, Sophie 63–4
Oliver Twist 63–4

Our Friends in the North 137
Oyelowo, David 14, 16

Palmer, Geoffrey 91
Parker, James 112
Paterson, Peter 44
Patterson, Bill 37
Pawson, Lara 111–12
Peaky Blinders 9
Pearson, Harry 76
Pennies from Heaven 57
Penry-Jones, Rupert 15
Peppard, George 54
Perfect Spy, A 13
Persuaders!, The 127
Pharoah, Ashley 7, 65, 83
Phelps, Sarah 63
Pidduck, Julianne 108
Piglet Files, The 13
Piper, Helen 92
Play for Today 137, 154
Poldark 9
Police 94–5
Potter, Dennis 2, 57, 72, 104
Powell, Michael 69
Pressburger, Eric 69
Preston, John 44, 80–1, 97
Pride and Prejudice 100, 101, 107, 142, 153
Prime Suspect 72, 93, 135, 142–3
Prisoner, The 12, 59, 65
Psychos 12
Public Broadcasting Service (PBS) 48, 99, 102, 104, 126, 118
Pulver, Lara 15, 30, 124, 129

Quantum Leap 65
Quatermass II 124

Radford, Ceri 111
Raison, Miranda 15
Rampling, Charlotte 150
Ramsey, Terry 124
Rathbone, Basil 115–16, 132
Rayner, Jay 62
Rebus 136
Red Riding 98
Redford, Robert 53
Rees, Jasper 62

Reilly: Ace of Spies 13
Remains of the Day, The 109
Rififi 52
Rimington, Stella 17
Ripper Street 9
Roberts, Les 142, 144
Rogues, The 53
Rosenthal, Jack 3
Ruth Rendell Mysteries, The 33, 34
Ryan, Maureen 112

Saint, The 118
Sandbaggers, The 12
Scarman Report 91
Scott, Andrew 129
Shameless 9
Shaps, Simon 46
Shayler, David 17, 28
Sherlock 1, 7, 8, 103, 115–33, 153, 154
Shetland 142
Shrimsley, Robert 26
Silent Witness 72
Simm, John 67
Simon, David 7
Simon, Hugh 30
Singing Detective, The 2, 57, 72
Skyfall 132
Sliders 65
Smiley's People 13, 153
Smith, Maggie 103
Softly, Softly 72
Sorcher, Ron 52
Sorkin, Aaron 7
Sosnovska, Olga 15
Southcliffe 142
Special Branch 72
Spooks 1, 6, 8, 11–31, 51, 56, 84, 111
Spooks: The Greater Good 29–31
Spooner, Dennis 103
Stephens, John 74
Stephenson, Ben 7, 11, 117
Starsky and Hutch 92, 127
State of Play 9, 153
Sting, The 53, 54, 58, 59
Street, The 9
Strong, James 142, 144
Study in Terror, A 125
Suschitzky, Adam 77
Sutcliffe, Thomas 44, 62, 81, 124

Sweeney, The 29, 67, 72–3, 94
Sweet, Matthew 26

Tennant, David 136, 143, 146
That Seventies Show 68
Thatcher, Margaret 78, 91, 139
Thaw, John 75
Thomas, Heidi 7, 9, 114
Thompson, Mark 3–4
Thompson, Stephen 124
Till Death Us Do Part 79
Tilly, Chris 125
Tinker, Tailor, Soldier, Spy 13, 15, 19, 135, 153
Torchwood 137
Torchwood: Miracle Day 52
Tunnel, The 9
Turner, Stephanie 94
Twin Peaks 65, 140

Upstairs, Downstairs 100, 101, 105, 108, 112

Vangelis 89
Vaughn, Robert 51, 52
Vertue, Beryl 118
Vertue, Sue 118
Vice, The 72, 136
Vincent, Sam 29
Viner, Brian 97
Vox 127

Wainwright, Sally 9
Waking the Dead 72
Walker, Nicola 19
Wallander 81–2, 117, 139
Walton, James 26, 44, 62
Ward, Mike 80
Warren, Marc 54
Waterman, Dennis 73
Wednesday Play, The 1, 137, 154
Weeks, Honeysuckle 36
Wertham, Fredric 128
WGBH-TV Boston 102, 118
Whedon, Joss 7
White, Liz 69
Whittaker, Jodie 136
Wilmer, Douglas 120
Wilson, Andy 14
Wilson, Benji 27
Wire in the Blood 136
Wizard of Oz, The 71, 72
Wollaston, Sam 80, 97–8, 111
Wolstencroft, David 14

Yesterday's Girl 81
Young, Gig 53

Z Cars 72
Zweites Deutsches Fersehen (ZDF) 135